Beyond Sex Roles

Beyond Sex Roles

*A Guide for the Study of
Female Roles in the Bible*

Gilbert Bilezikian

BAKER BOOK HOUSE
Grand Rapids, Michigan 49506

Scripture quotations identified RSV are from the Revised Standard Version of the Bible. Copyright © 1946 and 1962 by Division of Christian Education of the National Council of Churches in Christ in the United States of America.

Scripture quotations identified NIV are from the Holy Bible: NEW INTERNATIONAL VERSION. © 1978 by the New York International Bible Society, used by permission of Zondervan Bible Publishers.

Scripture quotations not identified as to version indicate that the RSV and NIV translations are essentially identical—or that the indicated verse has been quoted in the author's own words.

Printed in the United States of America

To
men and women
in quest of obedience
to
Holy Writ

Contents

Preface

Several years ago, I became associated with a church-related institution of higher learning where one of the administrative departments was headed by a pompous and bombastic man. It soon became evident that this person was incompetent and that his work was quietly being done by one of his assistants, a gracious woman gifted with genius-level intelligence and a phenomenal capacity for hard work. Eventually, the man was removed from his position (not without some institutional thrashing) and replaced by the woman who, now freed from hindrances, established a model operation. Since that time, she has been called to serve in a much larger institution where she has been promoted to the highest position in her area of service.

However, at the time, the administrative action that resulted in the change was severely criticized by people who objected to a woman occupying a position of authority over men. Since I was held responsible for the action, I was confronted with the need to examine my views of female roles in the light of scriptural teaching.

Several years later, due to a health problem in our family, it became necessary for me to bring my wife, Maria, and our four children—with ages ranging from five to eleven—back to the United States from an educational assignment in the Middle East. I then returned overseas alone and remained there for the better part of a year, finishing the assignment to which I had committed myself. During that year, Maria had to act as a single parent to four small children in the face of incredible difficulties. She was magnificent (and still is!). She handled crisis after crisis with confidence and equanimity. She managed children, household, and finances with competency and in manifest dependency on divine strength. I had occasion to return for two brief visits during that period. Every time, I went back overseas with a sense of admiration for her, and with the humbling conviction that had the roles been reversed, I would have been crushed by the responsibilities she was carrying out so gallantly. When I finally finished my term overseas and returned home to my family, I knew that the dynamics of our family life would change. By what right could I appear again and impose myself as her supervisor and chief decision-maker, when she had demonstrated superior capabilities in those very areas where I was supposed to lead her?

The next major development that forced me to grapple with the teaching of the Bible on this subject occurred as the result of church involvement. Some ten years ago, I was privileged to have a part, along with a small group of visionary students, in the founding of a church that we had carefully designed to reach the secular, unchurched suburban population in a residential section of the greater Chicago area. From its heroic beginnings in a movie theater, the group grew rapidly into a congregation of several thousands, engendering a sophisticated network of powerful ministries housed in ample physical facilities. But, along with the blessing of growth came the problem of leadership. Since the congregation consisted mainly of new Christians, the formidable leadership potential it represented would require years to develop. In the meantime, the few of us who carried the burden of teaching, training, coordinating, strategizing, and policy making were getting mercilessly burned out. Although we desperately needed to expand the number of elders, we did not have enough qualified men to do so.

It was at that point in time that we realized how effectively God had used the female members of the original team from the pioneer days of the church. Among us were several godly, committed, gifted women, both housewives and career persons, who seemed to have been providentially prepared for the challenges of leadership. But is it biblically legitimate to appoint women as elders? The general feeling among us was against such a move. However, the elders decided to make a decision based not on "feelings" but on the teaching of Scripture. There followed a period of three years devoted to the individual and corporate study of the biblical data and of their various interpretations. This study was supported with practically every book and article written on the subject. Recognized biblical scholars were also consulted, including opponents of female leadership. Some of the result of that long inquiry is contained in this book.

The desire to write a book on this subject was actually prompted by a rather trivial incident that took place a few years ago. I had been invited by a Christian radio station to debate sex roles with a woman nationally known as an ardent proponent of female subordination. What was supposed to be a debate became a vehement female monologue on the necessity for women to remain silent. Every time I would try to say something, the lady would interrupt and engage in a long discourse, oblivious to my helpless gestures signaling to her that

I wanted to place a word in edgewise. Here was a woman with no credentials as a teacher, trying forcefully to teach a huge radio audience and myself that women were not supposed to teach men or assume authority over them. The irony and the frustration of that experience made me hope that what I had not been permitted to state over the air, I might be able to put down in writing some day.

The occasion came with the granting of a sabbatical leave by the institution where I teach, to the administration of which I hereby express deep gratitude for making a semester available for this project. The real motivation behind this work is the realization that many Christian women and men are struggling with the issue of female roles in biblical definition, and that they are willing and capable of becoming directly involved in a discussion that has remained too long the privileged domain of scholars and popular media preachers.

The study-guide format is designed for either individual investigation or group work. I once wrote a book on the Gospel of Mark that is read mainly by mossback scholars like myself. With this one, I will make a deliberate effort to avoid using scholarly jargon and the display of pedantic citations, foreign-language quotes, and references to Hebrew and Greek that discourage lay people from interacting with biblical research. My aim is for the nonspecialized reader to be able to follow the discussion step by step, to evaluate arguments, to consider alternative views, and to arrive at independent conclusions. In the course of the discussion, it will be necessary to deal with some matters of a technical nature. Such considerations will be entered separately in notes gathered at the end of the book. But the bulk of the work will consist of a reverent examination of the texts of Scripture pertinent to female roles.

Since alternative interpretations need to be considered, divergent viewpoints will be cited and dealt with in the notes. A multitude of books written from a perspective opposite to the present study is available. Since it would be impossible to interact with each one of them within the scope of this work, I have chosen one of the most representative among them, James B. Hurley's *Men and Women in Biblical Perspective*, which has been acclaimed as "a magnificent piece of scholarly work" and praised for "its erudition and meticulous reasoning" (back cover). I have found that Hurley has read widely on both sides of the issue and has assembled in his exposition the most significant arguments that are commonly used in support of the authority/subservience pattern for male/female relationships in church and family. For the sake of convenience and brevity, I will dialogue mainly with Hurley's work.

Introduction

T he basic premise of the interpretative method followed in this book is that God's revelation of Himself and of
His will is progressive. His original purpose for mankind was
reflected in the institutions of creation as they are described in
Genesis 1 and 2. However, the introduction of sin through the
fall of Adam and Eve caused the disruption of God's creation
order (Genesis 3 through 11). Then, God established a covenant
with Abraham and his descendants (Genesis 12 to the end of
the Old Testament), in preparation for the new covenant (the
New Testament) which fulfills God's original creation purposes.
This order provides the natural outline for the contents of this
book. It may be summarized with a continuum of three words:

Creation—Fall—Redemption

Everything contained in the Bible relates to the concepts
represented by those three words. *Creation* refers to the divine

initiative that resulted in establishing the cosmos and, within it, a privileged environment that would provide a context for human life. The formation of human beings is presented in the Bible as both the ultimate creative achievement of God and the very purpose of His creative endeavors.

The *fall* refers to the temporary thwarting of divine purposes that resulted from human mutiny against God's will. The fall created multiple disruptions in the original design of creation. Those disruptions affected all aspects of human life and of the environment without destroying them completely.

The word *redemption* points to that aspect of God's nature that refuses to abandon fallen humans to the consequences of their rebellion. Out of love and with persistency, God established a program to reclaim human beings so that His original creation purposes could be worked out in their lives and in their corporate destiny. It was necessary for this redemptive program to be addressed to persons, since human sin and death are very personal realities. For this reason, God introduced this program through the instrumentality of the person Abraham. He and his descendants were intended to prepare the way for the universal expansion of the scope of God's redemption. God's activity in relation to Abraham and his descendants is properly called the "old covenant" since its purpose was to set the stage for a fulfillment that it could only anticipate in faith and foreshadow in its institutions.

The second stage of God's redemptive plan was one of fulfillment realized in what is called the "new covenant." Its intent was to restore the original purposes of creation through the ministry of Jesus Christ and in the new community that He established, the church. This restoration of God's will was initiated at the first coming of Christ. It will find its final consummation at His second coming, when the negative effects of the fall will be completely obliterated and the new community becomes the eternal community.

The concept of paradise is popularly and appropriately used to refer to conditions prevailing at both extremities of history. Paradise evokes the Garden of Eden at the very beginning. It also designates the destination of the redeemed at the very end. "Paradise regained" reclaims what was lost in the beginning. The story of humanity's fall and redemption is contained between the polarity of the two paradises.

This understanding of biblical history furnishes some tools for the conduct of our study. The first tool is an outline that unfolds naturally as we follow the creation-fall-redemption model. The divisions of this simple outline will enable us to raise appropriate questions relative to the topic of our study and to provide the proper scriptural contexts for obtaining the answers. As we ask, "What was the nature of male/female relations in God's original design of creation?" we will search the first two chapters of Genesis for the answer. In order to discover what happened to those relations at the fall, we will address ourselves to the account of the fall in the third chapter of Genesis. We will then have the bulk of the Old Testament in which to trace the nature of female roles in the old covenant. As we turn to the New Testament, we will be able to determine the norms set for female behavior in the economy of redemption, first through the ministry of Christ, and finally in the ministry of the apostolic church as reflected in Acts and the Epistles. This outline will enable us to ask the right questions and to address ourselves to legitimately concordant biblical texts for the answers.

The second advantage to be gained from following the creation-fall-redemption pattern is the discovery of a method of Bible interpretation that emanates from the Bible itself. The lack of an agreed-upon method of biblical interpretation provides the explanation for the confusing multiplicity of contradictory views held by people who have a common respect for the authority of the Bible. Cultural modes, religious traditions, personal biases, contemporary world views, and other influences can all contribute to the shaping of the method of interpretation that one applies to the Bible. As a result, equally well-meaning believers draw divergent conclusions from the study of the same biblical texts.

However, once the distinctive character of each phase of the creation-fall-redemption model is recognized, a coherent method of interpretation emerges from the Scripture itself. The basic tenet of this method is that biblical texts that pertain to each phase (creation or fall or redemption) are to be interpreted within their specific frame of reference. This eliminates the hodgepodge method of taking verses from various time frames and bringing them together to make them say in collage what they do not teach in their original settings. As ridiculous as it seems, this scissors-and-paste approach to the Bible is often popular among the very people who claim to honor the Bible as God's Word. They need to remind themselves that respect of the integrity of each text requires that it be interpreted in relation to its historical setting or its particular canonical context.

Similarly, the distinction between "preparation" (old covenant) and "fulfillment" (new covenant) is of momentous importance for the interpretation of the Bible. Because its function was to prepare and to foreshadow, the old-covenant revelation remained incomplete. It pointed toward a fullness of revelation that it did not yet possess. This fulfillment occurred with the advent of Jesus Christ, who is Himself the fullness of the divine Word. Consequently, for Christians, the ultimate revelation of God is located in the ministry of Christ and of the apostles He commissioned to teach on His behalf.

The implications of this fact become obvious: the New Testament possesses a finality that comprehends and supersedes the teachings and institutions of the Old Testament. Both Old Testament and New Testament reflect different stages of the process of God's revelation, but for Christians the ultimate court of appeal is the New Testament.

Such distinctions, which pertain to the very structure of the Bible, will guide us into maintaining a correct approach to its interpretation. As we carefully proceed with our study, the advantages of this method will become self-evident. It will help control our proclivity to read our own ideas into the text of the Bible and to impose our human traditions upon it. Instead, we should be able to hear the Bible speak a clear message and to have it provide us with the guidance we need.

1

God's Creation Design

Genesis One

In majestic strokes and with cosmic cadences, the first page of the Bible sets forth the story of God's dealings with mankind within the designs of creation. The beginnings of human history are correlated to the beginnings of time itself, and human life is described as the glorious culmination of God's creative endeavors.

The creation account moves swiftly from the development of infinite space to the establishment of the heavenly bodies surrounding the earth and of the earth itself. Then God causes the earth to produce the vegetable kingdom, while land and sea combine to bring forth animal life.

It is precisely at this point that a break occurs in the story. A dramatic change is noted in God's method of creation. Up to this point, God had spoken and His will had come into being. Each phase of creation was accomplished through verbal command, by remote control as it were. But God's approach to the creation of humans is different.

First, there is a pause of deliberation (v. 26) as God determines to make human beings in His image and to assign to them the task of exercising dominion over the earth. It is only after this statement of purpose that God is shown proceeding with the creation of man and woman as beings distinctively invested with His image. This unique feature pertaining to the creation of humans receives further amplification in chapter two of Genesis. But we can already draw some valuable lessons from the account in chapter one.

Genesis 1:26 (RSV)

> "Let us make man in our image, after our
> likeness; and let them have dominion. . . ."

Lesson: God determines to make "man" (singular), but refers to "man" as "them" (plural). The same phenomenon occurs in verse 27. These seeming anomalies are not grammatical errors in the Hebrew text. They reflect the fact that the designation "man" is a generic term for "human beings" and that it encompasses both male and female. This fact is made especially clear in Genesis 5:2 where the word *man* designates both male and female: "He created them male and female; at the time they were created, he blessed them and called them 'man' " (NIV).[1]

Thus, when God declares, "Let us make man in our image . . ." the term *man* refers to both male and female. Both man and woman are God's image-bearers. There is no basis in Genesis 1 for confining the image of God to males alone.[2]

Lesson: Since God is one, the plural self-designation for God ("let *us*"; "in *our* likeness") may seem strange. Various explanations have been offered for this usage. But in the light of

Genesis 1:1–3, where God is described as Father-Designer of the cosmos (v. 1), as nurturing, protecting Spirit (v. 2), and as creative Word (v. 3), the plural pronouns used for God seem to refer to the multipersonality existing within the Triune God. In other words, God in His whole being, with the active participation of the three persons of the Trinity, is involved in the creation of humans. Inevitably, something of the plurality that characterizes the nature of God will be reflected in His image-bearing creatures. That man comes as male and female is the reflection of an essential aspect of the Trinity within the being of God.[3]

Genesis 1:27 (RSV)

> "So God created man in his own image,
> in the image of God he created him;
> male and female he created them."

Lesson: From intention (v. 26) God moves to action, as the moment for the creation of humans arrives. The design calls for "man" (singular) made in His image (note the double parallelistic emphasis on the "image"). Then the divine decree crystallizes into action and (surprise!) the result is not one person but two. The original order called only for the creation of "man"; but because the product had to conform to the specifications of the divine image, "man" inevitably came as male and female.

In other words, the male/female sexual differentiation reflects realities contained within the very being of God and derived from Him as His image. Femaleness pertains to the image of God as fully as maleness. God is neither male nor female. He transcends both genders since they are both comprehended within His being.[4]

Genesis 1:26, 28

"Let them have dominion."

Lesson: There is a very close connection between humans possessing the image of God and the divine mandate for them to have dominion over the earth. By virtue of the fact that they bear God's image, humans are delegated to exercise some of His authority over creation. They are authorized to act as God's commissioned agents.

The repetition of the mandate to rule the earth in verse 28 highlights the importance of this concept for the definition of roles that man and woman play vis-à-vis the created order. Since both man and woman bear the image of God, they are both assigned the task of ruling the earth, without any reference to differentiation on the basis of sex. The text gives no hint of a division of responsibilities or of a distinction of rank in their administration of the natural realm. They are both equally entitled by God to act as His vice-regents for the rulership of the earth. The lack of any restrictions or of any qualifications in their participation in the task implies roles of equality for man and woman.

Lesson: The statement also calls attention to the authority structure delineated in the first chapter of Genesis. Because of His Creator rights, God allocates spheres of authority. He assigns limits to the firmament, to the water, to the earth. He sets boundaries to the process of reproduction in order to preserve the integrity of each genus. He ordains specific environments for the proliferation of each species. He gives the celestial bodies "for signs and for seasons and for days and years." He establishes the sun and the moon "to rule over the day and over the night." He carefully structures the ecological chain between humans and plants, and between animals and plants (vv. 29–30).

He prescribes in detail human rulership over the fish of the sea, over the birds of the air, over every living thing that moves over the earth including cattle and creeping things, and over all the earth (vv. 26, 28).

The whole created universe—from the stars in space to the fish in the sea—is carefully organized in a hierarchy of order that is meticulously defined in Genesis 1. And yet, there is not the slightest indication that such a hierarchy existed between Adam and Eve. It is inconceivable that the very statement that delineates the organizational structure of creation would omit a reference to lines of authority between man and woman, had such a thing existed. Man and woman were not negligible or incidental happenings in the story of creation. They constitute the climactic creative achievement of God. Consequently, the definition of authority structures between man and woman would be at least as important as the definition of their authority over birds, fish, and cattle. This is all the more so since the biblical text describes hierarchical organization as an element intrinsic to creation. But nowhere is it stated that man was intended to rule over woman within God's creation design. The fact that no reference is made to authority roles between man and woman in a text otherwise permeated with the concept of hierarchical organization indicates that their relationship was one of mutuality in equality and that considerations of supremacy of one over the other were alien to it.[5]

Genesis 1:28 (RSV)

"Be fruitful and multiply, and fill the earth and subdue it. . . ."

Lesson: God's procreation mandate (the command to reproduce and to populate the earth) offers an added explanation for the sexual differentiation between man and woman. Its purpose was not for one sex to dominate the other. To the contrary, through their harmonious union, man and woman were to fulfill God's command to establish human rule over creation. Because both man and woman are involved in procreation, both contribute cooperatively to the earth's being subdued. The sexual differentiation was partly intended by God to provide humans with the means to exercise dominion over the earth they were to populate. There is nothing in the text to indicate that the purpose for the sexual differentiation was structural or that it was intended for half of the population to govern the other half. Instead, the sex difference is shown as being instrumental for man and woman to effect together their God-ordained mastery over the earth. In this shared partnership they are equal. Their equality is further emphasized in the second chapter of Genesis, where the additional and even more basic reason for the sexual differentiation is given as mutual fulfillment (Gen. 2:23–24).

To summarize in plain language: In the Genesis 1 account of God's creation design, neither maleness or femaleness connotes a disparity in rank or function. Both man and woman bear the image of God, so that their sexuality is the reflection of different aspects of the Creator's personality. As a result, they both share equally the God-assigned task of creation rulership without any intimation of role distinctions.

Genesis Two

Although it is sometimes called the second creation story, this chapter is not repetitious of the first. It reenforces the teachings of chapter one and provides some new insights. A quick glance at its contents reveals that this text focuses essentially on the final phase of God's creative acts, the forming of man and woman. It is the sixth day of creation being replayed in slow motion and as a close-up, revealing details that serve to amplify and to reaffirm the lessons of the first chapter. Therefore, it is necessary to conduct a careful examination of the key statements of this chapter.

Genesis 2:18 (NIV)

"It is not good for the man to be alone. I will
make a helper suitable for him."

Lesson: By any standards, Adam had it made in Eden. He lived in the midst of a garden landscaped to his taste (v. 8); he had immediate access to all the food he needed (v. 9); he had private swimming pools and streams for fishing and canoeing (vv. 10–14); he owned mountains of fine gold and precious stones (v. 12); he had an occupation to keep him active and in good physical shape (v. 15); and he was given the animal kingdom for leisure and pleasure (v. 19). However, in spite of such opulence, Adam was not fulfilled.

Adam's plight was that while he remained alone, he was only half of the story. The image of God in him, itself the imprint of the triune nature of God, yearned for the presence of his female counterpart without whom there was no fulfillment. This does not mean that fulfillment can only be found in marriage. Quite to the contrary, the Bible teaches that believers who can manage singleness find greater fulfillment in lives of celibate service than if they were married.[6]

The plight of Adam attests to the fact that God has created humans as social beings and that each person needs other persons for self-definition. Human beings are just as complementary to each other today as Adam and Eve were to each other in Eden. In his magnificent solitude, Adam was incomplete—because maleness does not automatically impart completeness. The full expression of humanity necessitated the creation of woman, not as a sublime afterthought or as an optional adjunct to independent and self-sufficient male existence, but as the indispensable counterpart to man in God's perfect creation. In God's very words, without woman creation was "no good."[7]

Lesson: God's resolve to make Adam a "helper suitable for him" reveals an additional imperative for the creation of woman. Adam had been given assignments that required the assistance of a helpmate. According to Genesis 1, he was supposed to "multiply, fill the earth and subdue it." Evidently, these tasks called for a partner ("helper") complementary to him ("suitable for him"). The performance of God's creation mandate required the cooperative participation of both man and woman.[8] From this perspective, man is not more important than woman. Without woman, man would have been helpless and unable to fulfill his God-given mission.

Lesson: There was a time when uninformed teachers of the Bible seized upon the word *helper* to draw inferences of authority/subjection distinctions between men and women. According to them, *helper* meant that man was boss and woman his domestic. Fortunately, the study of the use of the word *helper* in the Old Testament has dispelled such misconceptions. It is now a matter of general knowledge that this Hebrew word for "helper" is not used in the Bible with reference to a subordinate person such as a servant or an underling. It is generally attributed to God when He is engaged in activities of relief or rescue among His people.[9] Consequently, the word *helper* may not be used to draw inferences about subordinate female roles. If anything, the word points to the inadequacy and the helplessness of man when he was bereft of the woman in Eden.

Genesis 2:21–22 (RSV)

"So the Lord God caused a deep sleep to fall upon the man, and while he slept took one of his ribs

> and closed up its place with flesh; and the rib
> which the Lord God had taken from the man he
> made into a woman and brought her to the man."

Lesson: The method used by God for the origination of woman is certainly the most bizarre element of this chapter. Until this point, every living organism had been drawn by God from the *ground*. "Out of the *ground* the Lord made to grow every tree" (v. 9); "out of the *ground* the Lord God formed every beast of the field and every bird of the air" (v. 19); "God formed man of dust from the *ground*" (v. 7). The trees, the animals, and man himself derived their origin from the ground. Once God decided to create woman, it would appear that He would follow the same procedure and make Eve in the same manner He had formed Adam—out of the dust of the ground. A consistent method had been established. Since God wanted to form another human being, all He needed to do was to repeat the same procedure.

Instead, God had recourse to a strange cloning operation that demonstrated beyond the shadow of a doubt the essential identity between man and woman. Had Eve been made out of the ground, there might have existed some ambiguity about the integrity of her human nature. After all, animals had also been taken from the ground. She might have been human but to a lesser degree than man. However, since she was taken from Adam, there was no confusion possible about her full participation in his humanity. She was made from the same material as his own body. From one being, God made two persons.

There is no justification for the derivation of Eve from the body of Adam to be viewed as a sign of her subordination to him. Such a theory might have had a chance of being true if she had been made out of the ground like the plants, the animals, and Adam himself. But the story of Eve's creation teaches

precisely the opposite lesson. Unlike Adam, she was made out
of human flesh already in existence. Humanity twice refined,
she is at least his equal.

Lesson: Some Bible expositors interpret the chronological
primacy of Adam (the fact that he was formed before Eve) as
a warrant for male supremacy over woman. Since such a theory
is neither stated nor implied in the Genesis text, they attempt
to prove their point by resorting to the dubious methods that
we described earlier as biblical collage systems. They try to
force upon the creation text an irrelevant birthright regulation
that they pull out of the Mosaic legislation.[10] Or, turning to the
New Testament, they draw ill-fitting parallels between the preeminence of Christ as "first-born" to Adam as first-formed
human.[11] In either case, not only is the method of such ap-
proaches questionable but the results are so farfetched that the
arguments become self-defeating. There is no evidence in the
creation text for the temporal primacy of Adam to be interpreted as supremacy or rulership. Such a concept is present
neither in the Old Testament nor in the New.[12]

As a matter of fact, a close scrutiny of Genesis invalidates
such a theory. As soon as primal origination becomes a norm
that confers dominance to the first in line, both Adam and Eve
fall under the rulership of animals. According to Genesis 1,
animals were created before humans. Therefore, they should
rule over humans. The absurdity of such a theory is evident.[13]
Temporal primacy of itself does not confer superior rank.

The argument for male superiority drawn from Adam's primacy easily boomerangs against itself. The logic of the sequence of the days of creation moves from the void of
nothingness to increasingly sophisticated modes of existence:
brute matter, the vegetable realm, the animal kingdom, human
beings. If Adam were considered the prototype of humanity,
Eve would qualify as its supreme expression. Her formation
would have brought God's works of creation to completion,

moving from His image made from clay to its perfected du-
plication made from man.

However, neither was the creation of Adam God's practice
shot at making humans, a sort of unveiling of the clay model
that anticipates the formation of woman. Nor is woman the
second sex. Both men and women (not just "all men") are
created equal. And if "we hold these truths to be self-evident,"
it is because they were first taught in the Good Book.

Nowhere in the creation story (or in the remainder of the
Bible) is man commanded to rule over woman, or woman
denied equality with man because of man's original primacy.
We can state categorically that the creation text attaches no
hierarchical significance to the fact that man was created before woman. Its purpose is to show that both man and woman
were uniquely made of the same human substance and that,
as a result, they enjoyed, prior to the fall, a relation of full
mutuality in equality.[14]

Genesis 2:22 (RSV)

"And the rib which the Lord God had taken from
the man he made into a woman and brought her
to the man."

Lesson: God who knows everything knew that the animal
parade was a charade. The text makes this plain when it states
that God brought the animals to the man "to see what he
would call them" (v. 19). In naming the animals, that is, in the
process of determining their definition and their function in
relation to himself, Adam discovered his own uniqueness as a
human being. Like Robinson Crusoe on his island, he was the
only one of his kind. He recognized that the animals belonged
in a different category of living beings, since "there was not
found a helper fit for him" (v. 20).

The naming of the animals served to set the stage for the magic moment of the first encounter between Adam and Eve. In this case, God simply "brought her to the man," without any expectation of his naming her. God knew that Adam would immediately recognize her humanity. The exercise of naming the animals was necessary, but it would be superfluous for the woman. Because the woman was drawn from his being, Adam would identify her instantly as the only other human present in the garden.

God's introduction to Adam of the animals as potential "helper" had a didactic purpose. It was intended as a teaching device. God's presentation of the woman to Adam was conclusive. It had the finality of a wedding rite, as suggested in verse 24. This difference in God's method of introducing the animals and then the woman to Adam emphasizes again the unique identity between man and woman within their essential humanity.

Genesis 2:23

> "At last, this is bone of my bones and flesh of my
> flesh; she shall be called woman because she was
> taken out of man."

Although there is no indication given to the effect that God expected a particular kind of response from Adam as He did when he brought the animals to man, yet Adam proffered a spontaneous expression of recognition the moment he saw the woman. He identified her as his alter ego, much like his female twin. With evident relief he exclaimed, "Bone of my bones and flesh of my flesh." The identity indicated by this phrase is so complete that common usage has adopted it to describe bonds of consanguinity that exist between parent and child rather than marital ties.

But Adam's expression of wonderment reached beyond the

recognition of mere physical identity. He also added a sentence indicating the woman's participation in the fullness of his own humanity. She was wo/man as he was man. She was identical to him with a wee plus, a complementary difference that would combine with his own humanity to make hers complete as well.

In the preceding verse, God was described fashioning Adam's rib into a new creature already designated "woman" (v. 22). Adam did not have to sit down, lay his chin in his hand à la Rodin, and wonder what kind of creature was being presented to him and what he might call her. He knew instantly that the new being was human, and he readily made his own the designation that God had already placed on her in the creative act described in verse 22.[15] With a joyful exclamation, Adam acknowledged his recognition of the deeper meaning of the divine initiative. For him, the creation of woman had marked the completion of humankind.

Adam's exclamation shows that he was in tune with God. He understood that God was presenting him with a being like himself, the companion perfectly suitable for him, his equal.[16] The course of God's creative endeavors had found its appropriate culmination with the making of the woman. She was God's ultimate achievement, taken out of man and made in God's image, the fusing of human beauty distilled to its graceful essence with mirrored divine perfection, the sudden presence that caused the man to marvel in a whisper, "At last!"

Genesis 2:24 (RSV)

"Therefore a man leaves his father and his mother and cleaves to his wife, and they become one flesh."

The conjunction *therefore* links together Adam's statement (v. 23) and the application the author of Genesis derives from it. From the statement that affirms the essential identity between male and female, the author draws universal norms. The foundational nature of this text holds far-reaching significance for male/female relations. The fact that both Jesus and Paul appealed to it in their own teachings testifies to its importance.[17]

Lesson: The marital bond is designed by God to take precedence over concern for the cohesion of a man's original family. He is allowed to break away from the parental circle to establish a new independent relationship. According to this text, the parents' role remains passive. The man takes the initiative to remove himself from his parents; he goes to his bride and joins her in the marital bond. The man's freedom of action in moving away and making his own choices does not reflect a family organization dependent on a father-ruler. Under a strictly patriarchal system, the father-ruler would be the one making those decisions; the new family would be aggregated to the patriarch's family, and it would remain under his authority. The independence enjoyed by the man in getting married and forming a separate "one flesh" entity argues against a patriarchic structure of the family as God's intent for the prefall economy of creation.

Lesson: Singularly, nothing is said of the bride's relationship with her own parents. She seems to be a free agent, in command of her own life. In this verse, the woman represents the stable point of reference. It is the man who moves toward her after leaving his parents. He attaches himself to the woman. She is not appended to his life. He is the one who adds his life to hers as he "cleaves" to her. The procedure of a man's separating from his father and cleaving to his wife reflects anything but a patriarch-dominated society.[18]

The contrast between this creation model and the conditions that resulted from the fall is striking. After the fall, once the patriarchic pattern of societal organization became institutionalized, it was the bride who moved away from her home and who joined her husband within his father's household and under his jurisdiction. Abraham's command to his servant illustrates the point. "Go . . . and take a wife for my son Isaac" (Gen. 24:4, RSV). The same order might have been given for the acquisition of a piece of property, a horse, a chariot, or a pair of sandals. Such a condition is worlds apart from the creation ideal reflected in Genesis 2:24.

Lesson: It should be noted that the "one flesh" designation is applied uniquely to a couple. Parent and offspring are not a "one flesh" entity. As a matter of fact, the parental bond is destined to be broken, since "a man will leave his father and mother" (NIV). But, by definition, the union of the "one flesh" couple is indissoluble. Paradoxically, the blood relationship of parent and child is only temporary, but the union of two strangers becomes permanent and it is designated as "one flesh."

The question arises as to why the biological bonds between parent and child cannot be described as constituting "one flesh." The answer to this question is to be found in the levels of interdependency within each relationship. The concepts of reciprocal dependency and mutuality in equality are intrinsic to the doctrine of oneness. Role differences exist between parent and child that do not exist between spouses. A child is unilaterally dependent on his parents. Normally, his parents are not dependent on him. Because of this disparity, he cannot be treated as an equal by his parents. Therefore, he is not "one flesh" with them and, once he becomes independent, may leave them. However, because husband and wife are mutually dependent in a relationship of equality, they "become one flesh" and their bond is characterized by permanency.

Again, the teachings of this text show that the notions of hierarchical distinctions or differences in rank between man and woman were completely absent in God's creation design.

Genesis 2:25

"And the man and his wife were both naked and
they were not ashamed."

Lesson: Nakedness in the garden is mentioned as a concluding affirmation of the goodness of God's creation. It signified the unhindered freedom of humans in relation to each
other and before God. Community meant a total sharing of
intimacy that rendered the violation and exploitation of another's personhood impossible. The indispensable context for
such reciprocal participation in the goodness of the body was
a relationship of complete mutuality of which sexual union
was only one of the components.

Lesson: The story of the fall in Genesis 3 reveals that the
need for privacy is the result of sin. It is sin that separates
humans from God—hence the need to hide among the trees
(v. 8)—and from each other—the need for fig leaves (v. 7).
Because of His mercy, God protects the rights of sinners to be
spared being discovered in the shame of their alienation by the
gaze of another sinner—He makes them garments of skin and
clothes them (v. 21). The stare of the voyeur gives to one rebel
power over another to which he has no claim. Even in sin,
humans have an equal right to hide the misery of their
separateness.

Whenever the principle of equal rights is denied and one sex
is subjected to another, a natural outcome is the denial of the
right of privacy for the subordinated party. Violation and exploitation ensue. The obscenities of rape, prostitution, and por-
nography are the sinful results of male dominance. To strip a
woman naked and hold her down under the power of a knife,
a fistful of money, or the glare of a camera is the supreme
expression of man's rule over woman. Such rulership was not
a part of God's creation ideal.

To summarize in plain language: The teachings of the second chapter of Genesis confirm and expand upon those of chapter one. They provide a rationale for the essential unity of human nature in male and female. They also show that in God's creation idea, man and woman were expected to enjoy a relationship of mutuality in equality. There is nothing in Genesis 1 and 2 that provides even a hint of a disparity of nature or rank between man and woman.

2

Sudden Death

The Fall—Genesis 3:1–6

Since the tree of the knowledge of good and evil that had been planted in the midst of the garden played an important part in the story of the fall of Adam and Eve, it is necessary to consider its significance.

Genesis 2:16–17 (RSV)

"And the Lord God commanded the man, saying 'You may freely eat of every tree of the garden; but of the tree of the knowledge of good and evil you shall not eat, for in the day that you eat of it you shall die.'"

Lesson: This much-maligned tree was actually placed by God in the garden to benefit Adam. As it stood there, without

39

anyone eating of its fruit, it was already the "tree of knowledge," exercising its teaching function. It was the "tree of knowledge" by reason of the prohibition placed upon it.

Quite often the tree is viewed as a means of testing Adam's obedience, as a malevolent device designed to make him trip, as a trick perpetrated by God upon humans for some mysterious motive hidden within the inscrutable ways of divinity. Such a view is demeaning to the character of God. The definition of the tree shows that it was provided by God to fulfill a positive function. It was the visible reminder to Adam of his humanity and therefore of the necessity to keep himself subservient to God as his Creator.

As a source of knowledge, the tree pointed to two possible paths: the way of happiness and the way of misfortune. The way of happiness was to be found in Adam's discerning the creation rights of God and submitting to them. God had granted Adam total freedom except for one limitation: that his freedom be exercised in dependency upon God. The way of misfortune would open before Adam should he attempt to dismiss God and substitute his will for God's will. Such an attempt to declare his independence from God would alienate him from the source of his existence and result in death.

As a provider of "knowledge," the tree reminded Adam that in order to function properly according to God's design and in order to remain true to his own humanity, he should never aspire to be God. He was made in the image of God, but he was not God. He was made by the Creator, but he was not his own creator. He was to live within the sphere of the sovereignty of God. By its very definition, the tree signaled to Adam the danger of competing with God for supremacy in his own life. The moment he would attempt to substitute his own authority for God's sovereignty, he would become an abnormality, a freak. He would become dehumanized to the point of obliteration ("the moment you eat of it you shall die").

In other words, the tree was a symbol of the one authority

structure that permeates all reality and gives it meaning: there is only one God, and to be truly human is to recognize His sovereignty and submit to Him. The tree provided the warning. Man's rejection of divine sovereignty would result in the loss of his humanity and would ultimately lead to non-being.

Lesson: In the two opening chapters of Genesis, there are only two references to human relationships that involve authority. God is sovereign over humans in that He commands Adam, and places the prohibition of the tree upon him. The other authority line is also clearly spelled out. God tells man and woman to subdue the earth and to have dominion over its animal inhabitants (1:28). This authority structure may be schematized in this manner:

God

Adam and Eve

nature

Conspicuously absent in Genesis 1–2 is any reference to divine prescriptions for man to exercise authority over woman. Due to the importance of its implications, had such an authority structure been part of the creation design, it would have received clear definition along with the two other authority mandates. The total absence of such a commission indicates that it was not a part of God's intent. Only God was in authority over Adam and Eve. Neither of them had the right to usurp divine prerogatives by assuming authority over each other. Any teaching that inserts an authority structure between Adam and Eve in God's creation design is to be firmly rejected since it is not founded on the biblical text:

God
Adam
Eve
nature

Genesis 3:1

> "Now the serpent was more crafty than any of the
> wild creatures that the Lord God had made. He
> said to the woman, 'Did God say, "You shall not
> eat of any tree of the garden" '?"

Lesson: Why did the tempter approach the woman and not
the man? If Adam was boss in the garden, it would have made
more sense to go to him directly. By addressing himself to the
lesser in command, the tempter would be taking the risk of
Adam's interference as the authority figure, or of wasting his
efforts in case Adam refused to participate in Eve's downfall.

On the other hand, if Adam was indeed in command over
Eve, the tempter would get both by obtaining his fall. If the
tempter was facing a hierarchical situation between Adam and
Eve, he obviously addressed himself to the wrong party. But the
fact is that the tempter was not dealing with a chain of command in the garden. Either one of the two would do for the
tempter to gain an entrance into their lives. Adam's willingness
to follow Eve's example and to take of the fruit she gave him
confirms the absence of predetermined roles in the garden.
The alternative pattern of Adam's directing Eve's actions
would have required the temptation to begin with him. This
was obviously not the case.

Lesson: The tempter, being the most clever among his kind,
rightly perceived that the greatest amount of resistance would
come from the woman. So, he concentrated his attack upon
her in the expectation that if she fell, Adam would follow suit.
He was proven right in that Eve put up a good fight whereas
Adam fell instantly, without saying a word. The fact that Eve
faced the tempter's challenge with a greater degree of authority
than Adam confirms the observation that God had not weighted
the advantage of decision-making power in Adam's favor.

Lesson: The most obvious reason for the tempter's attack being focused on Eve was her vulnerability. This vulnerability was not the result of a weaker character, as is often suggested.[1] It had to do with the circumstances surrounding the moment when God gave Adam the prohibition to eat from the tree.

As the dialogue between Eve and the tempter indicates, her knowledge of the prohibition had been obtained secondhand, through the mediation of Adam.[2] At the time when God gave Adam the prohibition, he was alone in the garden. She was not yet in existence. She was still in his chest, twelve inches below the tear in his eye. As a result, she had not heard God give the command. She had not been part of the living experience of God's putting the tree off limits. For her, the prohibition was a matter of theoretical knowledge. She was a victim of the second-generation-believer-fadeout syndrome.[3]

Having received the instruction secondhand, Eve was ill-prepared to discern the tempter's lies. Because Adam had received the instruction directly from God, he was more likely to understand the tempter's intentions. Consequently, in this particular matter, Eve was the less-qualified individual to make the decision. Adam had been directly taught by God. As a late-comer on the scene, she had been taught by Adam. Adam's personal experience of the prohibition made him more competent to face the tempter's onslaught. He possessed the added resource of being able to refer himself back to the moment of encounter with God and to the frightful warning about death that accompanied the prohibition. Shrewdly, the tempter ignored Adam and challenged the less-knowledgeable Eve. Only by reason of specific competency and not because of hierarchical superiority, was Adam better prepared to discern and denounce the tempter's nefarious work. Eve should have referred the matter to Adam from the very beginning. Or Adam could have intervened and taken over as the better-qualified respondent. Instead, Eve faced the challenge alone and she was "deceived."

Again, we note that there is nothing, even in this tragic

phase of the story, to indicate that Adam acted or that he was entitled to act as Eve's ruler.

Genesis 3:4–5 (RSV)

"But the serpent said to the woman, 'You will not die. For God knows that when you eat of it your eyes will be opened, and you will be like God, knowing good and evil.'"

Lesson: In some traditions of Judaism and Christianity, the blame for the fall of humans is placed on Eve. She is portrayed as weak, faithless, easily perverted. By inference, the same guilt and characteristics are extended to all women.[4]

Such notions need to be examined under the microscope of Scripture. The story of the fall describes both Adam and Eve committing the crime that would result in disaster. But a careful investigation of the text shows that the motives and the process of the fall were different for each one of them.

At the moment of temptation, Eve was less informed than Adam. She had missed some significant learning experiences about God that had been available to Adam. Adam had seen God plant a garden and place him in it (2:8). He saw God make plants grow for pleasure, for food, and for knowledge (2:9–10). He saw God make available an abundance of waterways and riches of precious minerals (2:11–14). He received from God the commission to take care of the garden (2:15). Adam received from God the proscription regarding the tree of knowledge (2:16–17) and heard from God Himself the fateful words *evil* and *death* (2:17). Adam knew of God's desire to find him a companion (2:18). Adam knew he was the reason for God's creation of the animals, and he saw God bringing them to him to name (2:19–20). He also knew that God had engaged in an unprecedented act to form the woman (2:21–22), and once he saw the woman, Adam recognized the work of God's hands (2:23).

Adam was the beneficiary of God's revelation available in each one of those events. But Eve was not present at any of them. If she knew about them, it was only through hearsay. There existed between God and Adam a rich history of personal involvements that provided Adam with certainties and evidences not available to Eve. As a result, Eve was a more likely target for the tempter's assault.

The nature of the tempter's approach verifies that he had discovered her weak point: her relative lack of knowledge of God. He goes straight to the jugular in that he calls in question the character of God. Posturing as the liberator who takes sides with humans against a despotic divinity, he imputes to God oppressive motives for His prohibition of the tree. He knows that in this manner he might be able to discredit God in her eyes because of the very fact of her lack of knowledge of God. Even the promises he makes capitalize on Eve's lack of knowledge of God. He promises her immortality and a human impossibility—equality with God.[5]

The greater vulnerability of Eve does not suggest that God had made her stupid, wicked, or inferior to Adam. It resulted from the fact that she did not have access to the revelational opportunities that had enriched Adam's life prior to her existence.

Genesis 3:6 (RSV)

"So when the woman saw that the tree was good for food, and that it was a delight to the eyes, and that the tree was desired to make one wise, she took of its fruit and ate. . . ."

Eve's actions that immediately followed the tempter's en-
ticements attest that she was really convinced that she could
dispense with God. She was thoroughly deceived about the
relevancy of God for her life. Lacking adequate background
experience, she listened to the wrong teacher and was duped
by him.

Acting upon the tempter's inducement, she proceeded to
verify for herself the integrity of the forbidden tree. In the
process, she established some archetypal forms of philosophical
God-denial that have remained to this day.

1. "She saw that the tree was good for food." She jettisoned
revelation and decided to become sole judge of the matter; she
would believe what she could deduce from her own observation. Eve discarded revelation to rely solely upon her own reasoning, thus making herself and her own perception the
ultimate measures of truth. She believed only what she could
see, and she had seen the tempter and she could see the tree.
But, reportedly, she had not seen God. Because of her reliance
on sensory experience as the source of knowledge, she could
perceive only the goodness of the tree. Having dismissed revelation as a source of truth, she was oblivious to the evil potential of the tree. She knew only half of the truth. She was
"deceived."

Eve's approach sets a model for modern empiricism—the
world view according to which only physical reality can count—
and perhaps even for naturalism, according to which the processes of nature contain all the explanations of its existence.
God and revelation are necessary for neither of them. Unwittingly, Eve became the inventor of both.

2. Eve also saw that the tree was "a delight to the eyes."
Pleasure took precedence over revelation and became deter-
minative for conduct. Thus was born the philosophy of hedonism, which advocates the satisfaction of desire and the

gratification of the senses as being the ultimate value of human life.

3. Finally, Eve saw that the "tree was to be desired to make one wise." She already had a source of knowledge available, since God had spoken to Adam, and through him she had access to revealed information. But Eve aspired to becoming "wise" herself. She wanted the knowledge to reside in herself so that recourse to revelation would be unnecessary. In so doing, she would become "like God," knowing everything. This is the position espoused by utopian humanism, an understanding of humans that makes them the measure of all things and results in a self-deluded anthropocentric view of reality.

Alas, Eve does not stand alone in her desire for self-transcendence and equality with God. The belief that humans can dispense with God and the propensity to claim self-determination by ruling God out of consideration are universal evils.[6] Sometimes conscience rejects them, but too often our deeds affirm them. The aberrations attendant to empiricism, hedonism, and humanism touch the lives of each descendant of Eve, and none of us is entirely free from the grip of their power.

Both the dialogue with the tempter and the rationales given in the Genesis text for her subsequent actions indicate that Eve's downfall was not caused by weakness or stupidity, but that it was the result of an aggressive quest for Godlikeness. She fell victim to the misguided exercise of her highest human faculties. She was deceived.

Lesson: Questions have often been raised concerning the Bible's soft interpretation of Eve's offense. On one hand, Adam is made responsible for the introduction of sin and death into the world (Rom. 5:12–14; 1 Cor. 15:22), while Eve's sin is described only as her being "deceived" (2 Cor. 11:3; 1 Tim. 2:14). When God called Eve to account for her deed, she explained, "The serpent beguiled me, and I ate." And she was not questioned further (Gen. 3:13).

Our analysis has already provided some explanation for Eve's being deceived.

1. There is no evidence of God's having revealed Himself to Eve in person before the fall. She had a relatively limited knowledge of Him.

2. She was vulnerable to error because her information regarding the tree was obtained by transmission and not directly from God.

3. She was encouraged by the tempter to doubt God and to play God, as we are all prone to do.

An additional explanation becomes apparent. When Satan assumed the tempter's disguise, he appeared in the familiar form of the serpent—but endowed with supernatural faculties. Not only could he communicate with Eve but, as the content of the dialogue indicates, he displayed supernatural knowledge about God, about humans, about the tree, and about future results of present actions. The apostle Paul notes in one context that "the serpent deceived Eve by his cunning" and that "Satan disguises himself as an angel of light" (2 Cor. 11:3, 14). Eve was deceived in that she was not able to see through the disguise of this supernatural manifestation, masquerading as a benevolent ally. She was led into error by none other than God's archenemy, a powerful supernatural opponent. Adam was led into error by his wife.[7]

Genesis 3:6 (RSV)

"... she took of its fruit and ate; and she also gave some to her husband, and he ate."

Lesson: Adam's conduct throughout the encounter between Eve and the tempter remains a source of bafflement. Some scholars compare the feisty, brainy, confrontational involvement of Eve to the lethargic presence of Adam and draw disparaging conclusions about him. They point out that his sole activity consisted of grasping the fruit offered to him and eating it without raising questions, as if he were in a state of moronic stupor, like a zoo baboon that catches a banana and chews on it distractedly. Such an assessment of Adam is to be rejected for several reasons.

1. Adam was no imbecile. Like Eve, he had been created in God's image. His intelligence was comparable to hers.

2. His answer to God when called upon to account for his disobedience reveals the reason for his seeming passivity during the temptation (3:12). He had been carefully preparing a defense designed to implicate Eve and make her responsible for what happened. Not that he wanted to discredit her, but he knew that there were extenuating circumstances for her disobedience. He had none.

So, Adam allowed Eve to act out his own emancipation fantasy. The fact that he also ate of the fruit attests to the fact that he, like Eve, had yearned for Godlikeness. However, because of his long-standing friendship with God he could not bring himself to take an initiative in regard to the tree. Eve's embroilment with the tempter provided the occasion to participate in her sin and to use her as a pretext, in the hope that the blame would fall upon her.

Consequently, while Eve was getting inveigled by the tempter, Adam refrained from interfering. His silence was one of assent. Premeditation became evident in his readiness to take of the fruit from her hand and to eat it after her without raising any objection.

3. For this reason, the Bible lays the blame for the fall at the feet of Adam. He sinned knowingly. He was aware of the meaning of his defiant gesture and yet participated in the rebellion against God. The less-experienced Eve is said only to have been "deceived." This means that she did not sin willfully. She was fooled into making a fateful error of judgment.

Although both sinned, the fact that God held Adam responsible for the fall and pronounced upon him the sentence of
death should inspire caution to people who are prone to place
all the blame upon Eve. The views that Eve brought sin and
death into the world and that women are inferior beings because of it cannot be documented from the Bible.

To summarize in plain language: The dynamics of the drama
of the temptation do not exhibit the existence of a hierarchical
relationship between Adam and Eve prior to the fall. By virtue
of the fact that Eve was less informed than Adam regarding
the forbidden tree, her sin is described as one of bad judgment.
She was deceived. Because he had been the original recipient
of God's prohibition, Adam's participation in the revolt carried
greater significance.

The Consequences of the Fall—Genesis 3:7–4:19

Before the fall, God had warned Adam that "in the day that
you eat of it you shall die." Once the fall was consummated,
the irruption of death was inevitable. The enemy had been
invited by human rebellion to intrude into God's world. In their
attempt to gain freedom from God, Adam and Eve had befriended the author of death. They had unwittingly triggered
a catastrophic upheaval that invaded all areas of their lives,
and the effects of which were to reverberate through the ages.

The intrusion of death in the midst of life caused devastating
reversals in the relationship of humans with God, within their
own social structure, in their vocational lives, and in the ecological realm. Since our concern in this study is with
man/woman relations, we shall focus mainly on the effects of
the fall on Adam and Eve's relationship.

Genesis 3:11 (RSV)

"He said, 'Who told you that you were naked?
Have you eaten of the tree of which I commanded
you not to eat?' "

Lesson: The fact that God summoned Adam before Eve to
bring him to account for the fall has been interpreted by some
people as a proof that Adam was in charge of Eve in the Garden
of Eden. A careful examination of the text invalidates this
interpretation.

Adam understood very well that God was addressing him
as an individual and not as Eve's representative. Although both
of them had been hiding from God, he explained only his own
behavior and not that of Eve: "*I* heard, *I* was afraid, *I* was
naked, *I* hid *myself*" (v. 10). And as God proceeded to question
him further, he was speaking to Adam himself, pointedly excluding any reference to Eve. Both Adam and Eve had discovered their nakedness as the result of sin, but God singled out
Adam to inquire, "Who told you [Adam, second-person sin-
gular] that you [Adam, second-person singular] were naked?"

The context of God's next question to Adam reveals why God
summoned him first: "Have you [Adam, second-person sin-
gular] eaten of the tree of which I commanded you [Adam,
second-person singular] not to eat?" As the sole recipient of
God's original order prohibiting consumption from the tree,
God asked Adam to give an account of himself. That order had
been given to Adam as a personal prohibition (2:17 is also in
the second-person singular) when Eve was not yet formed. It
was therefore to be expected that Adam would be first in line
to account for his disobedience. God did not ask him any questions about Eve. Her turn would come. She would have to
speak for herself, as a person in her own right.[8]

Genesis 3:12

> "The man said, 'The woman you gave me to be
> with me, she gave me fruit of the tree, and I ate.' "

Lesson: Adam's answer to God confirms the accuracy of our commentary on the previous verse. Adam made no reference to Eve's having eaten of the fruit or to her having eaten of it first. In admitting that *he* ate, he recognized that *he* disobeyed the divine order that had been communicated directly to him and to him alone.

Lesson: However, Adam did refer to Eve in his answer, in a manner that demonstrates the frightful degree of deterioration that affected their "one flesh" relationship as a result of the fall.

Normally, Adam's answer to God's question, "Have you eaten of the tree?" should have been a contrite "Yes." Far from acting as a "spokesman" or as a "priest" for Eve as some claim he was, Adam became her accuser, as he tried to absolve himself by incriminating her. Instead of owning up to personal guilt, he recited a history of the temptation that was intended to hold others, both God and Eve, responsible for his fault. His despicable answer may be paraphrased, "I assumed you knew what you were doing when you gave me a wife, who gave me the fruit, which I naturally ate."

Obviously, this cowardly subterfuge was not acceptable to God. When the promised sentence of death fell upon Adam and Eve, it was pronounced not on Eve but on Adam (3:19).

Genesis 3:13 (RSV)

> "Then the Lord God said to the woman, 'What is
> this that you have done?' The woman said, 'The
> serpent beguiled me, and I ate.' "

Lesson: God turned to Eve and called on her separately to account for herself and for her responsibility in the fall.[9] Consistent with God's approach to Adam, it could be expected that God would have asked Eve the same question He addressed to Adam: "Have you eaten of the tree I commanded you not to eat?" But God knew that He had never given that command to Eve. Any information she possessed about it had been communicated to her by Adam. Consequently, God asked her instead to describe what happened: "What is this that you have done?" Eve readily admitted having been deceived by the serpent without trying to lay the blame on someone else. She might have tried to incriminate God by saying, "The serpent that you created so subtle, he told me to eat, and I ate," or again, "That man you gave me for a husband, he never interfered. In fact, he approved of my action." But, as the saying goes, she stood there and took it like a man.

Genesis 3:15 (NIV)

"[The Lord God said to the serpent,] 'I will put
enmity between you and the woman, and between
your offspring and hers; he will crush your head,
and you will strike his heel.' "

Lesson: The promulgation of the curses upon the serpent and the soil and the judgments upon Eve and Adam constitute the most tragic portion of the Bible (3:14–19). They read like a grim litany of woes dominated by the somber specter of death. The only element of hope this passage contains appears in connection with the mention of the offspring, or seed, of the woman. The promise is given by God that the descendant of the woman will bruise or crush the head of the serpent. This statement is often interpreted as a prediction of the conquest of Satan by Christ. The grip of death upon humans and their world has become so tenacious that the redemptive work of Christ will also entail suffering ("you will strike his heel"). The deliverer from death will Himself experience the ravages of death.

Genesis 3:16

"I will greatly increase your pains in childbearing, in pain you will bring forth children. Your desire will be for your husband, and he will rule over you."

Lesson: There are some obvious omissions in the woman's sentence:

1. Whereas both the judgment upon the serpent (v. 14) and upon the man (v. 17) begin with the "because you have . . ." formula, no such denunciation is stated for the woman. After she readily admitted having been deceived (v. 13), she was not questioned further. It appears that the woes that will befall her are not intended as a special retribution against her. They seem to represent the impact upon her life of changes that will occur in her environment with the advent of death. She does not receive the heavier sentence because she was not guilty of the heavier offense. She had not sinned willfully; she had only been deceived. However, now that death is present, she will also fall under its multiple effects.

2. No "curse" is pronounced on the woman. Although there is obviously a relationship of cause and effect between her sin and her sentence, it is not designated a "curse," as is the case for the serpent (v. 14) and for the ground, which becomes man's own curse (vv. 17–19).[10]

3. The woman is not reproved for having assumed leadership in the garden. Evidently, the content of her initiative was wrong. But no objection is raised to the fact that she, as woman

or wife, took the freedom to instigate action and invite her husband to follow her. Nowhere in the text is there an indication that she is taken to task because she failed to abide in her place within a presumed authority structure.[11]

Lesson: The woman's judgment consists of three statements of facts.

1. Because death has permeated all realms of life, suffering as a preliminary form of death will be allowed to mar the process of life from its very beginning, in childbirth. Adam is told that the ground that once produced fruit of its own will now produce it through suffering. Conversely, human reproduction will be subject to pain. Life will go on after the fall but, because of the pressure of death, it will be a struggle from its very beginning.

2. Probably because the woman was entrusted with the childbearing function, she will yearn for the "one flesh" union that defined the family prior to the fall (2:24). Her desire will be for her husband, so as to perpetuate the intimacy that had characterized their relationship in paradise lost. But her nostalgia for the relation of love and mutuality that existed between them before the fall, when they both desired each other, will not be reciprocated by her husband. Instead of meeting her desire and providing a mutually supportive and nurturing family environment, he will rule over her.[12]

3. As a result of their severance from God, Adam and Eve suddenly found themselves in an environment pervaded with the reality of death. Whereas prior to the fall they were both subject to God who alone had authority over each of them, they now had to cope with new masters. God was the primary source of their lives. Having dismissed Him through rebellion, they became subject to the secondary sources of their lives, each to his or her own primeval element. Adam became subject to the soil from which he had been taken. Eve became subject to Adam from whom she had been taken. Adam's toil will

make him slave to the ground that will eventually engulf his life. And Eve's life will now be ruled by the slave.[13]

The fall had spawned the twin evils of woman's suffering in labor and of man's laboring in suffering. As a result of Satan's work, man was now master over woman, just as the mother-ground was now master over man. For these reasons, it is proper to regard both male dominance and death as being antithetical to God's original intent in creation. Both are the result of sin, itself instigated by Satan. Their origin is satanic. In the "curse," God acknowledges their inevitable reality as the product of the fall, without ever sanctioning them as His design. The "he shall rule over you" should not be viewed as prescribing God's will any more than death may be regarded as God's will for humans. The statement acknowledges the emergence of a disaster that resulted from the very sin against which God had forewarned Adam. Significantly, the redemptive promise of the woman's bearing children and of her seed's crushing Satan immediately precedes the pronouncement on male rulership. Indeed, in the community of redemption, God's original design of mutuality in equality shall be restored.

Genesis 3:17 (RSV)

> "And to Adam he said, 'Because you have listened
> to the voice of your wife, and have eaten of the
> tree of which I commanded you, 'You shall not eat
> of it,' cursed is the ground because of you. . . .' "

Lesson: God sentenced Adam for having listened to the voice of his wife when she induced him to eat the fruit, instead of having obeyed God's command prohibiting it. Adam's fault was not to have listened to his wife, but to have listened to his wife as she countermanded God's order. The idea could be paraphrased: "Instead of acknowledging My sovereignty alone and treating Eve as your mere equal, you followed *her* leading rather than Mine. You both assumed My sovereignty for yourselves." Adam was not reproved for allowing Eve to assume leadership; he was rebuked for having followed her in her state of disobedience to God.[14]

Lesson: The advent of death upon the human scene affected different parts of God's creation in various ways. The serpent and the ground became cursed. The woman died to herself as she fell under the rule of man. But the full force of the power of death fell upon Adam. Although Eve will also experience death, he is singled out in the Genesis text as the one who pioneered the return to the now-cursed ground to become dust.[15]

The ground once ruled by man now rules him and eventually absorbs his being. His domain becomes his cemetery; his throne becomes his grave. And in his pilgrim journey toward the grave, he is afflicted with pain, itself a harbinger of the death that will inevitably devour his being. With the environment cursed and human life doomed, the disaster is complete. The only ray of hope in the statement of the curse appears in relation to the woman. In Adam all die, but Eve, as the mother of the living, shall bring forth life—and from her seed will issue redemption.

Genesis 4:19 (RSV)

"And Lamech took two wives. . . ."

Lesson: God's original marriage ordinance had been for the pair to become "one flesh." The entrance of sin in human life dislocated the "one flesh" union into a ruler/subject hierarchy. It took only six generations from Adam to Lamech for hierarchy to disintegrate into polygamy, the showcase of male dominance in the fullness of its sinful expression.[16]

With the deterioration of the "one flesh" union, the family

became a mini-monarchy. It was inevitable that the male ruler would multiply the number of his female subjects until rulership attained the hideous apotheosis of King Solomon's harem of a thousand wives. The ruler of woman becomes the owner of woman. And the owner of woman becomes the owner of women. Such is fallen man that ownership of a desirable possession inevitably elicits the collector's greed. For a collector, two is better than one, and a thousand better than two.

To summarize in plain language: The fall had catastrophic consequences for the relationship between God and humans. The humans became alienated from God, and each one of them assumed primal dependency on his or her original element. Adam's life became subject to the ground from which he had been taken, and Eve's to the man from whom she had been taken. The ruler/subject relationship between Adam and Eve began after the fall. It was for Eve the application of the same death principle that made Adam slave to the soil. Because it resulted from the fall, the rule of Adam over Eve is viewed as satanic in origin, no less than is death itself.

The fall has displaced God from a position of exclusive sovereignty over Adam and Eve. Their lives have become subject to the forces of death unleashed on the cursed environment.

Creation Design	The Fall	
God	God	nature
Adam and Eve		Adam
nature		Eve

3

The Old-Covenant Compromise

The Dark Side

With the appearance of sin, God's brand-new, shiny, sparkling world of creation became infiltrated with the ugly power of Satan which wove its destructive network of death into the very fabric of life. The "subjection to futility" that resulted from the coexistence of Satan's "bondage to decay" alongside the life-sustaining power of God created an ambiguous situation of tension that will be resolved only at the end of time.

In order to implement this final resolution, God initiated the program of redemption. The active phase of redemption began with God's call to Abraham, the progenitor of a community that would dissociate itself from Satan and opt for God and the life characterized by "the glorious liberty of the children of God." Thus initiated, the program of redemption came to fulfillment in the ministry of Jesus Christ and in the establishment of the new community, the church. The work of redemption

59

will reach final consummation when the new community enters eternity, while everything that has suffered decay under the foul touch of Satan is purged away from God's presence with the annihilation of death itself (Rom. 8:18–25).

In this chapter, we are concerned with the phase of God's redemptive program that is called the "old covenant." This was a time of preparation for a fulfillment that would come only with the ministry of Jesus Christ. Consequently, as a time of transition, the old covenant reflected a dual set of characteristics. On one hand, the effects of the fall were very much in evidence within the old-covenant community. For instance, although they had been chosen by God to be His people and be governed by spiritual leaders and by the Law as given to Moses, the old-covenant people rejected God as their king and set themselves under political monarchs who led them into repeated periods of national apostasy and defeat (1 Sam. 8:8; 10:19; 12:17). This is the dark side of the old covenant.

On the other hand, since God was using the old-covenant people as an instrument to accomplish His redemptive program, there appeared in its life many positive features that prepared the way for the coming of the Redeemer and for the restoration of God's original creation purposes in the life of the new community. This is the bright side of the old covenant.

This situation of tension—resulting from the presence in the old-covenant period of both negative factors derived from the fall, and of positive elements pointing to redemption—is characteristically reflected in male/female relationships. As we now examine female roles in the Old Testament, we will discover that the data fall in either one of two contradictory but parallel currents. One has its sources in the creation design and runs in the direction of the community of redemption. The other current finds its origin in the fall and shows the devastating impact of the satanic perversion of God's creation ideal for male/female relations.

It is the paradoxical coexistence of those two opposite currents that constitutes the old-covenant compromise. Divine commandments enscripturated in the Old Testament were laid down to curb and contain the consequences of the disruptions that accrued from the fall. Out of divine mercy and in anticipation of the new creation, God's word was applied to sinful conditions such as polygamy, patriarchy, adultery, and so on, not to condone or endorse such evils but to limit the damaging effects of those inevitable results of the fall. Likewise was violence curbed. By placing a limit on retaliatory practices (only one eye for an eye, only one tooth for a tooth, only one life for a life, cf. Exod. 21:23–24), the Old Testament legislation attempted to bring under control the murderous tendencies of fallen human nature (cf. Gen. 4:23–24) without endorsing violence as a way of life among humans. Jesus and the texts of the new covenant make it clear that the restoration of the creation purposes of God in the new community has invalidated many provisions of the Old Testament legislation by fulfilling their intent. In the community ruled by love, the law of the talion (Exod. 21:23, 24) becomes superseded and is therefore abrogated (Matt. 5:38–39). The same is true for Old Testament regulations limiting the evil impact of polygamy, patriarchy, adultery, and so on. As will be shown below, such legislations have been rendered obsolete in the new covenant by the total rejection of these practices, as conditions not acceptable within the new community.

We will now examine a few evidences of the negative pressure of the fall on the old-covenant community relative to the role of women.

Polygamy

One of the most vicious perversions of the "one flesh" principle brought about by the fall was the practice whereby males acquired more than one wife. (Technically the word is *polygyny.* However, we are using the more popular term *polygamy,* which means "several marriages.") Once male dominance transformed the creational relationship of equals into one of superior to subordinate ("he shall rule over you"), it was inevitable for wives to be regarded as conveniences and providers of posterity. For the master, the more the better.

This odious practice was adopted by the founders of the old-covenant community. Abraham had several wives and concubines (Gen. 16:3; 25:1–6). His grandsons followed in his footsteps: Esau married three wives (Gen. 26:34; 28:8–9), and Jacob's twelve sons, born of four different mothers, became the progenitors of the twelve tribes of Israel (Gen. 29; 30).

The practice of polygamous marriages persisted through the centuries. Gideon the Judge is reported as having had thirty wives and at least one concubine (Judg. 8:30, 31). King David kept adding wives and concubines to his household despite consequent family troubles that plagued him all his adult life (2 Sam. 3:2–5; 5:13–16; 20:3). His son Solomon established the biblical record with seven hundred wives and three hundred concubines (1 Kings 11:3).

This enumeration might suggest that the practice of polygamous marriage was confined to a few men of privileged position. The fact that bigamy was recognized as a legal fact in the Old Testament indicates that it was practiced by common people as well (Exod. 21:10; Deut. 21:15–17).

The concept of polygamy is irreconcilable with the original marriage ordinance that called for a man to leave father and mother and join himself to his wife (not "wives") so that they would become "one flesh" (Gen. 2:24). Evidently, the radical disruption of this family ordinance as it occurred at the fall opened the door wide to the monstrosity of polygamy as husbands assumed the position of rulers over their wives.[1]

Patriarchal Oppression

As the primal male became ruler of the household after the fall, other breakdowns were bound to take place within the "one flesh" relationship. The fact that the Old Testament word for husband (*baal*) was also used for "master," "owner," and "lord" gives some idea of the status of wives in regard to the "ruling father" (patriarch). The Old Testament is replete with a multitude of reported practices and incidents that describe the unfortunate consequences of the patriarchy for women within the family and in other areas of societal life. They were often treated with little regard for their persons, for their claims, or for their wishes. They were generally excluded from playing significant roles in public functions and in the civic and religious life of the community.

The Old Testament legislation regarding contractual engagements and individual decisions made by various members of the family provides an appropriate illustration of the oppressive nature of the patriarchal system (Num. 30). According to this passage, commitments made by a wife both prior to her marriage and after her wedding could be overruled by her husband (vv. 6–15). There is no indication that a wife enjoyed the same privilege in regard to her husband, or that the husband's abrogation required the concurrence of his wife.

Likewise, the decisions of a young woman living in her father's house could be nullified by him (vv. 3–5). Male offspring do not seem to have been subjected to the same restrictions, and a man's decisions were not subject to the approval of his wife (v. 2). Naturally, once a woman became a widow or a divorcée, she could assume responsibility for her commitments, since she ceased being under the jurisdiction of father or husband (v. 9). However, the legal status of a married woman was that of a child in relation to the ruler of a house. She did

not enjoy a greater degree of independence than her own
daughter (v. 16).

Simply stated, the legal rights of the women of a household
could be arbitrarily exercised by its male ruler without their
consent and against their will.[2] This lack of reciprocity in the
decision-making process, and the subjection of the women to
the master of a household, made possible the inhumane family
structure where a father could sell his daughter as a servant
(probably to double up as a concubine) under religious sanction, as if she were a piece of his property (Exod. 21:7).

Double Standard on Adultery

The "one flesh" union of the creation ideal is predicated
upon the principle of an exclusive relationship of sexual intimacy between spouses. Obviously, the cooperation of each
spouse is necessary for a relationship committed to monogamy
to be successfully maintained. The ideal of mutuality in equality provides the best possible conditions for the natural implementation of the "one flesh" commitment. In such a
relationship, both spouses have a share of responsibility in generating and sustaining a climate conducive to mutual fidelity.

However, the difference of status between men and women
that resulted from the fateful "he shall rule over you" of the
fall would inevitably produce inequities in the area of sexual
behavior. Such inequities are indeed reflected in the old-
covenant legislation on adultery, which is summarized in
Deuteronomy 22:13–30.

Since a married man was ruler over his wife, her unfaith-
fulness violated his property rights.[3] It was a crime punishable
by death. Therefore, an adulterous wife was put to death (v. 22).

Since a married woman was not ruler over her husband,
she had no rights over him. Consequently, his adulterous behavior did not constitute a crime against her. As a result, the

old-covenant law prescribed no penalty against an unfaithful husband. His extramarital relations were not considered an offense against his wife.

A man was subject to capital punishment if he had sexual relations with a married or betrothed woman, since he violated his male neighbor's possession (vv. 22–27). However, the violation of a single woman was not punishable by death, since she was not the possession of a husband (vv. 28–29).

A man, even married, pursuing extramarital relations with a prostitute or an unattached woman was subject to no penalty, since he was not violating any man's daughter or wife.

This one-sided definition of adultery gave enough latitude to male permissive practices for prostitution to become a persistent affliction in the history of the old-covenant people. Although the Old Testament contains numerous references to harlots and to harlotry as an image for religious apostasy, nowhere is the practice of prostitution explicitly condemned or prohibited. The warnings concerning the evils of prostitution (Prov. 7; 23:27–28) and the few restrictions placed upon it only emphasize its prevalence in Old Testament times. Such restrictions included prohibitions of sacred or temple prostitutes (Deut. 23:17), of the wages of prostitution presented as offerings (Deut. 23:18), of daughters of priests becoming prostitutes (Lev. 21:9), of fathers forcing their daughters into prostitution (Lev. 19:29), and of daughters becoming prostitutes when they were still in their father's house (Deut. 22:21).

Trial by Ordeal

One of the most grievous manifestations of the double standard that characterized marriage litigations in the old covenant concerns a practice that was common among ancient people, the trial by ordeal. A case law dealing with such a trial is described in Numbers 5:11–31.

The procedure concerns a woman suspected of adultery by her jealous husband. The alleged offense cannot be attested by witnesses, since the presumed offender was not caught in the act. The trial is conducted by a priest who has recourse to a cereal offering intended to bring the case to God so as to make Him the judge in the matter. The outcome of the trial is to be considered as a verdict coming from God. This practice illustrates again the unequal treatment administered to wives in the context of male rulership.

1. A guiltless wife was at the mercy of a hateful or unjustifiably jealous husband. She was defenseless in any refusal to expose herself to opprobrious and demeaning inquisitions.

2. Once a wife was declared not guilty, there was no provision made for compensating her for the abuse suffered.

3. There was no punishment meted out to the unjustly suspicious husband for his accusations.

4. Only husbands had access to this procedure. A wife who suspected her husband of misconduct was helpless. She had no recourse in overt cases of adulterous behavior on the part of her husband, much less for behavior arousing suspicion.

5. The final statement of the text summarizes our point: "The man shall be free from iniquity, but the woman shall bear her iniquity" (v. 31, RSV). This was the privilege of the ruler.

Divorce Legislation

As might be expected, when the "one flesh" union breaks down into a ruler/subject relation, the subordinate member may be discarded and replaced with ease. The Old Testament illustrates this point with several cases of husbands who put away their wives (Gen. 21:8–14; Judg. 14:20; 15:2; 1 Sam. 25:44; and so on), and with references to the minimal procedure required for a man to effect a divorce (Isa. 50:1; Jer. 3:1, 8).

The latter find their point of origin in a piece of Old Testament legislation outlining the simple method to be followed by a husband divorcing his wife (Deut. 24:1–4). Because of the inequities intrinsic to the patriarchal system, the divorce statutes were overwhelmingly one-sided in favor of the husband. He alone had the power to initiate a divorce. Husbands could divorce their wives at will, but the reverse was not possible. There existed no procedure and there were no grounds for a married woman to press for divorce. The cause for its instigation by husbands was so vaguely defined—"because he has found some indecency in her" (v. 1), or if her second husband "dislikes her" (v. 3)—that any pretext could be used to dismiss an unwanted wife. The divorced woman had no recourse for appeal or for financial support from her former husband. She was thrown out with a bill of divorce in her hand.

Jesus gave an objective assessment of this practice and of its causes when He told His contemporaries that Moses had made the divorce concession to his people because of their "hardness of heart," and that divorce was incompatible with God's creation ideal for the "one flesh" family (Matt. 19:3–8).

Moses' legislation on divorce was actually provided to protect wives from the arbitrariness of their husbands. The intent was to slow down the divorce rate by requiring a cause for divorce, as minimal as it may appear now, and by requiring that a legal document be given to the divorced wife so that she could account for her married years. When he laid down this legislation, Moses was in fact trying to contain the depredations caused by divorce. As permissive as it may seem, the intent of the legislation was to curb the abusive practice and reduce some of the damage it caused.

The necessity for such a concession in the Mosaic Law illustrates the vicious use to which the rulership principle was put by men, as it gave them the power to dispose of their wives without concern for their desires and without retribution for their own injustice.

To summarize in plain language: In its time, the old covenant provided the best possible situation for God to establish a community that would be responsive to His will. However, the depredations caused by the fall were so severe that they defiled the life of the covenant people in some of its most sacred expressions. The marriage ordinance provides a case in point. All the advantages of divine revelation and of moral guidance available to the old-covenant people did not suffice to help them recover the reciprocity that had prevailed before the fall. Man continued to rule over woman under the cover of a depraved family structure that dehumanized both.

The Bright Side

Fortunately, the dismal conditions described in the previous section reflect only one aspect of the old covenant. Indeed, the gradual unfolding of God's redemptive program needed to take into realistic account the degraded situation that had resulted from the fall. Consequently and by necessity, the old-covenant period was a time of partial accommodation to sinful realities as a way of achieving their resolution in the new covenant.

However, because the old covenant was a time of preparation for the new age, it also contained several elements that bridged the gap between creation paradigms and their anticipated restoration in the new covenant. These positive elements of the old covenant were the lingering effects of the goodness of God's creation ideal, pointing to the new creation in Christ. As might be expected, relations between the sexes were included among such signs of a redeemed future. The old covenant gave many indications that the time of male rulership would come to an end, and that men and women would be able to enjoy again the parity for which they had been created. We will adduce two kinds of evidence from the Old Testament that pointed in this direction. The first concerns the assumption by women in the old covenant of positions of rulership in religious, civil, and domestic life. The second is the recovery of the goodness of monogamous, equalitarian marriage.

Female Authority in Religious Life

The prophetic ministry was the highest religious function in the old covenant. The priest entered the presence of God on behalf of the people, but the prophet went forth from the presence of God to the people. The people spoke to God through the priest, but God spoke to the people through the prophet. The mantle of divine authority was worn by the prophet more than by the priest. Interestingly, while the old-covenant legislation made no provision for the appointment of female priests, several female prophets ministered during that period.

The priesthood had originally been appointed through the legislation laid down by Moses, who was himself a prophet (Deut. 18:15–19; 34:10). Later, it became the duty of prophets to act as correctors to the priests and to stand in judgment against them and their temple practices in times of spiritual and cultic defection (Isa. 1:10–17; Jer. 7; Amos 5:21–27; and so on). Prophets had authority to appoint kings, to denounce their wrongdoings, and to pronounce their demise (Saul and David, for example). A major segment of the biblical record consists of the authoritative message of the prophets. Only a prophet could stand and declare, "Thus saith the Lord. . . ."

Although statistically the majority of the old-covenant prophets were male, the Bible refers to several prophetesses and describes them as exercising the same kind of authority in the religious sphere as their male counterparts (Miriam, Deborah, Huldah, and so on). The story of Huldah will suffice to illustrate our point.

Desiring to know the fate of his nation, the reformist King

Josiah commanded the high priest and several of his notables to inquire of the Lord on his behalf. They could have gone to either Jeremiah or Zephaniah, both of them contemporaries of King Josiah. Instead they went to the prophetess Huldah, herself the wife of a second-rank temple officer. She delivered to them a scathing denunciation of the religious corruption of the nation and a powerful prediction of doom that motivated the king to effect profound changes in the religious life of the people (2 Kings 22:11—23:25). Thus, the spiritual leadership of a woman used by God to teach His will to the king, to the high priest, and to her contemporaries affected the history of the whole nation.[4]

Female Authority in Civil Life

The Old Testament recounts the stories of several women who have altered the course of history (Rahab, Esther, Ruth, Athaliah, and so on). We will focus on the case of Deborah, which is found in the Book of Judges, chapters four and five.

The story begins during one of the down phases of the apostasy-oppression-repentance-deliverance cycles, when the people were "crying to the Lord for help" (Judg. 4:3). They indeed had much to cry about, since their enemies had been oppressing the northern part of their country for twenty years, and they were doing it with an armored cavalry of nine hundred chariots of iron.

The people were facing three kinds of difficulty: religious disintegration, military defeat, and lack of competent political leadership to resolve the troubles of the nation. God's answer to this desperate plight in that male-dominated patriarchal society was a woman. Her name was Deborah (which means "honey bee" in Hebrew). As prophetess, she assumed spiritual leadership; as "judge" she exercised judicial and political power;

and eventually she became involved in directing on the field the strategy for a decisively victorious battle.

Probably because she was a spokesperson for God as a prophetess, Deborah served also as a political guide and as a one-woman supreme court (4:4–5). As her leadership affirmed itself, she became disturbed at the unchallenged domination of her people by their enemies and felt called to take the matter into her own hands. The commander in chief of the Israelite army was a powerful fellow by the name of Barak (which means "lightning" in Hebrew). But he was too fearful of the enemy to consider any military action against them.

Deborah summoned Barak to come to her and he readily complied with her request. As General "Lightning Bolt" Barak, dressed in full military regalia, came lumbering into the presence of Judge "Honey Bee" Deborah, one of the most surprising dialogues contained in the Bible took place. Deborah told the general that he should go to fight a battle at a specific location. She promised him that God would grant him the victory. The general refused to move unless Deborah accompanied him— to which she readily agreed.

On the day of the battle, Deborah gave a final pep talk to the still-timorous Barak and signaled the moment for the engagement to begin (4:14). Not only did the battle end in total victory for Deborah and Barak, but as a final irony, the fleeing enemy commander was killed by Jael, another woman. The story was immortalized in a very ancient but beautiful poem (Judg. 5) that lays the victory at the feet of two women, Deborah and Jael (vv. 6–7, 12–15, 24–27). And the land was at peace for forty years.

Female Authority in Marital Life

If a woman were to assume spiritual or civil authority over a whole nation, it stands to reason that her husband would

also come under her authority, since he would be part of the
people under his wife's jurisdiction.[5] Even more specifically, the
Old Testament shows instances of wives who took over the
leadership of their households, so that their husbands followed
their orders and advice. Thus, Abraham, the man presented in
Scripture as the model of faith for all believers, obeyed Sarah
several times (Gen. 16:2, 6; 21:10–12)—even as Sarah is cited
in the New Testament as an example of wifely obedience (1 Pet.
3:6). As a case study of female authority in marital life, we will
now look at the record of a wife who authoritatively overruled
her husband's decisions, and who took an independent course
of action designed to reverse them, all under God's blessing.
The story is found in 1 Samuel 25.

There was this wealthy but ill-mannered rancher who had
a beautiful, intelligent, and sensitive wife. He was called Nabal
(which means "fool"), probably in deference to his reputation
as an ill-tempered bully. His wife's name was Abigail, which
means "source of joy." There was also David, roaming the coun-
tryside with his men and getting desperate for a square meal.
In exchange for protection afforded to Nabal's flocks and personnel, David politely requested some provisions for his men.
Nabal flatly and insultingly refused to practice hospitality. Abigail learned that David and his men were preparing to attack
the estate as a result of her husband's obduracy. She hastily
devised a scheme to avert disaster.

Unbeknownst to her husband, she sent several loads of supplies to David including lamb meat, wine, and sweets. Then
she surreptitiously went out in the country to meet him. Predictably, David and Abigail became very impressed with each
other. She apologized profusely for her husband's stupidity.
David exclaimed, "Blessed be the Lord, the God of Israel, who
sent you this day to meet me!" (v. 32, RSV) and thanked her for
her discreet initiative in coming to him. Upon returning home,
Abigail waited for her husband to recover from a drunken revel

and brought him up-to-date on the dangers that had almost befallen him. Shortly after, "the Lord smote Nabal; and he died" (v. 38). When David learned that Nabal was dead, he praised the Lord and married the beautiful widow.

Obviously, the narrator of this account did not find it objectionable for a wife to take it upon herself to revoke her husband's orders, to dispose of household supplies without his permission, to go secretly in the country to placate a young and handsome warrior, to praise him obsequiously when her husband had called him a runaway slave, and to try to win his favor when her husband had ruled him out of consideration. David, as designated king (1 Sam. 16:1–13), commended Abigail for having acted independently, in contradiction to her husband's expressed will, and told her, "I have hearkened to your voice" (v. 35). David recognized Abigail's independent behavior as being in conformity to God's will (vv. 32–34). And when God Himself intervened, He did not punish Abigail for disobedience to her husband, but released her permanently from Nabal's tyranny.[6]

Such stories demonstrate that women were not always "subordinate authorities"[7] in old-covenant times. Men could also be subordinated to their decisions. The tension that exists between such positive views of female roles and the male-rulership principle of the fall becomes sharper with Old Testament perceptions of the goodness of monogamous marriage as a relation of mutuality in equality. Two of these will be considered.

The Song of Solomon

Beyond matters of composition, sources, purpose, and interpretation of the "most beautiful song" (which is what "Song of Songs" means), this poem—The Song of Solomon—is to be noted for two features. The first is obvious in that the Song consists of a graceful, emotional, highly lyrical celebration of conjugal love. The precise meanings of many of its symbolic expressions escape us today, since references are made to contemporary mystical and mythical imageries, to erotically suggestive parallels drawn from the realm of nature, from geographic locations and architectural landmarks. But enough of the Song is intelligible to recognize in it a strong affirmation of the enjoyment of human sexuality in the context of complete mutual freedom and reciprocity.

The setting is similar to the pristine goodness of creation in its Edenic innocence, when a world untainted by evil was sparkling, bejeweled with primal dew. The man and the woman frolic in complete abandon, free spirits cavorting through gardens, vineyards, and green hillsides as they seek each other's desire and fulfillment. Although many subtle games of love are being played throughout the poem, there is never any hint of manipulation, of domination, or of disparity in rank and status. The terms of endearment reflect deference and reciprocity. Admiration for the beauty of the human body is mutual, and access to the physical being of each other is unhindered. The leitmotif of the song summarizes well its content: "My beloved is mine and I am his."

The second feature of the Song is less obvious because it resides in what the poem does not say. As captivating as the love story between Abigail and David may have been, it contained a tragic flaw. Both protagonists were presented as strong, spirited, self-reliant individuals. Those qualities were precisely the cause of their attraction to each other. David acknowledged the boldness and the rightness of Abigail's initiatives, and he "hearkened to her voice." But as romance found consummation in marriage, this reciprocity was lost and their relationship became defiled by the sin-generated principle of male rulership. As she received David's proposal, Abigail is reported to have "bowed with her face to the ground, and said, 'Behold, your handmaid is a servant to wash the feet of the servants of my lord.' " And the text adds that "David also took Ahinoam of Jezreel; and both of them became his wives" (1 Sam. 25:41–43, RSV). Here a beautiful love story is sullied by male dominance and its nefarious effects.

Such a tragic flaw is never present in the Song of Songs. If mentioned at all, the Solomonic harem is removed far beyond the horizon of the poem. The admiring, supplicant, wooing tones of the male protagonist do not match his rank of king and assumed male privilege. There is no coercion or violation of the woman's will. The numerous names and lovers' designations are endearing and tender. There is no manipulative reference to titles, to power, to authority, and to thrones. The humble estate of the woman is never held against her. God's *shalom* permeates the whole story.[8]

We believe that the Song of Solomon was included in the canon of Scripture because it celebrates conjugal love in its generic state. It miraculously catches a glimpse of the divine intent for the ways of man and woman together, above and beyond their fateful separation as ruler and subject. As such, it may be considered a poetico-dramatic commentary on the original charter of God's definition of male/female relations found in Genesis 2:23–24. The fact that the poem is signed by the most notorious polygamist in biblical history can only enhance the miraculous nature of its message.

The Strong Wife

The Song of Songs describes the relationship of intense intimacy that characterizes a couple united in the embrace of equalizing love. However, it does not address the issue of the outworking of such a relationship in daily domestic life. Fortunately, there is in the Old Testament another poem, this one authored by a woman, that describes in some detail the roles held by a capable woman in an environment of marital trust and harmony.[9] This text will be surveyed verse by verse to draw its significance for our topic. Our comments should be followed with Bible in hand, opened at Proverbs 31:10–31.

Verse 10. The literal meaning of "good wife" in the Hebrew text is "woman (capable) of strength." Appreciation for such a wife is comparable to the desirability of the "wisdom" that cannot be purchased for all the treasures of the world (*see* Job 28:12–19).

Verses 11–12. Her husband has confidence in her. He respects her judgment and her independent decisions since she has proven herself competent and beneficial to the household.

Verses 13–14. She is a good businesswoman, whose range of activities extends far beyond her house. She keeps her house well supplied with materials and food.

Verse 15. She is diligent and competent in the management of resources, personnel, and responsibilities in her house. She is the provider of food for the household.

Verse 16. She has funds available so that she can deal in real estate and invest in productive ventures. "Fruit of her hands" refers to earned income that she can invest.

Verse 17. She is confident in her own strength. She gets ready for action and flexes her muscles ("girds her loins" and "makes her arms strong," RSV). The word *strength* used in this passage (*'az*) is the one used numerous times for God's strength, especially in the Psalms (21:1, 13; 28:7, 8; 29:1, and so on), and for strength communicated by God to His people (for example, 29:11; 68:35; 84:5). The expression *to gird one's loins* is used of males ready to accomplish some demanding task (1 Kings 18:46; 2 Kings 4:29; 2 Kings 9:1; Jer. 1:17; and so on).

Verse 18. She is a successful businesswoman and works late hours. She manages for herself an independent career.

Verse 19. She also handles domestic skills competently.

Verse 20. She is sufficiently affluent to extend herself to the poor and thus fulfill a major concern of Old Testament spirituality.

Verse 21. She provides well for her household and protects it against adversity.

Verse 22. She takes good care of herself, dressing with dignity and refinement.

Verse 23. This is the only reference to the "activities" of the husband! The implication is that he is well respected in the community because of his wife's industry and competency. (*See* vv. 11–12.)

Verse 24. She is a "working wife" as she combines career and housekeeping. She is her own salesperson who deals directly with the merchant to whom she takes her goods.[10] Her home is the base for her business operations. In an economy of cottage industries, there were no shops, factories, offices, and hospitals in the modern sense of those terms. However, her professional activities take her occasionally away from her home.

Verse 25. She rejoices at the confidence and security that she derives from her labor and her independent achievements. Note again the use of male traits to describe her, as in verse 17.

Verse 26. She is gifted with wisdom (*see* the "value of wisdom" in v. 10 above), so that she can dispense "faithful instruction" (NIV). The businesswoman/housewife can also be an able teacher.

Verse 27. She is the vigilant supervisor of her household. The total list of her accomplishments indicates that she is the one responsible for making the managerial decisions affecting the life of her home.

Verse 28. She has good relationships with the other members of the family, with her children and husband.

Verse 29. Her husband affirms the superior qualities of his wife, and he acknowledges that there are many other women like her. Although she is the best among them, many other women can boast the same status and achievements.

Verse 30. The secret of her success is not external beauty, which is only skin-deep, but the fact that she is a godly person.

Verse 31. Give her the rights that belong to her! She should enjoy the benefits of her labors (*see* v. 16 above) and receive credit for her achievements. She has a right to receive the same respect from the community as her husband does. She is to be praised "in the gates" (RSV), as he is known "in the gates" (v. 23).[11]

This text extrapolates at the level of everyday life the implications of the relationship described in the Song of Songs. It anticipates the restoration of the original pattern of husband/wife relationships that prevailed in creation prior to the fall. It also accomplishes a verse-by-verse demolition of the male-rulership system that issued from the fall, by showing God's ideal for women—to share fully in the responsibilities pertaining to the governance of community life in the family.

To summarize in plain language: The mixture of negative and positive elements make of the old covenant a time of compromise between the pressures of the creation ideal and of the fall. Signs of both are present in an uneasy accommodation that marks the passage from the disastrous effects of the fall to the new age of redemption, when God's purposes of creation are restored so that all things are made new.

4

The New Creation in Christ

As we turn to the New Testament, we discover that a victorious proclamation rings through it like a clarion call: Christ has brought about a "new creation; the old has gone, the new has come!" (2 Cor. 5:17, NIV). The new age has dawned with the advent of Jesus. He has inaugurated the fullness of redemption. He has created the community of reconciliation, God's family: the church.

The fundamental difference between the old-covenant people and the new-covenant family is the reversal of the effects of the fall within the latter. Inside the old community there was the tension of two contradictory currents, running parallel but working against each other. In the new community peace prevails. The effects of the fall are being conquered by Christ, and the line of continuity that flows from God's creational design determines the life of the church. As a result:

Where there was the loss of Eden and alienation from God, there is a family of reconciliation where all may call God their Father (Gal. 4:4–7).

Where there was terror in the face of the great violator of Eden, death itself, now there is the quiet assurance of eternal life (John 11:25–26).

Where work had been a curse, it now becomes a blessing (2 Thess. 3:12–13).

Where bread was eaten in hardship and sorrow, it now becomes a sign of God's bounty to be shared together (Acts 2:46).

Where the curse had predicted "he shall rule over you," the gospel ordains that "husbands should love their wives as their own bodies" (Eph. 5:28, RSV).

Although it is true that the dark, sin-polluted current from the fall is still running during the church age, it exists in the world outside of the new community. If there is a tension for the new-covenant people, it is the tension between the kingdom of God in the church and the kingdom of Satan in the world, not a tension within the community itself, as was the case for the old covenant. And the promise of the first coming of Jesus is that the elimination of the dark side will become complete at His second coming, when Satan and death are annihilated and the sin-defiled world is replaced with the new heaven and the new earth (2 Peter 3:13).[1]

Having said this, we must quickly admit that there are occasions when the old tension between the two currents might appear within the life of the church. Whenever the church fails to model the original creational purposes of God and becomes "worldly" in that it accepts within its life elements of the fall that still prevail in the world, it slips back into a compromise situation and loses something of its integrity as the new com-

munity. Therefore, it is very important for all aspects of the life
of the church to be brought into conformity with the will of
Christ, who laid its foundations through His ministry and
teaching.

Since our concern in this study is to face the issue of the
impact upon female identity of the new creation in Christ, we
need to raise the following question: Did Jesus base His definition of male/female relations in the creation ideal, or in the
realities of the fall—or did He settle for some kind of compromise between the two?

It would have been easy for Jesus to derive His directions
from the institutionalized traditions of the environment in which
He lived. This environment was no longer the old-covenant
compromise milieu as we found it in the Old Testament. Long
before Jesus' time, the old Hebrew religion of Moses and the
prophets had been replaced by a new religion called Judaism,
which was based on the traditions of the scribes and Pharisees,
frequently mentioned in the Gospels as the opponents of Jesus.
In this new religion, the dark side of the old-covenant compromise had taken over almost completely. Women were generally viewed as being responsible for the evil in the world.
They were strictly segregated from the social and religious life
of their communities as inferior and unteachable creatures,
and they were mercilessly oppressed within the seclusion of
their fathers' or husbands' homes.[2]

Jesus' understanding of His mission led Him in the opposite
direction. Jesus was not a radical by temperament. His disposition was to accept, to forgive, and to heal gently. He did
not have the personality of an assertive revolutionary firebrand.
Yet he took a firmly countercultural stance on many issues, not
because of a volatile, reactionary character, but because His
mission was to oppose that which violated the will of God.
Consequently, on this issue of female roles and feminine identity, Jesus felt compelled by His convictions to affirm creation

and to repudiate the fall. To answer our question above, Jesus
solidly based His definitions of persons and His directives for
male/female relations in the creation ideal. As a result, He
fearlessly demonstrated in His actions, teachings, and example
His rejection of the male-rulership principle. There is much
evidence in the Gospels for Jesus' special concern for the restoration of women to the position of human dignity that Eve
occupied in creation, before the fall. We shall now survey some
of this evidence.[3]

Unnoticeable Women

Compared to literary works of the same epoch, the Gospels
contain a relatively high number of references to women. Except for vulgar ancient comedy pieces, the Gospels are unique
in presenting a great variety of situations that involve women.
Remarkably, not in a single case is a woman denigrated, re-
proached, humiliated, or cast into one of the lewd stereotypes of the day. Males, especially establishment-type, power-
wielding men, are often the object of severe castigations, but
not women. Jesus' treatment of them is always solicitous and
supportive, as if He were assuming responsibility toward them
for a long history of derogation and compensating for it with
an outpouring of divine love.

Predictably, Jesus sees the unnoticeable women—the little
gray shadows who make themselves invisible so that every-
where they can blend into the background, the inconspicuous
silent sufferers who can only think of themselves as negligible
entities destined to exist on the fringes of life. Jesus sees them,
identifies their need and, in one gloriously wrenching moment,
He thrusts them to center stage in the drama of redemption
with the spotlights of eternity beaming upon them, and He
immortalizes them in sacred history.

Peter's Mother-in-Law—Matthew 8:14–15

Jesus entered that house with his close apostle-friends (*cf.*
Mark 1:29). It must have been a most important meeting between the Lord and His first disciples. Yet we do not know
anything of what Jesus did in that house except one. Jesus
ministered to a woman's need. Her fever was called "fire in
the bones" by the rabbis. As Jesus took her hand and assumed
her suffering (*see* 8:17), she witnessed to His power in two
ways. She "arose," thus pointing to His resurrection power,[4]
and she immediately made herself available to Him as a disciple by ministering to His needs.

The Woman with a Hemorrhage—Mark 5:21–34

All this woman wanted was to steal the blessing and fade
away. In vain she had spent all her substance to retain the life
that was ebbing out of her. She knew she was a terminal case.

Jesus was a powerful man. But He was surrounded with all
those important people, the ruler of the synagogue and his
entourage. This woman had no rights, no claims, and hardly
any hope. She wanted to touch Him, steal the blessing perhaps,
and quietly slip away unnoticed.

She touched, and instantly two things happened. She was
healed and she was discovered. She fell to the ground, consumed with grief, wishing she had chosen death instead. But
Jesus was leaning toward her, and He lifted her in His arms
calling her His "daughter." He gave her His love and sent her
away whole.

The Daughter of Jairus—Mark 5:35–43

This was only a child and a girl, at that. She had been
comatose, precariously crisscrossing the line between life and

death (in Matt. 9:18 she is reported by her father as having already died). With the mortality rate as high as it was among the young, she was doomed to be one more statistic, had they kept any. But Jesus went. They told Him it was too late, because she had died. Jesus went on. They mocked Him. He kept going. When He saw the body, He took her hand. It must have felt so tiny and cold in the Carpenter's powerful grip. He wanted to assume her death and to communicate His life to her. She "arose." In the excitement, He noticed that the little girl was hungry. So He told them to hurry up and give her some lunch. Then He left.

The Widow of Nain—Luke 7:11–17

There was this widow in a remote little town nestled in the wrinkle of a hillside in Galilee. She and her son were the only survivors of her family. But he had died, and they were taking him to the same place where her husband had been buried. The procession was outside the gate, almost gone when Jesus arrived. He had seen many funerals. People died all the time. But then, among the wailing women, Jesus saw the mother. He recognized her by that special sorrow that crushes a hurt mother with haggard, voiceless despair. And suddenly, it became imperative that she stop weeping. With the command, "Arise!" He gave the bewildered son back to his mother, as the great prophet had done long before. And they all knew that God had a special love for the little widow with one son in Nain of Galilee.

The Crippled Woman—Luke 13:10–17

After a synagogue service, Jesus discovered that behind the women's partition there was a woman who had heard Him without seeing Him. The problem was not just the partition but the fact that she was bent over and could only see the ground a few feet ahead. But Jesus saw her and He felt her pain in His own body. Since eye contact was not possible, Jesus laid hands upon her and freed her from the power of evil. On the Sabbath she praised God.

But there was one fellow who was not praising God at all. The ruler of the synagogue, the defender of the Sabbath, took it as an affront that he had not been consulted on the propriety of healing on the holy day. Since he was too cowardly to confront Jesus, he rebuked the woman for being healed on the Sabbath by haranguing the whole congregation.

Outraged by such callousness, Jesus called the ruler a word he would never forget until his death, and upbraided him for thinking more highly of his traditions and of animals than of the hitherto crippled woman. Furthermore, Jesus told him that God had made the Sabbath precisely for the purpose of defeating Satan by bringing release to a crippled woman, since she was no less a descendant of Abraham than the ruler himself. Evidently, before God, she was as important as the hypocrite's rulership, his synagogue, and his Sabbath.[5]

Women as Faith Models

In a culture where women were to be neither seen nor heard, Jesus presented them as models of faith to His listeners, who could always hear teaching in which women were presented as corrupting influences to be shunned and disdained. In His teaching, Jesus used women as examples to emulate.

The Widow of Zarephath—Luke 4:24–26

Jesus reminded the people in the synagogue in Nazareth that in the days of the great prophet Elijah, it was a woman—and a Gentile woman to boot—who became the exclusive recipient of God's mercy in a time of crisis. The old-covenant people who had a concept of exclusivity about their divine privilege were completely bypassed. Likewise, God's visitation in Christ will benefit those who are receptive like the widow was. The murderous denizens of Nazareth were to learn from the Gentile widow.

The Queen of the South—Luke 11:31

This time the Gentile woman in Jesus' teaching is not a poor widow but a majestic queen. She had been more responsive to Solomon's wisdom than Jesus' contemporaries were to God's momentous revelation in Jesus Christ. Not only should the queen be regarded as the model of faith, but she as a Gentile woman would stand in judgment over men, the compatriots of Jesus who rejected Him. A woman will be given judgment over a whole generation of men and condemn them for their spiritual obduracy.

The Woman Finding the Lost Coin—Luke 15:8–10

There is a man seeking his lost sheep. Likewise, there is a woman looking for a lost coin. Both of them model the joy in the heavenly courts of God for a sinner who comes to repentance. In this parable, like the good shepherd, the woman is found worthy of illustrating the fruits of the gospel mission and its eschatological joy.[6]

The Persistent Widow—Luke 18:1–8

The widow who obtained justice in a desperate case by virtue of her sheer persistency is a model for believers who may be tempted to cease praying and to give up before the end. The woman is more consistent in pursuing a wicked supercilious judge than some Christians in trusting their benevolent God in the face of the eschatological woes. The woman teaches Christians how to face persecution in full reliance on God's faithfulness.

The Poor Widow's Offering—Luke 21:1-4

The widow who brings the totality of her belongings to God is set as an example of devotion and faith. She loves God enough to give Him all, and she trusts Him sufficiently to rely on His providence for survival. God values her pathetic gift to a higher degree than the gifts of the rich. Although these are vastly more substantial, they do not witness to either love or faith. Again, a woman, insignificant by worldly standards, is used by Jesus to teach a spiritual lesson to the disciples.

The analysis of these passages shows that Jesus had no qualms about women being cast in the role of didactic models for the people of His time or for the Christian community today. In His own teaching ministry, Jesus made use of women as teachers.

Undoing the Fall

The fall had inflicted devastating results on male/female relations. The unity, solidarity, and harmony of Eden had given way to separation (Gen. 3:7), recriminations (v. 12), and domination (v. 16). Despite the launching of God's redemptive program with Abraham, those negative effects of the fall persisted within the old-covenant period. They became particularly grievous with reference to the domination of one sex by the other, as evident in one-sided legislations relative to adultery, divorce, polygamy, and other evil practices.

As Jesus established the new community, He designed it to model God's enduring creational purposes. He made sure that the abuses that had remained through the dark side of the old covenant would be eliminated in the new community. Thus the church would become the haven of unity, solidarity, and harmony that Eden had failed to sustain.

Redefining Adultery—Matthew 5:27–30

What had been done with the commandment against adultery is only too well known. Adultery had essentially become a female sin. Men could usually commit adultery with impunity, but it was unmercifully prosecuted when a woman was found guilty of it. (Although textually questionable, the pericope in John 7:53—8:11 provides an ancient illustration of this dichotomy.)

With a single stroke, Jesus condemned the iniquity and resolved the inequity. The iniquity resulted from the violation of the "one flesh" principle. Jesus went to the root of the problem by denouncing the lecherous attitude of predatory men who look at a woman and see a body instead of a person, and who degrade her as a lust object to satisfy their craving to possess and dominate.

The inequity had derived from a double standard that made it possible for the perpetrator of the act to rationalize away his own involvement and to join in inflicting punishment on the victim. By this reasoning, might makes right. Rulers can justify themselves, but their subjects are defenseless. The verdict is always on the side of rulers, since they are the ones who sit in judgment and make things happen. With squinty glances, they "check out the chick." If the subject stirs their fantasy, they pursue the "conquest" until their lust is satiated and she suddenly becomes a "slut." If she does not cooperate, she is dismissed with a shrug as a "dog" or a dingbat. Either way, the subject is the loser. Rulership confers upon men privileged rights of ownership that empowers them to consider any woman fair game for the satisfaction of their lust.

Jesus' solution is magnificent in its simplicity. He cuts across legalisms and casuistry by requiring a radical change of heart that will make it unnatural in the Christian community for a man to want to exploit or degrade a woman. This change of male mentality toward women may be so difficult to achieve, due to agelong socializations, that its attainment is akin to self-mutilation. Indeed, giving up the myth of male privilege may be as demanding as plucking out an eye or cutting off a hand. But Jesus couched the requirement in the form of a command, and He promised hell as the alternative to obedience.[7]

Divorce Revoked—Matthew 5:31–32

As it was practiced in Jesus' time, divorce put wives at the mercy of their husbands under the cover of the Mosaic legislation. In order to alert His followers to the dehumanizing implications of such practices, Jesus had recourse to violent language.

He showed that men who discard their wives reduce them to the status of whores. For such husbands, wives become disposable items, throwaway playthings to be used for a while and dismissed. The man who will put out his wife has the heart of an adulterer (Matt. 19:3–8), since he sleeps with someone he intends to treat as a whore.

The man who marries a woman who has thus been passed around encourages the infernal cycle. He further robs her of what may be left of her dignity by making her once more the victim of legalized wife-swapping. He marries a woman whom someone else has treated as a whore; and he will himself treat her like a whore by dismissing her. As secondhand automobiles lose their value each time they are passed down from owner to owner, so the wife trade-in system savages the divine image-bearing nobility of women by reducing them to the level of a public adulteress.

By addressing His thunderous disapproval to men, who alone had the power to initiate divorce, Jesus made it clear that they should accept the blame for the deplorable practice so as to make amends and correct it.[8]

Redemption for Prostitutes—Luke 7:36–50

The Pharisee was correct in assuming that the perfume offered to Jesus by the harlot was purchased with income from her prostitution. And as she expressed her love to Jesus, she gave the only kind she knew, the erotic enfoldments of her trade. And Jesus accepted both.

The Pharisee evaluated Jesus' accepting response to the woman by his own standards. He assumed that Jesus was enjoying the prostitute's effusions and that He was exploiting the opportunity for selfish advantage. Therefore, he concluded that Jesus was no prophet.

The Pharisee looked at the harlot, and he could see only a fallen woman. Jesus looked and saw only the repentant sinner. For the Pharisee, the harlot was unredeemable. For Jesus, it was the self-righteous Pharisee who was unredeemable.

Point by point, Jesus compared the penitent attitude of the harlot to the haughty aloofness of the Pharisee, and He pronounced the words of divine forgiveness on the woman. Finally, He let her go, rehabilitated in God's *shalom*. Thus, He demonstrated once more that God's unconditional acceptance of sinners may be conditioned only by their rejection of His acceptance.

Later, Jesus would tell the assembled leaders of the Judaic establishment that harlots were far ahead of them in entering the kingdom, because they believed while the leaders rejected

Him (Matt. 21:31–32). Paradoxically, the very women who had been crushed into infamy by the heartless exploitation of the rulers became the exemplars of faith chosen by Jesus to shame the rulers.

Monogamous Marriage Vindicated—Matthew 19:3–12

In an attempt to discredit the authority of Jesus, the Pharisees challenged Him again, this time about His views on divorce. They tried to pit Jesus against Moses, so that He would come out the loser.

Indeed, faced with the realities of the fall, Moses had given a concessionary ruling on divorce. Likewise, the Pharisees, in order to legitimize divorce, drew their definition of marriage from the fall. Since man was ruler, he alone had the power to determine who should be his wife and for how long. Divorce was the ruler's option.

In His answer, Jesus showed that He refused to endorse the fall as a basis for the definition of marriage. The fall had produced a satanic parody of God's original design. Consequently, Jesus' answer hopscotched over both the old covenant and the fall to base His definition of marriage squarely in the creation ideal. For Jesus, the normative source of teaching on marriage was to be found in Genesis 1 (*see* Matt. 19:4) and Genesis 2 (*see* Matt. 19:5). Anything altering marriage thus defined was the result of the "hardness of heart" that set in after the fall; but "from the beginning it was not so" (v. 8, RSV).

Once the Pharisees had left, Jesus' own disciples came to Him in a state of shock. They had accurately understood the teaching of Jesus about the "one flesh" principle, about the equity that existed between man and woman in creation, and about its negative inferences on divorce. But the concept of male advantage was so ingrained within their beings that they offered this staggering observation: "If a man is going to be stuck all his life with the same wife, he's better off not getting married at all" (v. 10).

Jesus agreed that celibacy could be a high priority option for some of His followers. However, He also made it clear that celibacy should not be considered as a means of escaping the responsibilities of lifelong monogamous marriage, but that it should be viewed as an enhanced opportunity for serving the kingdom of God and as a response to God's calling for some individuals to remain single—"He who is able to receive this, let him receive it" (v. 12, RSV).[9]

The bottom line of this exchange between Jesus, the Pharisees, and the disciples is that in the age of redemption, the frame of reference for the definition of male/female relations is the creation story in Genesis 1 and 2. The fall and its consequences are to be seen as aberrations that have been resolved in the ministry and teaching of Jesus Christ. He reemphasized God's creation standards and made them normative for the new community, thus abrogating the authority structure that had been spawned by the fall along with other scourges afflicting fallen human life. Like the Master Himself, the members of the new community are so to define their relationships as to affirm creation (Gen. 1 and 2) and repudiate the fall (Gen. 3).

Equal Opportunities

Jesus trained twelve disciples as the pioneer task force that would initiate the gospel mission. But His discipling ministry was not limited to these twelve men. There were several other groups of people and individuals who were beneficiaries of Jesus' teaching ministry and who were commissioned along with the Twelve to fulfill the gospel mission (Luke 10:1–22). Jesus issued His call for discipleship to great multitudes (Luke

14:25–27), while individuals such as Joseph of Arimathea (John 19:38) and, later, the woman Dorcas (Acts 9:36) were also called "disciples." In this section, we will discover that Jesus called both men and women to follow Him in discipleship and that He expended Himself to teach them and involve them in His service without regard for sexual differences.

The Sisters of Jesus—Matthew 12:46–50

At certain times during His ministry, it became necessary for Jesus to assert His independence vis-à-vis close relatives, from the fear that they would compromise His mission by interfering with it. This passage relates one of those instances. While establishing some distance between His overanxious relatives and Himself,[10] Jesus used the occasion to teach a lesson about the composition of the new community and the requirements for being a part of it.

Pointing to His disciples, He identified them as His true relatives, His real "mother and brothers."[11] The difference between His biological family and His new spiritual family was the obedience of the latter to the will of His Father in heaven. Because God was His Father, those who identified themselves with God through their obedience became part of the same family that Jesus and the Father formed together. They were gathered into the community of the disciples. And these included not only the Twelve but also anyone else who met the condition of obedience. He or she became "brother, sister, mother" to Jesus. Whereas the story began with references only to the mother and brothers of Jesus, His call to discipleship was extended to "sisters" as well. Jesus took special precautions to make sure that younger women, not just surrogate mothers, realized that they were included in His call to become disciples. This special mention was all the more remarkable since women in general, but especially young women, were excluded from taking an active part in the religious life and institutions of contemporaneous Judaism.

Real Blessedness—Luke 11:27–28

Overwhelmed by Jesus' teaching, one of His hearers made an ejaculation of praise that gave Jesus an opportunity to teach an important lesson.

Jesus picked up on the strange statement from the woman for several reasons. She had not praised God. She had not pronounced Jesus' presumed father "blessed," as might have been expected. She had not even proffered thanks for His mother as a person. She had only recognized the biological function that had brought forth Jesus, as she invoked blessedness on a womb and mammary glands.

Perhaps she was saying with a tinge of envy, "Your mother is fortunate. Having had a child like you gives significance to her life. I wish I could have been your mother. My life might have amounted to something. We women are only baby machines. Once in a while, one of us will luck out and produce a winner. Your mother has something to be proud of."

Jesus' answer conveyed two lessons. The first is that to be a disciple—that is, one who learns ("hear") the word of God and practices it ("keep")—is more important than being the mother of Jesus. This lesson was a follow-up on the incident previously surveyed, which is also found in Luke (8:19–21). The second lesson derives from the fact that Jesus offered the statement as an answer to the woman in order to meet her specific need. In effect, Jesus was telling her, "You can become a disciple. Your life can find that new significance which is available to all who learn the word of God that I teach, and obey it. Motherhood is fine; but discipleship is the real blessing. And it's open to you. You cannot be My mother. But you can be My disciple. And that is much better."

The woman's statement reveals something of the feminine mind-set at the time. Although her beatitude was cast in the form of a Hebrew synecdoche (a part represents the whole, as in Luke 10:23), the fact that she could only relate the ministry of Jesus to the significance it had for His mother bespeaks of a benighted view of women's role in life. In His answer and with one sentence, Jesus catapulted women along with men, both shoulder to shoulder, to the cutting edge of God's program for the redemption of the world.

Choosing the Best—Luke 10:38–42

In the writings of Luke, to sit at someone's feet is the position of the receptive disciple (see 8:35 and 39! Cf. Acts 22:3). While Mary was learning from the Lord, Martha was acting as a serving disciple. Of the two sisters, Martha was fulfilling the role traditionally assigned to women. She was busy with her pots and pans and getting increasingly exasperated at her sister's "unconventional" behavior. She probably had tried to attract Mary's attention by sending subtle distress signals in the secret code language peculiar to each family (that any observant guest can quickly detect). But when Mary refused to budge, Martha finally burst in and appealed directly to Jesus. She rebuked Him for condoning such behavior and demanded that He send Mary to the kitchen where she belonged. Instead of complying, Jesus pointed out to Martha the futility of most of her pursuits, and He cited Mary as the person who had made the right decision, one that would prove of lasting value. Although Mary had turned upside down the role traditionally assigned to her as a woman, she had rightly chosen the way of commitment to discipleship that no one would be able to take away from her, even if he tried.

Women Disciples—Luke 8:1–3

If a disciple is to be defined as a follower, a student, and a servant, the women who traveled with Jesus and the Twelve during His itinerant ministry certainly qualified for the designation.

This overt participation of women in the latter part of the ministry of Jesus established an audacious precedent in the Palestinian world at that time (confirmed in Mark 15:41). The disciples' amazement at the fact that Jesus had dared to speak to women in a public place at an earlier stage of His ministry gives a measure of the prejudices that had to be overcome (John 4:27).

The courage of the women is to be admired as much as Jesus' initiative in establishing this ministry. But then, they were unusual women. They had been delivered from the power of Satan, some in a spectacular manner. Mary Magdalene had been bound sevenfold when she was liberated by Jesus. She followed Him to the cross (Matt. 27:56) and to the tomb (v. 61). She saw the tomb empty (Luke 24:10) and was the first to see the risen Christ (John 20:18).

Joanna was a married woman, the wife of an officer in the household of Herod the king. She and her husband, Chuza, had probably decided that if Simon Peter could leave his wife and household to obey Jesus' call to discipleship, so could she.

Susanna must have been known to Luke's readers as a prominent Christian in the early church, since no information is provided about her except for the fact that she was one of the women who supported Jesus' ministry financially. Apparently, some of the women disciples were persons of sufficient means to enable Jesus and His group not to be concerned about their expenses.

The bold initiative of involving women in His ministry was doubtless carried out with sufficient tact and precautions not to create a scandal among the very people whom Jesus wanted to reach. Yet, by its very existence, it made a cogent statement about the nature of female roles within the emerging new community of which the Twelve and other followers of Jesus constituted the predictive microcosm.

Privileged Opportunities

The Gospels show that whenever possible and while remaining mindful of the cultural constraints of the day, Jesus gave women special opportunities to play a primary role in the main events of His redemptive ministry, such as His birth, miracles, outreach missions, death, and resurrection.

The First Female Beneficiaries—Matthew 1:3, 5, 6

The genealogy placed at the beginning of the Gospel of Matthew serves several purposes. Primary among them is the author's intent to show the integrity of Jesus' Abrahamic ancestry and of His royal credentials as a descendant of David. But certainly the most astounding feature of this family tree is the inclusion of four women in addition to Mary. Not only was this an unusual occurrence in Jewish family trees, but the identities of the women give cause for reflection.

All four of them were women who had been victimized in what we called the "dark side" of the old covenant, the negative elements that had prevailed from the fall. Tamar had been the subject of a sordid story of oppression and incest that one would rather forget. Rahab was a Canaanite prostitute who, by faith, cast her lot with God's people. Ruth was a Gentile woman, widowed early in her married life, who found her destiny bound up to the purchase of a field. The identity of the fourth is given obliquely by the mention of her Gentile husband,

Uriah, who was murdered in the cover-up of the adulterous pregnancy that resulted from the sexual harassment of his wife by the king of the land.

These all died without knowing that their tarnished lives would be rehabilitated through their participation in the ancestry of the Savior. By giving them specific mention, Matthew singles them out as the first unlikely beneficiaries of the retroactive effects of the salvation that their divine descendant made available to all those who believe. Although unworthy by birth or conduct, each one of these women was chosen by God to serve and to be remembered as that ancestress of Jesus, whose mission it became to defeat the oppressive results of the fall that had marred their lives.

The First News of the Incarnation—Luke 1:32–35

The revelation of the fullness of time when God would send forth His Son to be born of a woman was first made to that very woman. It was not her father, the high priest, the ruler of the synagogue, a male prophet—and not even the man to whom she was betrothed—who received the annunciation. The angel of God came to Mary in person, and in lofty terms drawn from the prophets of old he opened before her the cosmic panorama of God's design.

Realizing that the burden of the redemption of the world was made dependent upon her, Mary said, "I am the servant of the Lord." As servant of God she joined a long and noble tradition of men and women who had been singularly called to do great things for God. And because both she and God together were giving the world its Savior, she exclaimed, "Henceforth, all generations will call me blessed" (v. 48, RSV). And another woman, Elizabeth, inspired by the Holy Spirit, confirmed, "Blessed are you among women, and blessed is the fruit of your womb!" (v. 43, RSV).

The First Miracle—John 2:1–11

The miracles of Jesus were not mere wonder-working feats. They were "signs" of the presence of the new age inaugurated with the advent of Jesus. Because this was the deeper meaning of the first miracle accomplished by Jesus, it manifested His glory (v. 11). In other words, the water-into-wine miracle revealed His role as the fulfiller of the new age. Significantly, both a man and a woman were the beneficiaries of this first miracle, since it took place in the context of their wedding celebration. Thus, a woman became instrumental in providing the occasion for the first manifestation of Jesus' eschatological glory.

The First Samaritan Convert—John 4:7–42

When Jesus assigned His followers the universal mission, He commanded that Samaria should receive the gospel before they reached out to the ends of the earth (Acts 1:8). It would have been too easy for them to bypass Samaria, even unintentionally.

During His own ministry, Jesus prepared the future mission to the Samaritans with three reported visits, the first of which was especially productive. Since the first result of that campaign was the conversion of the Samaritan woman, it may be said that a woman became the prototypical convert of the universal gospel mission.

Amazingly, this woman whom Jesus treated with extreme deference was a pathetic creature who had been abused by men and treated as a harlot. She had been married five times and dismissed in divorce five times. The last fellow who had picked her up did not even bother marrying her. Her past was so checkered and her conscience so burdened that when she rushed back to her village and told her compatriots, "This man told me all that I ever did," they became immediately convinced that He must be a fantastic prophet. They came to Jesus, heard Him for themselves, and they believed that He was indeed the Savior of the world. As a result, the first Samaritan convert became also the first missionary of the new age.

The First Gentile Convert—Matthew 15:21–28

Earlier in His ministry, when Jesus discovered how willfully impervious some of His hearers remained to repentance, He pronounced judgment on their cities and declared that if corresponding Gentile cities had received the same visitation, they would have repented in sackcloth and ashes (Matt. 11:21–22). In Jesus' estimation, the nearby cities of Tyre and Sidon stood as Gentile territory par excellence, as they were inhabited with people who might be more receptive to His ministry than was His own nation.

In this passage, Jesus is shown making a trip to that very district of Tyre and Sidon and being faced with the challenge to perform a ministry of healing on behalf of a Gentile woman. The seemingly indifferent attitude of Jesus to the woman's plea and the strange dialogue that followed are not to be interpreted as reluctance on His part to minister to Gentiles or to a woman. The focus of the story is the faith of the woman, which Jesus later describes as "great." In His transactions with her, Jesus' intent is to bring into the open the woman's understanding of His ministry. Does she treat Him like a passing Jewish wonder-worker, or does she have a perception of the universal scope of His mission? Jesus engages her in a dialogue that will draw out her convictions and provide an opportunity to teach a lesson of racial inclusiveness to the intolerant disciples. By playing the devil's advocate in favor of anti-Gentile prejudice, Jesus causes the woman to admit that Gentiles have a share in salvation, although in chronological sequence it comes first to the Jew.

The woman has perceived and confessed the true nature of His messiahship and admitted that it transcends human segregations, so that each person, Jew or Gentile and man or woman, may benefit from it. Jesus discovers in the woman the faith that He had not found in Chorazin and Bethsaida, and He establishes her in sacred history as His first convert in an area identified by Himself as the Gentile world.

First Resurrection Teaching—John 11:23–27

This time, Martha has been forced out of her kitchen by one of the inevitable tragedies of life.[12] Her brother, Lazarus, has died.

On various occasions, Jesus had made references to His resurrection and also to the eschatological resurrection. But on this day, Martha becomes the recipient of the most emphatic, the most explicit, and the most comprehensive teaching on the subject of resurrection as Jesus declares to her, "I am the resurrection and the life" (v. 25). Martha becomes the first person in history to be given an understanding of the correlation between the person of Jesus ("whoever lives and believes in me"), His own resurrection from the dead ("I am the resurrection"), and the final resurrection ("though he dies, yet shall he live"). Martha's confession indicates that she understands accurately the teaching of Jesus. She recognizes His lordship ("Lord"), the mystery of His messianic mission ("you are the Christ"), His divine nature ("the Son of God"), and His ministry as the fulfillment of divine purposes ("He who is coming into the world").

Then, at the request of the two women, Jesus proceeds to bring back to life the man who had been buried for four days, thus verifying in action the truthfulness of the momentous teaching first entrusted to Martha.

First Perception of the Cross—Mark 14:3–9

If Martha was the first person to be taught the significance of Jesus' person in terms of resurrection, her sister, Mary, was the first to understand the meaning of the death of Christ.

The anonymous woman of Bethany is identified as Mary in John 12:2. While her sister was again busy serving at community banquet organized to honor Jesus on His way to Jerusalem for the last time, Mary took it upon herself to do once more the unconventional thing. In a manner reminiscent of the prostitute's offering to Jesus in the house of a Pharisee (Luke 7:36–50), Mary brought a vase of costly perfume and used it to anoint the head and the feet of Jesus.

When some remonstrated at the apparent waste of money, Jesus explained His understanding of her act with five statements:

1. "She has done a beautiful thing to me" (v. 6). Mary's gesture goes deeper than an expression of respectful conviviality: "She is not just giving Me the usual greeting with a very expensive ointment. Her action is very personal, and it has a profoundly spiritual significance."

2. "You will not always have me" (v. 7). Mary has realized that a crisis looms ahead, and she knows that time is short. She is expressing her love while she still can.

3. "She has done what she could" (v. 8a). She knows that tragedy is inevitable: "The forces of evil that have been unleashed against Me are so powerful, and the nature of My messiahship is such that she does not even try to interfere. Giving Me a last joy is the extent of what she can do. She feels powerless, just as I am powerless to stop the fateful events that lie ahead."

4. "She has anointed my body beforehand for burying" (v. 8b). In effect, "She has developed sufficient perception in the sacrificial nature of My ministry to realize that My life will

soon be taken away by violence. What may seem like a festive offering is actually a burial anointment that lets Me know she also knows the end is near. She is already mourning over My death before it happens because, of all the people who surround Me, she alone has understood that there is no greater love for anyone than expending one's life for the sake of others. What she now does for Me is a prophetic parable of what I will do for the world on the cross."

5. "And truly, I say to you, wherever the gospel is preached in the whole world, what she has done will be told in memory of her" (v. 9, RSV). Thereby Jesus teaches that what may seem like the end shall become the glorious beginning of a movement that will confront the world with the power of the gospel. And wherever the gospel is preached there should be the special remembrance of this woman who was first, and probably alone, in acquiring an understanding of the cross before it happened: "So, I ordain that what took place here today become immortalized in the worship and the liturgy of the church, so that future generations of believers will continue to learn from Mary, whose love sustained Me through the last days of My ministry on earth."

First to Witness the Resurrection—Matthew 28:9; John 20:16

On the night of His arrest, Jesus was abandoned by the disciples, who scattered and fled (Mark 14:50). During His execution on the cross, the same women disciples who had followed Him in Galilee were gathered watching, clustered together in a huddle of despair (Matt. 27:55–56; Luke 23:49–56). They were present when Jesus' body was entombed. They were also the ones who came to the grave early on the third day to complete the embalming of the body.

But, as they arrived in the early dawn, they discovered the

tomb open and empty. Soon after, they saw Christ Himself, touched Him, and worshiped Him. They became the first humans to witness and experience the reality of the risen Christ.[13]

The First Witnesses to the Resurrection—Matthew 28:10; John 20:18

The women disciples were the first persons to be commissioned by Christ as the messengers carrying the epoch-making news of the resurrection. This function of "witnesses to the resurrection" later became a favorite self-designation of the apostles and the early Christians (Acts 1:22; 2:32; and so on). It was the reward of the loyal female disciples, who had accompanied Jesus to the place of crucifixion and stayed with Him through the horror of His execution, to be entrusted by Him with the most powerful message that has ever impacted the world: "He is risen."

This rapid listing of exceptional roles played by women in the crucial events of the life of Christ suggests that He made deliberate choices concerning the place of women in the economy of redemption.[14] The message conveyed by those decisions is not to be found in mere chronological primacy (which according to Jesus is of no advantage; *see* Matt. 20:16), but rather in the fact that women were given a foundational and a prominently constitutional role in the history of redemption by Jesus Himself. Any subsequent reduction of the conspicuous involvement of women in the community of redemption could be perpetrated only in violation of the will of its divine founder.

The Abrogation of Rulership

Much of the teaching of Jesus concerns the life of the new community that would emerge as a result of His ministry. Jesus anticipated and gave directions concerning a multitude of issues that pertain to individual and collective Christian life. This legacy of teaching that He committed to the disciples indicates that Jesus was particularly concerned about laying a strong foundation for the organizational structure that He expected Christian communities to adopt. He repeatedly defined His conception of the use of authority in Christian communities and provided guidelines for the structuring of such communities.[15]

There are basically two Christian communities: the local church and the family.[16] Since the teaching of Christ applies to both, it is obvious that it also has a direct bearing on male/female relations. In this section, we shall trace some of the main emphases of Jesus on the use of authority and on the role of dominant individual leadership in Christian communities.

Who Is the Greatest?—Matthew 18:1–5

Some disciples had apparently approached Jesus with this question but, as Mark indicates (9:33–37), He waited until the whole group was present to teach on the matter. The embarrassed silence of the disciples was an expression of guilt. They realized that Jesus would not approve of the contest they had engaged in to determine which of them was chief disciple. According to their observation, a group like theirs was supposed to be hierarchically structured. The rabbis ranked their disciples according to a pecking order over which they exercised absolute control. The synagogue was a carefully stratified community. The political system under which the disciples lived was rigorously structured under the autocratic rule of the emperor.

Jesus had called the disciples to His service in order to prepare them for a great mission, but He had failed to organize the group as they expected, by appointing a chain of command. This method, or the seeming lack of it, was so foreign to the disciples' experience that they had resolved among themselves to correct the deficiency on their own. Their socialization was such that they could not operate outside of the notion that "somebody's got to be in charge." So they had decided to designate the "greatest" among them as their leader. But the competition among them was so fierce that they had failed to agree on a leader. Jesus caught them at this point and gave them two lessons on the nature of leadership in Christian communities.

1. *Mark 9:35*—He who aspires to a position of preeminence should constrain himself to take the lowest rank and to act as a servant to the very people he wants to rule. Instead of seeking to rule others, disciples should desire to practice servanthood. Instead of telling others what to do, they should do it for others.

2. *Matthew 18:3–4*—If he was a typical Middle East child, the little boy who suddenly became the center of attention in the midst of an impressive-looking group of adults must have been completely overwhelmed by the situation. Pointing to the diffident and unpretentious attitude of the child, Jesus told the disciples that unless they gave up their ambitions and became as meek as the child, they could not enter the kingdom, much less become leaders in it. True kingdom greatness is not to be achieved through rank, position, and leadership but by accepting the placement of oneself in a position of inferiority and dependency in regard to others. The new community is composed of people who are all willing to assume the status of children. People who view themselves as rulers are not even included in the kingdom of God.

Jesus turned upside down the disciples' worldly, pagan view of community organization as a pyramid of power. He showed them that greatness was achieved in Christian communities by serving at the very bottom.

Who Makes the Decisions?—Matthew 18:15-20

Jesus' pronouncement on true greatness left unanswered the question regarding community structure. With no dominant individual (the "greatest") to rule the group, how would decisions be made? The answer to this question appears in the immediate context, with the teaching on adjudication procedures between contending parties within the Christian community.

In a hierarchical society where power is exercised from the top down, the aggrieved parties submit their differences to the highest accessible authority. Thus, a judge, a priest, a king, or a patriarch makes a ruling that becomes binding for the contestants. But, according to Jesus, this is not how the church is to function. Since the congregation is not ruled by a leader, decisions are made by community rule. After exhausting the preliminary steps of recourse to personal confrontation and brotherly mediation, the contesting parties submit their case to the congregation, whose decisions become binding. The decisions made on earth by the Christian community receive divine approval (v. 18),[17] because Christ is spiritually present among the congregation, providing guidance during its deliberations (v. 20).

According to Jesus, the appropriate locus for authority rests within the congregation and not in a leader above it. Jesus smashed the pyramidal concept of ecclesiastical authority and replaced it with participatory consensual community rule. He denied any one individual the right to arrogate the power to control other persons in Christian communities, which power belongs to Him alone.

"It Shall Not Be So Among You"—Matthew 20:20-28

Among several similar teachings, this passage contains the clearest statement of Jesus on the exercise of authority among

Christians. It explicitly forbids any one individual to assume authority over another in a Christian community. A hierarchical authority structure is legitimate in the pagan world but is prohibited among Christ's followers.

Verses 20–21. The request of the Zebedee brothers as formulated by their mother reveals the mentality behind it. Jesus is viewed as a potentate who will eventually occupy a throne similar to that of the Roman emperor. The two brothers wish to be the ones who will sit next in command, participating in Christ's rule.[18]

Verse 22. In His answer, Jesus points to the brothers' complete misunderstanding of His mission, which is one of suffering and self-sacrifice. Discipleship requires participation in His suffering-servant ministry rather than vying for positions of power.

Verse 23. By deferring to the Father the matter of honorific placement in the kingdom, Jesus gives it an eschatological reference and removes it from relevance to the community on earth.

Verse 24. The anger of the ten other disciples betrays the same kind of misunderstanding regarding the nature of the new community. Had they recognized the futility of the brothers' request they would have dismissed it with laughter as a preposterous expectation. Their sensitivity indicates that they actually believed that the two brothers could have succeeded in obtaining an advantage over them. As far as they were concerned, the two best seats were up for grabs, and the brothers had almost beat their peers in securing those seats for themselves.

Verse 25. The turmoil among the disciples causes Jesus to engage in a special teaching session (this is the meaning of "Jesus called them to him and said" [RSV]). He traces the source of their misunderstanding to the fact that they are carrying over into the community of believers an authority structure that belongs in the secular world. So He analyzes for them the nature of the practice of authority among pagans. Their model is the imperial form of government, whereby emperor, kings, governors, and rulers are organized in a tight hierarchy that enables them to use their power from the top down as they "lord it over" the people they administer and "exercise authority" over them.

In this passage Jesus neither denies the legitimacy of political power nor decries its abuses. Caesar has rights (Matt. 22:21), and Christians are to submit to his temporal rule (Rom. 13:1–7; 1 Peter 2:13–17). But Jesus makes it clear that such authority structures belong among the Gentiles.

Verse 26. "It shall not be so among you . . ." (RSV). The one-man rule that characterizes the governance of pagan collectivities is absolutely forbidden among Christians. No Christian is to "lord it over" other believers, and no one among them is to "exercise authority over them." Christ's prohibition of the practices cited in the previous verse could not have been worded more clearly or in more absolute terms.

This does not imply that anarchy is to prevail in the two Christian communities of church and family. As Matt. 18:17–18 prescribes, authority is indeed to be exercised in Christian communities, but only on the basis of participatory consensual community rule. Christ refuses to allow any one person to assume in church or family the authority that belongs to Him. Both the congregation gathered together and husband and wife bowed together receive the mind of Christ. His authority may be usurped by self-styled autocratic leaders only in violation of His will.

Verse 27. With the prohibition Jesus offers positive advice: the desire to become dominant should be overcome by assuming the attitude of a servant and by taking the position of a slave. Servants and slaves do not control others. They allow others to control them. The attitude of servant and the position of slave are Jesus' antidotes to the poison of dominant individual leadership.

Verse 28. In order to emphasize the point and to teach how such servanthood is to be practiced, Jesus cites His own example as one who gave up the highest position of equality with God to take the form of a servant and to give His life for others. If Christ, who is rightful Lord, can act as a servant to the point of self-sacrifice, how much more must His followers, who are nothing but servants.

In a society intoxicated with the spirit of competition and driven by upward mobility obsessions, Jesus establishes a community of disciples who seek the status of servants and who aspire to downward mobility, so as to make themselves available to each other in sacrificial service and devote themselves to the fulfillment of the needs of others.

Idolatrous Concepts of Leadership—Matthew 23:1–12

Jesus warned His followers against the danger of allowing the pagan model of hierarchical government impersonated in "the rulers of the Gentiles" and "their great men" to infiltrate the structures of Christian communities. But the same pattern of dominant individual leadership existed also in the Judaic religious establishment that was the immediate background of the disciples. As a consequence, there was a danger that the Judaic authority structures might be duplicated in the life of the Christian community. Jesus gave very strong warnings against such an eventuality. Some salient features of those warnings are reported in this passage.

According to *verses 1 and 2*, the teaching of the Judaic teachers is legitimate as long as it reflects the authority of Moses and not their own. A teacher's authority does not reside in himself but in the Word of God. His role is merely to dispense the revealed teaching. Whenever a teacher arrogates to himself divine authority, his leadership becomes idolatrous (as a God substitute), and the following abuses ensue:

Verse 3. As the leader assumes authority in himself, he becomes the source of his teaching. Since he controls the teaching, the teaching does not control him. As a result, he treats himself with immunity to his own teaching. He lays down the law heavily upon his charges, but he absolves himself from practicing it.

Verse 4. Because power tends to corrupt, the strong individual leader becomes arbitrary and oppressive. He makes demands upon others that he refuses to fulfill himself.

Verse 5. Since this pattern of deceit might impugn on his credibility, the dominant leader has to put on a good show. He carefully stages his performance and his appearance so as to impress others with his respectability.

Verse 6. He craves for every sign of deference given to him, as a reassurance that he is successfully deceiving the people under his leadership.

Verse 7. His ego requires constant gratification and the fawning adulation of his victims.

In order to prevent such deplorable conditions from developing in the Christian community, Jesus made some sweeping prohibitions:

Verse 8: Against autocratic teaching. Jesus recognizes only two levels in the hierarchy of teaching authority. The first is Himself: "You have one teacher." The other is made of all the disciples, recipients of His teaching: "You are all brethren." Therefore, no follower of Jesus may usurp the title *teacher* in the traditional religious sense, as if he were the self-empowered source of authoritative teaching. In the Christian community the teaching ministry is entirely different. The Christian teacher is only a proclaimer of Christ's teaching, never of his own. As a mere proclaimer of the Master's message, the teaching disciple does not occupy a status higher than the rest of his brethren. He is only one learner, transmitting to other learners the words of the Teacher.

Verse 9: Against autocratic rulership. In the Christian communities no one should claim the authority over believers that belongs only to God as their Father. In Judaic tradition, the patriarchs and venerable worthies were called "father." A father had the right to rule his children's lives, but mature Christians are not to be treated like children by any self-appointed father-figure. That kind of authority belongs only to God, whose children we are. God is the only legitimate Father-Ruler over the lives of adult Christians.

Verse 10: Against autocratic leadership. This particular Greek word for "leader" is found only in this verse in the New Testament. However, it is used in classical Greek with the meaning of "leader," "guide," or "master" (not in the sense of slaveowner but of tutor/teacher). Jesus predicted that wicked men would rise within the Christian community, taking upon themselves the prerogatives of Christ in order to lead the faithful astray (Matt. 24:4–5, 24). Such defections begin when the authority that belongs to Christ is conferred upon human leaders (1 Cor. 1:12) or usurped by super-apostles (2 Cor. 11:5). Jesus' solution to the subtle danger of falling prey to strong individual leadership is simple: Christians should reject any leader that would attempt to muster a following and treat these people as *his* followers. Christians follow only one leader, Christ Himself.

It was precisely to prevent such abuses that the New Testament insists on team leadership (plurality of elders) in Christian communities. Jesus sent out his disciples in groups of two (Mark 6:7). The apostle Paul pursued his missionary endeavors surrounded with teams of co-workers, and he co-authored or co-signed his Epistles whenever possible. As churches were established, the leadership was entrusted in each one of them to a group of pastors rather than to one individual leader (Acts 11:25–26; 13:1; 14:23; and so on). Those leaders were to act

as models to the community rather than domineer over it
(1 Peter 5:3). Within the family, both parents were responsible
for leadership (Eph. 6:1; Col. 3:20). Numerous times, Christian
communities were exhorted to remain vigilant in preventing
the rise of individual leaders to positions of power that belong
only to God and in rejecting idolatrous definitions of leadership
(Rom. 12:3–8; 1 Cor. 4:1–2; 2 Cor. 11:13–20; and so on).[19]

From denunciation of abuses and prohibition of idolatrous
practices, Jesus moves to positive prescriptions designed to preserve the integrity of Christian leadership:

Verse 11. Some people are naturally gifted as born leaders.
They stand out in the community as the "greatest." Those are
the very people who should exercise care in avoiding authoritarian and assertive behavior. They should make their gifts
available to others as servants rather than as masters. Whether
in church or family, the "greatest" should provide leadership
by empowering others for participation rather than by wielding
authority over them. A servant does not wield authority; he
submits to it. A leader is a servant. The true leader submits to
the authority of the group.

Verse 12. This statement is often found in both the Old and
the New Testament. It touches on the very essence of interpersonal dynamics in God's universe. He who said, "I will ascend
to heaven" was "cut down to the ground" (Isa. 14:12–15, RSV).
But He who "did not count equality with God a thing to be
grasped" became "highly exalted" (Phil. 2:5–11, RSV). Those
who use the community of faith for self-promotion and self-
aggrandizement will receive divine retribution. But those who
subject their interests to the common good will inevitably be
rewarded.

Christian leadership is not a case of somebody telling other
people what to do. Leadership is someone getting together with
one or more persons to determine what God wants them to
do. As such, leadership is always a community enterprise—

never an individual assertion. A leader is a team worker, not an order giver.

"All Authority Has Been Given to Me"—Matthew 28:16–20

As might be expected, the last command of Jesus subsumes the thrust of His whole ministry and reveals His purpose for the full scope of history. The striking feature of this final statement is its peremptory tone. Jesus had "directed" the disciples to the encounter; He affirms His universal "authority"; He orders them to "go," to "make disciples," to "baptize," to "teach" new disciples who are to "observe" that which He had "commanded." There is no exchange, no dialogue, no questions asked. The tone is terse and martial. The disciples are to receive the summons and to proceed with the execution. The risen Christ has taken command of human destiny.

Verse 18. As a result of His death and resurrection, Jesus has assumed supreme rulership. All authority finds its definition in Him, since He alone is Lord. He commissions disciples but without committing His authority to them. He alone remains in charge.

Verse 19. The task of the eleven disciples is to make more disciples like themselves. Jesus pointedly does not replace Judas, the missing disciple. The numerical integrity of the original group is unimportant to Jesus, since disciples will multiply by the thousands. It was after Jesus' ascension and prior to the coming of the Holy Spirit at Pentecost that the Eleven awkwardly attempted to select a twelfth member by resorting to the roll of the dice (Acts 1:26). But, for Jesus, the preservation of the original unit was irrelevant, since the disciples would scatter and generate more disciples like themselves. The Eleven would eventually disappear among the multitudes of new disciples they were to induct into the Christian faith.

Verses 19–20. The method for making disciples among the nations was twofold:

1. The disciples were to baptize new converts as a sign of their entrance into a newness of life characterized by a personal relationship (this is the meaning of "in the name of") with the fullness of the divine being in Father, Son, and Holy Spirit.

2. The original disciples were also to teach the new disciples all that Christ had commanded them. The teaching was not their own. It was the "command" of Christ. He maintained His authority within the community of new disciples by their adherence to His teaching. The original disciples were not vested with any autonomous authority. They were only communicators of the command of Christ. They were transmitters of His message. Whatever authority they manifested pertained uniquely to the teaching of Christ. New disciples who transmitted the teaching of Christ would become just as authoritative as the original disciples. The authority resided in the message, not in the men and women who took it to the world.

Verse 20. The final word of Jesus is that He will be present with the disciples in all generations until the end. He will accompany them and vouchsafe the authority of their message under the cover of His sovereignty.

The significance of this statement lies as much in what it omits as in that which it emphasizes. In His parting words, Jesus gives no hint of the necessity for an authority structure among His followers. There is no appointment to command positions, no delineation of hierarchies. No one is designated as supervisor over the other disciples or as ruler of the new community. *Au contraire*, Jesus states that He will remain with the disciples to exercise Himself that authority which belongs to Him alone.

Later, as the church grew and spread throughout the world, it became necessary to organize the local communities and to recognize gift specializations within them. But in keeping with the mandate of Jesus to the Eleven, the Book of Acts and the Epistles bear witness to the fact that the church was careful to establish authority structures that were participatory and collective rather than predicated on individual authority figures. Thus, the New Testament church kept faith with the consistent teaching of Jesus, who had maintained the dual principle of leadership as a corporate function and leadership as servanthood, even at the crucial moment of the commissioning of disciples for the conquest of the world.

The Supreme Example—John 13:1–17

Jesus utilized His last and most intensely dramatic moment of intimacy with His disciples to teach them in deed the proper attitude of a servant-leader within the community of faith. By washing the feet of the disciples, He placed before them a binding precedent, the practice of which remains the necessary condition for receiving blessedness (v. 17).

Washing the feet of the members of a household was considered so menial a task that Jewish servants were not required to perform it. It was relegated to Gentile slaves. The author emphasizes further the incongruity of Jesus' action by reminding his readers in verse 3 of Christ's awareness of His universal supremacy ("knowing that the Father had given all things into His hands") and of His divine origin and destination ("He had come from God and was going to God"), just prior to describing His rising, taking a towel and a basin, and washing the disciples' feet. Peter's horrified recoil gives an accurate measure of the enormity of the deed.

The crux of the story resides in the lesson that Jesus draws from His action. It could be paraphrased: "If I, your Lord and Teacher, have been a servant to you, how much more each one of you who is neither Lord nor Teacher should feel obligated to be servant to others. Don't you ever think of yourselves as

being too great to act as servants. Being equal among yourselves, you cannot aspire to be greater than I am, and behold,
I was your servant" (vv. 14, 16).

In our day, the supreme irony is to watch a mitered primate
of the church dressed in resplendent ecclesiastical vestments
rinse with holy water, over a golden basin carried by a couple
of priests, the antisepticized foot of a subordinate priest, himself prostrate before his superior's throne, humbled under the
weight of such an honor. Shifting from the sublime to the
mundane, there seems to exist a strange reverse correlation
between the foot-washing ritual of the bejeweled churchman
and the attitude of the Christian husband who leaves a room
strewn with his dirty socks and underwear for his wife to pick
up—because he considers it her subordinate role to do so.

Both the church and the Christian home are under relentless
attack from the pagan world to forego their distinctive character as Christian bodies and to replace Christ's teaching with
the satanic legacies of the fall. In regard to role distinctions
within church and family, Christians need to be especially on
their guard so that they do not conform to worldly norms. Both
their thinking and their practice should be radically transformed through the renewal of their mind so that they can
discern the will of God and follow after that which is good,
acceptable, and perfect as it was delineated by Christ Himself
ever so clearly.

The foregoing survey of the most significant teachings of
Jesus on the subject of authority shows the extent of His concern
for the proper structuring of Christian communities. Forcefully
rejecting the implementation of pagan hierarchical models of
governance among Christians, He denounced the dangers inherent to the imperial/pontifical method of decision making
and warned against the idolatrous adulation that surrounds
individual authority figures. He also warned against the worldly
desire to substitute individual leadership for consensual deci-

sion making. Jesus viewed the exercise of authority as a collective responsibility where strong, gifted individuals make it their servant task to empower others in participating in the decision-making process and in generating general ownership in the decisions. He promised He would be ever-present with the community of believers to guide them and give them the cover of His authority whenever they would gather to seek His will in the multiple wisdom of heads bowed together in submission to Him.

Although Jesus made several references to marriage and family in His teaching, He never excluded the home as an exception from community rule. What He taught about authority roles among Christians applies to all Christians and to their lives within the complementary communities of church and family. It applies doubly to the family, since it is a microcosm of the church, the family of God. His order, "It shall not be so among you" (Matt. 20:26) is all-inclusive. It signals the abrogation among Christians of the rulership principle that had resulted from the fall.

To summarize in plain language: Jesus intruded into the sin-laden institutions of the world in order to release a new kind of life, an irrepressible ferment that would change men and women and empower them with the effervescent dynamic of the Spirit. Endowed with new powers, they would personify the new creation and establish the new community. In this community, men and women are called by God to occupy kingdom functions and to assume kingdom roles at maximum levels of involvement and visibility tolerable within their contemporary cultures. In multiple ways, Jesus established the principle of full access of both men and women to the responsibilities attendant to the harmonious functioning of the new community. Jesus taught His followers in word and deed to consider the gender difference irrelevant to the concerns and to the processes of the kingdom of God.

5

The New Community

The ultimate purpose of God in creation was to establish a community of persons made in His image who would be responsive to Him and responsible toward each other. Such a community existed in Eden but became disrupted at the fall. God's program of restoration that was initiated with the old covenant and accomplished in Christ finally came to fulfillment in the new community, the church. As such, the church represents the culmination of God's creational and redemptive purposes. It is paradise regained, with a plus that gives it the seal of permanency. It is the eternal community.

However, on this side of the great resurrection, the church remains in an ambiguous situation. It anticipates becoming the eternal community when it will be presented to the Savior in splendor, without spot or wrinkle or any defect, holy and without blemish. But while it remains on earth the church is vulnerable. False teachings, errors of judgment, cultural pressures, and adverse historical developments can cause God's people to conform to the world and to lose their distinctiveness. Thus, almost a millennium ago, the Christians in Europe banded together in huge masses and, in the name of God, launched some of the most violently imperialistic ventures the world has ever witnessed as they set out to conquer the "holy land" by the force of arms. Five centuries ago, the church established in the name of Christ a system of inquiry incongruously called the Holy Office, which developed a reign of oppression, terror, and murder that has made "Inquisition" a byword for tyranny and cruelty. A century ago, evangelical Christians were still fighting hard, sometimes with Bible in hand, to perpetuate one of the most dehumanizing practices generated by Satan from the very pit of hell, the institution of slavery. Today, some evangelical Christians are struggling to justify church and family structures that dehumanize the female half of their populations by placing it under the rulership of the male segment.[1]

More than ever, biblical Christians need to heed the admonition of the great apostle, "Examine yourselves to see whether you are in the faith; test yourselves. Do you not realize that Christ Jesus is in you—unless, of course, you fail the test?" (2 Cor. 13:5, NIV). Paul's reference to Jesus Christ in this context is relevant to our study. In the preceding chapter, we discovered the norms that Christ established as He grounded His doctrine of male/female relations in the patterns of creation. His teaching was characterized not only by a complete absence of instructions on authority structures between males and females, but also by the categorical repudiation of the validity of such concepts among His followers. In this last chapter of our study, we will discover that the early church, whose history is reflected in the Book of Acts and the Epistles, remained obedient to the vision and to the directions of Christ for the new community. The texts relevant to our topic fall naturally into three categories: inaugural statements, passages expounding the teachings of the church on female roles, and references to the practice of the church. We shall proceed with the study of those texts according to that order.

Inaugural Statements of the New Community

The great turning points in redemption history were prefaced with inaugural statements. The call of Abraham was set in the context of a divine declaration on world redemption (Gen. 12:1–3). The exodus from Egypt and the organization of the people of the old covenant were initiated with God's self-revelation as the great "I am" (Exod. 3:6–22). The conquest of the Promised Land was launched with the ringing promise of God's abiding support (Josh. 1:2–9). The prophetic ministry of the old covenant was dominated by God's commission to Isaiah (6:3–13). Mary's prophetic Magnificat saluted the incarnation (Luke 1:46–55). And Jesus' ministry began with the royal manifesto known as the Sermon on the Mount (Matt. 5–7).

The church of Jesus Christ celebrates its own birthday on two occasions. The first is collective and embraces all Christians of all times. It is the day of Pentecost. The second is individual and concerns each person at the moment of his or her inclusion into the body of Christ through confession of faith and baptism. Every time a believer is formally inducted into the church through baptism, the body of Christ celebrates a new birth into the kingdom of God. Predictably, the New Testament reports foundational inaugural statements formulated for each of those two occasions.

At the moments of the church's reception of the Holy Spirit (Pentecost) and of the reception of believers into the church (baptism), constitutional declarations are articulated about the nature of relations within the church, thus defining the distinctive nature of the new community as a body where equality and unity prevail. In Christ Jesus, those who were far off have been brought near. He has become their peace, having broken down the dividing wall of hostility, creating in Himself one new being instead of the two, thus making peace. They have been reconciled in one body, thereby bringing the hostility to an end (Eph. 2:13–16). Those two inaugural statements celebrate the newness of life in that one body, the recovery of the ideal of mutuality in equality.

Because of their programmatic character, the two statements contain direct applications to the topic of male/female relations in the new community. We will examine them separately in this section.

Pentecost—Acts 2:15–21

In order to make sure that the disciples would properly interpret their experience of the Holy Spirit at Pentecost as the extension of His incarnation, the risen Christ had given them a simple predictive object lesson. As He commissioned them to go and effect the ministry of forgiveness, He breathed on them and said, "Receive the Holy Spirit" (John 20:21–23). This manifest continuity between the ministry of Jesus and the presence of the Holy Spirit in their midst helped the disciples to apply in the life of the church community the teachings He had entrusted to them. As we shall see, this was true of the disciples' approach to the use of authority and to the equal access of believers to participation in the life and ministry of the church.

A considerable amount of emphasis is given in the account of Pentecost to the unitive power of the Holy Spirit. Men and women "numbering about a hundred and twenty persons" (Acts 1:14–15) were all gathered "together together" (deliberate redundancy in the Greek text, Acts 2:1). The hurricane sound surrounded *all* of them and *all* of them were singularly designated as recipients of the Holy Spirit with a living flame.

They were *all* filled with the Spirit and started speaking in a dozen foreign languages.[2] The meaning of this enablement was not only that the Spirit was giving them new powers to proclaim the gospel in all the world, but also and more importantly that the human race was again being united into one body. The scattering, and the ethnic and linguistic splintering that had occurred at the tower of Babel (Gen. 11:8–9), were reversed through the ministry of Christ. The divisions and the fragmentations that had resulted from the fall were finally overcome in the new community. Eden was being reborn.

Verse 16. Peter provides the proper explanation for the obstreperous conduct of the believers. They are not drunk. They celebrate the long-awaited fulfillment of the outstanding prediction concerning the Holy Spirit in the Old Testament (Joel 2:28–32). Peter exclaims, "This is it!"

Verses 17–18. The prophet Joel had anticipated a new age when God's presence would become universally available in the intimacy of each believer's life. Peter defines this age as the "last days."[3] The coming of the Holy Spirit inaugurates the beginning of the "last days" period. The words of Joel quoted on this occasion have the force of both an explanation for the exhilarating occasion and of a program for the newly born church. By making them his own, Peter gives to Joel's words the import of an inaugural speech.

"I will pour out my Spirit upon all flesh" (RSV). During the old-covenant period, the Holy Spirit had been occasionally and sporadically extended to selected individuals to perform designated tasks (prophet, king, artisan, and so on). But in the new age, the Spirit will make Himself available abundantly ("pour out") and universally ("upon all flesh"). "All flesh"— that is to say, people from all races and ethnic backgrounds, Jews and Gentiles—will benefit from the indwelling presence of the Holy Spirit.

Lesson: Racial distinctions are irrelevant in the church.

"And your sons and your daughters shall prophesy" (RSV).
Since the Spirit is given to *"all"* flesh," both men and women
become His recipients. But the spectacular news is that they
will both have access to the prophetic ministry. There were
prophetesses during the time of the old covenant. However,
compared to their male peers, their number was very small.
The change brought about in the time of the Spirit is that male
and female will receive the prophetic call without any discrimination. The disparities between male and female will be abol-
ished to the extent that both will model the energizing impact
of the Holy Spirit as symbolized in the prophetic ministry. Because the gift of prophecy is exercised under divine sanction,
it epitomizes divine activity in human life, and it authenticates
the person whom God is using as His mouthpiece. In the age
of the Spirit, the highest levels of ministry will be open to
believers without regard for gender.

Lesson: The sex difference is irrelevant in the church.

*"Your young men shall see visions, and your old men shall
dream dreams"* (RSV). In the new community, rank distinctions
predicated on age will be removed so that anyone, young or
old, can be used as a channel to provide divine guidance. The
visions of a young man will have as much validity as the dreams
of a venerable grandfather. The Holy Spirit will close the gen-
erational gap.

Lesson: Differences of rank are irrelevant in the church.

*"Yea, and on my menservants and my maidservants in those
days I will pour out my Spirit; and they shall prophesy"* (RSV).
The servant people who were at the lower echelons of the social
ladder will be promoted to the highest status in the new age.
Not only will they receive the fullness of the Spirit like their
superiors in the flesh, but they will also have access to the same
functions in the new community. They will prophesy like the
sons and daughters of their masters. The menservants will be
thus honored and so also will the only category of humans

below them, the lowly maidservants at the very bottom of the social heap.

Lesson: Class differences are irrelevant in the church.

Peter's appropriation of Joel's prophetic statement as the inaugural declaration of the church is of momentous consequence.[4] It links the emerging church to the expectations of the old covenant by showing that the church is the predicted outcome of the preparation laid out in "the law and the prophets." Thus, the developments taking place in the Pentecost community receive a historical warrant from God's promise to the old community. With the inauguration of the church, God's plan for the ages has come to fruition.

Peter's choice of this passage also serves to manifest the radical newness brought about by the new community. The pouring out of the Holy Spirit has an ennobling impact upon each individual receiving it. Accidents of birth, fortune, and rank become transcended by the elevating power of the Holy Spirit. The members of the new community are now bonded together in a relationship of mutuality in equality brought about by the empowering of the same Spirit. As a result, the old distinctions of race, sex, rank, and class pale into insignificance. What becomes important is the shared identity and the shared ministry of new-covenant believers.

Because of its far-reaching implications, Peter's restatement of Joel's prophecy should be allowed to govern our understanding of relationships within the church. As a key constitutional document of the church, this statement should be allowed to play a determinant role in the definition of relationship and ministries in the new community.[5] As we shall see in the next section, the practice of the apostolic church was in conformity to the expectations laid out in the inaugural speech of the church. Does the same obedience to God's commands characterize our present-day churches?

Baptism—Galatians 3:26–29

As God's great missionary to the Gentiles, the apostle Paul can also claim an inaugural statement in the Scriptures. The Epistle to the Galatians is considered by many to be Paul's first extant writing.[6] As it spells out the Christian case for justification by faith and freedom from bondage to the law, it has the ring of a manifesto. But in this study we are more particularly concerned with a segment of the Epistle that possesses the character of an inaugural statement, since it is formulated in connection with baptism, the individual rite of entrance into the church and of participation in its life. Many scholars believe that the actual wording of verse 28 is the transcription of a creed repeated during baptismal ceremonies in Pauline churches.[7] Whatever the case, Paul's use of the statement in its context has a definite correlation to baptism. Therefore, it has the force of an inaugural statement for the church each time a new believer joins the body of Christ.

The main motif of this passage concerns the new identity conferred by God upon believers. "All" who are in Christ become "sons [or children] of God" (v. 26). They receive baptism as a sign that they have "put on Christ" (v. 27). This means that they receive a new nature which is renewed according to the image of the Creator (*see* Col. 3:10). Out of their diversity, they join a community in which the members are "all one in Christ Jesus" (v. 28). Regardless of their racial ancestry, they become "Abraham's offspring" and therefore "heirs of the promise" to Abraham (v. 29).

This survey shows that the passage addresses the question of what happens to persons who by faith identify themselves with Christ. The apostle's emphatic answer is that they receive a new identity which they hold in common with other believers. In this passage Paul does not address the issue of who may become a believer. He has made that abundantly clear prior to this point. All who have faith, Gentiles included, qualify for the blessing (3:8–9, 14, 22). Here Paul is concerned with the result of their entrance into the life of faith. He shows that they receive a common identity that heals their segregations and their antagonisms as they are fused together into the unity of the body of Christ. The passage emphasizes their commonality as believers.[8]

Verse 28. The correlations between this statement and the contents of Peter's inaugural speech at Pentecost are striking.[9]

"There is neither Jew nor Greek [or Gentile]." When Jew and Gentile identify with Christ by faith, their spiritual allegiance takes precedence over their racial or ethnic distinctiveness. Because of their commonality in that one area of life which is of supreme importance to them, they are united in Christ. Their commitment has shifted from their Jewishness or Gentileness to the unity they have in Christ. They still remain Jew and Gentile, but such distinctions are immaterial to their equal participation in the life of the church.

Lesson: Racial distinctions are irrelevant in the church. Therefore, the practice of racial discrimination in the church is sinful.

"There is neither slave nor free." When slaves and freemen identify with Christ by faith, their spiritual allegiance takes precedence over their class or social stratification. Because of their commonality in that one area of life which is of supreme importance to them, they are united in Christ. Their self-definition shifts from their status as slave or free to the unity they share in Christ. They still remain slave and free, but such distinctions become immaterial to their equal participation in the life of the church.

Lesson: Class distinctions are irrelevant in the church. Therefore, the practice of class discrimination in the church is sinful.

"There is neither male nor female." When male and female identify with Christ by faith, their spiritual allegiance takes precedence over their maleness and femaleness. Because of

their commonality in that one area of life which is of supreme importance to them, they are united in Christ. Their sense of personal worth shifts from their maleness or femaleness to the unity they share in Christ. They still remain male and female, but such distinctions become immaterial to their equal participation in the life of the church.

Lesson: Sex distinctions are irrelevant in the church. Therefore, the practice of sex discrimination in the church is sinful.

Conclusion on the inaugural statements: The commanding prominence of those two statements as constitutional declarations of the church and their crystalline clarity endow them with normative power. Guidance for present practice should be drawn from the normative texts and not from any exceptional case.

These texts define the composition of the church and determine its functioning. But above all they stand against the formulation of value judgments and against the attribution of worth, rank, role, office, or participation on the basis of race, class, or sex. Together, they teach that Christian unity can be achieved despite diversity of race, class, and sex in the church. But they also teach that true unity cannot be achieved without equal opportunity for participation in the life of the church regardless of race, class, and sex.

Discrimination of any kind is a monstrous denial of the oneness of the church of Christ. The Scripture promises destruction for anyone who thus destroys the church, the temple of God (1 Cor. 3:16–17) and judgment without mercy to anyone who is found guilty of practicing discrimination within the body of Christ (James 2:1–13).

The Teachings of the New Community

In the previous section, we discovered that the perspective of the apostolic church as reflected in its constitutional declarations was consistent with the teaching of Jesus on the nature of the church and its government. Our study could legitimately stop at this point. The instruction given by Jesus and the directions offered by the two inaugural declarations of the church provide sufficient normative guidance to formulate scriptural policies for our present-day churches. But the Epistles contain a number of teachings pertinent to our topic, since they reflect the efforts of the early church to conform itself to the teaching of Christ. When we survey those passages, we will discover that both Paul and Peter were able to maintain a course consistent with the teaching of Christ and with their own inaugural statements, as they addressed specific female-roles issues in a culture hostile to the Christian principle of nondiscrimination.

Equal Rights in Christian Marriage—1 Corinthians 7:1–5

The Corinthian Christians had written Paul to ask for Christian perspectives on marriage and celibacy. The first two verses of Paul's answer summarize the theme developed in this whole chapter: marriage is honorable, but celibacy is preferable. Should celibacy with chastity be impracticable, the appropriate alternative is matrimony. However, matrimony should not be viewed as a halfway compromise with celibacy. By its very nature, the married state requires that it be fully lived out, once it is assumed.

Verse 3. "The husband should fulfill his obligations to his wife, and likewise the wife to her husband." Marriage entails a bilateral assumption of commitment. The husband has expectations that must be met by the wife. But the same is true of the wife. She has expectations that must be met by the husband. Although this verse does not spell out the nature of such expectations, it confirms the principle of marital mutuality.

A male-dominant marital structure is characterized by unilateral subordination of the wife. Thereby, the male has rights and expectations, and the wife is dependent on his direction and goodwill. He defines her expectations and meets them as he sees fit. Not so in a biblically defined marriage. The reciprocal obligations are symmetrical. The Revised Standard Version translates this verse appropriately: "The husband should give to his wife her conjugal rights, and likewise the wife to her husband." The content of such rights find their definition in God's definition of marriage as a "one flesh" union predicated on mutuality in equality.

Lesson: In a Christian marriage, both husband and wife have legitimate expectations that must be met by the other.

Verse 4. "The wife does not have authority over her own body, but the husband *does*; and likewise also the husband does not have authority over his own body, but the wife *does*." This New American Standard Bible translation gives a literal rendering of the Greek text. The importance of this verse for a biblical perspective on male/female relations cannot be overestimated.[10]

1. The statement concerns the exercise of authority between husband and wife. The Greek word for "authority" appears twice in the sentence in symmetrical constructions for husband and wife.

2. The statement defines the nature of the obligations referred to in the preceding verse as a reciprocal right of husband and wife to exercise authority over each other.

3. The statement displays a perfect balance of terms linked together by the strongest word available in the Greek language to convey the concept of equivalency and translated by "likewise." The addition of the seemingly redundant adverbial conjunction "also" emphasizes the complete correspondence between the two propositions.

The first half of the sentence in verse 4 is no news 'at all. In a male-dominated culture, the wife does not rule over her own body; the husband does. But the explosive newness that the gospel brings to marriage is that the reverse formula is also true. Both husband and wife have exactly the same right of rulership over each other.

It might be objected that the mutual submission required by the reciprocal exercise of authority concerns only matters that pertain to the "body," and that the corporateness described in this text applies only to a narrow range of a couple's experience. However, the context of the passage does not justify such a restrictive definition of "body." A few lines above, while discussing sexual sin, the apostle Paul exclaims, "The body is meant for the Lord, and the Lord for the body" (6:13). The close association established in this text between the Lord and the "body" endows this term with a meaning that transcends sexual relations. The "body" represents the totality of a person's being, responding to the Lord or to a spouse.

No doubt the sexual union of spouses is included as a part of their shared authority and mutual submission. But it should be remembered that far from being relegated to the fringes of marital life, the sexual union expresses a depth of relationship that images the union of Christ and the church. It is when husbands love their wives as their own bodies that they image the love of Christ for the church (Eph. 5:28–32).[11] Therefore, the frame of reference for the mutual exercise of authority and reciprocal submission described in this passage concerns the totality of the lives of spouses, including its holistic expression in the sexual union.

Lesson: This statement stands as a clear invalidation of the principle of male rulership that resulted from the fall. Male authority is replaced by a relationship of mutual authority and mutual submission that reproduces in the life of the Christian couple the restoration of pre-fall conditions.

Verse 5. The same pattern of mutuality in equality is at work in the decision-making process. The resolve to withdraw temporarily from the preoccupations of marital life to seek individual spiritual retreat is not to be imposed by either spouse's posing as spiritual leader to the other. It is a decision that must be made conjointly. This means that either husband or wife may take the initiative in proposing such a plan, and that either one may veto its execution. The dynamics of mutuality at work in such a relationship rule out any kind of authority/subordination model. Decisions are made on the basis of consensual partnership. A couple is not an army unit, so it does not need to be ordered by a commanding officer to run properly. It is not a business corporation, so it is not run by a boss. It is not a branch of government, so it conducts its affairs without the need for a ruler. Husband and wife together make up a body. They are a church in microcosm. This text demonstrates that the principles of government laid down for the church by Jesus apply to the life of the Christian couple as well.

Lesson: The fact that the decisions of a Christian couple are made by mutual consent indicates a relationship without disparities of rank.

Equal Rights in Mixed Marriages—1 Corinthians 7:14

This text addresses the problem that arises when one of the spouses in a pagan family becomes a believer. Paul's answer is that such a mixed marriage obtains validity in God's sight as if both spouses were Christians. The Christian identity of the believer brings the marriage into God's "one flesh" definition. Divine grace becomes potentially accessible to the unbelieving spouse (v. 16). Consequently, God views the offspring of such a couple as His children. He sanctifies the fruit of their physical union by treating them no differently than the children of a family where both parents are believers.

Such a role of mediation, whereby the Christian spouse represents the whole family before God, can be played by either male or female. If we were to use the imagery of priesthood, we might say that a female believer as well as a male believer can act as priest before God on behalf of the rest of the family. A Christian wife may thus exercise the same level of spiritual authority in her family as a Christian husband in his. Because of the liberating power of the gospel, a Christian wife can expect to exert the same kind of influence on the rest of her family as her husband would if he were the believer. According to Paul, spiritual leadership may be exercised irrespective of whether the Christian spouse is male or female.[12]

Lesson: The undifferentiated role of a male or female Christian spouse in a mixed marriage parallels Paul's definition of mutuality for a Christian couple (v. 4). In either case, male and female have equal access to the challenges and opportunities of married life.

Equal Rights in Christian Service—1 Corinthians 7:32–35

According to Paul, the primary vocation of a Christian is not to get married and reproduce. For some, Christian service entails marriage. For others who have the ability to remain single, marriage would constitute a hindrance to their "undivided devotion to the Lord" (v. 35). Therefore, Paul calls upon all Christians to consider singleness as a preferred option and to marry only if they do not have the gift for remaining celibate (vv. 1–2). Paul tells people who thus opt for singleness that he wants them "to be free from all anxieties" so that they may devote their attention to "the affairs of the Lord." This being the case, the "unmarried man is anxious about the affairs of the Lord" (v. 32, RSV). As a free agent, he can devote himself unreservedly to God's service.

In a patriarchal society, one may expect a man to be allowed the freedom to make his own determinations in respect to marriage and celibacy and to volunteer for Christian service.

Such independence in decision making and vocational choice is a male prerogative in a male-dominant social structure.

Because the church is not a male-dominant community, Paul grants the identical privilege to celibate women and even to a younger "virgin." Like their male counterparts, they may choose to remain single in order to devote themselves to "the Lord's affairs" (v. 34, NIV).

The activity of both male and female celibates is described with the identical phrase of pursuing "the affairs of the Lord" (RSV). It is not apparent from this text that any difference in role attributions existed in the early church on the basis of gender. Single women were able to act as independent agents, not deriving their identities from a spouse or a male relative. They could choose to devote themselves to Christian service on the same basis as their male counterparts.

Lesson: This text indicates that the early church did not perpetuate in its life the functional differentiations between male and female that were prevalent in its ambiant patriarchal society. Men and women were treated as equals in their service to the church.

Worship Protocol—1 Corinthians 11:2–16

Obviously, the compact nature of this passage requires that it be approached gingerly. By isolating two or three of its sentences and by attempting to draw lessons apart from the context, one could easily make them say the opposite of their intended meaning. The passage contains some significant clues that will aid its comprehension. They are: (1) the different symbolic meaning of man's physical head and woman's physical head; (2) the relevance of headcovering for worship; and (3) the significance of worship on earth to the world above.

By taking into account those key ideas, we will be in a better position to uncover the main teachings of this condensed argument. The following is a freely expanded rendition of its content:

> When believers stand to pray and prophesy in the midst of a worshiping congregation, they enter into the very presence of God and His angels. Anyone entering the presence of God should cover his or her head as a sign of respect for Him. The angels cover their faces before Him (Isa. 6:2), and humans should follow their example.
>
> However, man and woman represent different realities in the presence of God. When a man faces the heavenly courts in worship, he represents both divinity and humanity combined in his person. His physical head is a reminder of the activity of Christ in creation, and it reflects the image and the glory of God. Therefore, it should not be covered.
>
> Christian worship signals the recovery of the purity of God's creation design. As communication with a nontemporal God, worship causes the collapse of time. A man who stands before God is a reminder of Adam in the garden. He causes the telescoping together of the two moments of creation and redemption. The angels watch and see man reflecting divine glory (his head) and human dignity (his being) combined together. This glory should not be covered, since it reflects the divine nature.
>
> A worshiping woman stands in a different relation than man before the courts of heaven. Because of the circumstances of her creation, a woman's physical head is a reminder of her derivation from man. Eve's being was drawn out of Adam. She reflects the fullness of human glory, both in herself and in her face, which is a copy of Adam's appearance. Therefore, a worshiping woman stands in a privileged position to represent authentic, uncompounded humanity before God. Unlike man, she does not stand for both the divine and the human. In the presence of God and the angels, she possesses the authority to reflect the glory of unmingled human personhood. Consequently, woman is uniquely qualified to represent the integral participation of humans into worship. As she enters the presence of

God she places both man and woman in relation with God.
Therefore, like the angels, she should cover her head.

To this development, the apostle Paul adds two important considerations. The first is in the form of a disclaimer. He does not want his argument on the difference between man and woman in creation to be used for drawing implications of male advantage because of chronological primacy in the sequence of creation. So, he states that "in the Lord," man's birth dependency on woman balances woman's origination from man. They both came from God, and He alone has primacy (vv. 11–12).

The second observation concerns confirmations of Paul's argument from creation in both nature and church practice. Paul draws significance from the traditionally accepted long hairstyles of women and their ancient custom of wearing a headcovering in public. He uses those cultural factors as confirmations that reinforce his theological argument.

Later, in 2 Corinthians 3:12–18, Paul has recourse to similar concepts of worship, the covering, the image, and the glory to describe the eternal destiny of all believers without reference to sex or creational disparities—and to declare freedom from the figurative veil for all Christians, male and female. He bases such conclusions on spiritual revelation from "the Lord who is the Spirit," rather than returning to creation guidelines, to nature, or to church practice in congregational worship. In the presence of God, Moses had reflected the divine radiance without hindrance. The veil had been placed upon him only for the benefit of his fellow Israelites (v. 13). Likewise, the new "freedom" brought by the Lord (v. 17) enables believers to approach God with boldness (v. 12), so that they *all* become increasingly capable of reflecting the divine image and glory without the hindrance of veiled faces (v. 18).

With this general perspective, several lessons relevant to our topic of female roles may be drawn from the 1 Corinthians 11:2–16 passage under consideration.

Lesson: The variety of references to the word *head* in this passage indicates that its definition should be approached with a great deal of caution. The Greek word for *head* refers primarily to the upper part of the human body but, as suggested in the paraphase above, it also has a figurative meaning. English-speaking people might expect that this figurative meaning of *head* might be chief, boss, authority, ruler, since *head* is used in this manner in the English language. However, in ancient Greek as well as in many other languages, *head* does not have that meaning at all.[13]

In order to avoid possible misunderstandings, translators of the Bible should avoid using direct word equivalents when such words do not have the same meaning as in the original language. For instance, the ambiguity of the word *bowels* has caused translators to abandon it where a literal translation would result in an obscenity (Philem. 7, 12, 20; 1 John 3:17; and so on). The word *head* falls in the same category, since it conveys, as we shall discover from the biblical text itself, the idea of derivation, origin, starting point, and nurture. The concept might be better served by the expression *fountainhead* or *life-source*. Thus, in the perspective of creation it makes sense to say that Christ is the fountainhead of man's life, and that man is the fountainhead of woman's life. Likewise, from the perspective of the incarnation, God is the fountainhead of Christ's life.[14]

The interpretation of *head* as ruler or authority, when applied to our text, would change its meaning entirely. It would result in a chain of subordination moving from the top of a hierarchy of power to the bottom: God is Christ's ruler, Christ is man's ruler, man is woman's ruler.[15] This approach raises several problems,[16] not the least of which is the fact that Paul's precise sequential arrangement of the three elements of this verse shows that he is not building a chain of command.

As a careful, inspired writer, Paul knows exactly how to build a hierarchy on a scale of decreasing importance. Thus, in 1 Corinthians 12:28, he starts at the top with first, then second, third, and down. But in 1 Corinthians 11:3, he begins with Christ/man, which in a hierarchical structure should be in second position; he goes on with man/woman, which in a hierarchical structure should be in third position; and he ends with God/Christ, which in a hierarchical structure should be in first position. According to this theory, Paul would have dislocated his alleged hierarchy by arranging it in this order: second, third, first. It is inconceivable that Paul would have so grievously jumbled up the sequence in a matter involving God, Christ, and humans, when he kept his hierarchy straight as he dealt with the lesser subject of spiritual gifts in 12:28.

This difficulty constitutes an insuperable argument against the hierarchical interpretation of 11:3. However, when the Greek word for *head* is properly rendered as "fountainhead," the problem disappears. Then the three relationships are viewed as illustrating the principle of headship as source of being, and they naturally fall into their chronological sequence as per Paul's order: first, Christ/man with the creation of man; second, man/woman with the formation of woman; and finally God/Christ with the birth of Jesus.

We conclude that the sequence of relationships in verse 3 does not warrant a hierarchical view of this text. It conforms to a chronological sequence that is further confirmed in the remainder of the passage as it emphasizes the symbolic meaning of headship as original representation and not authority. The findings of our examination of 1 Corinthians 11:3 may be thus summarized:

Hierarchical View		Chronological View	
God Christ man woman	Christ/man ——————— (creation of man) first	man/woman ——————— (formation of woman) second	God/Christ ——————— (birth of Christ) third

Lesson: Sometimes, it is argued that the worship exercises referred to in verses 4 and 5 as prayer and prophesying were practiced privately or among small circles of believers, so that they refer to something other than congregational worship. This view is to be rejected on two counts:

1. By definition, the gift of prophecy presupposes a congregational setting. Although there are abilities designed to minister only to the individuals practicing them privately, "he who prophesies edifies the church" (1 Cor. 14:4, RSV). If there is no church, what happens is something other than prophecy.

2. According to Jesus, two or three people gathered in His name constitute a worshiping community, since He becomes present in their midst (Matt. 18:20). The number of persons participating is immaterial, and the fact that either a man or a woman may decide to pray or prophesy suggests a mixed congregation.

Worship consists of many elements. Only two are cited in this instance: prayer and prophecy. Did Paul pick those at random, or is there a particular reason for their choice? The answer to this question lies in the peculiar nature of these two functions. Because they involve direct communication with God and from God, prayer and prophecy constitute the essence of worship. By prayer, the worshiper, along with the congregation, gains an entrance into the very presence of God—who then responds by giving His word to the congregation through the person prophesying.

The significance of the prophetic function in the New Testament is akin to that in the Old Testament. It is endowed with the highest ascription of authority, since the church is said to be "built upon the foundation of the apostles and prophets . . ." (Eph. 2:20). The gospel of Christ, hidden for a long time, is now "revealed to his holy apostles and prophets by the Spirit" (Eph. 3:5, RSV). This revelatory function of the prophets is operative at the level of the local church since the purpose of prophesying is that "all may learn" (1 Cor. 14:31, RSV). In addition to this didactic dimension, prophecy served devotional and inspirational purposes as it was used for "encouragement and consolation" as well as for the more formal "edification" which implies a teaching ministry (1 Cor. 14:3, 4). In Paul's listing of the spiritual gifts, prophecy is mentioned at the highest level, second only to the apostolate.[17] It is to be noted that in Paul's graded evaluation of spiritual gifts in 1 Corinthians, prophecy, as one of the three "higher gifts" (12:28–31), is to be desired more than the other gifts (14:1).[18]

When the apostle Paul enjoined the faithful to seek the spiritual gifts, especially the gift of prophecy, he opened the opportunity to all believers (14:31). Had Paul intended to prohibit women from prophesying, this twice-repeated invitation (vv. 5 and 31) would have offered him a marvelous opportunity to state a restrictive clause. Instead, he cited approvingly the fact that women were engaging in full parity with men in the ministry of prophecy within "the churches of God" (11:5, 16). We conclude that women had access, under apostolic sanction, to the highest levels of ministry in the early church, and that equivalent ministries should likewise be accessible to women in the modern church.[19]

Lesson: Some people use verses 7–10 of 1 Corinthians 11 as the New Testament confirmation of the subordination of women on the basis of man's chronological primacy in creation (Gen. 2). They interpret this passage as teaching that for a woman the wearing of the veil was a sign of her subordination to male authority. By this reasoning, woman has a subordinate status in regard to man because she was created from him and for him. Therefore, when a woman worships, she must wear the sign of her subordination upon her head.

However, this interpretation is beset with several difficulties that invalidate such a superficial reading and invite us to treat the passage with greater care.[20]

Verse 7. Men and women represent different realities in relation to God. By virtue of his unmediated origination, man's presence in worship emblemizes his head as his spiritual Maker. Man's head represents "the image and glory of God," somewhat like the "glory of God in the face of Christ" (2 Cor. 4:6). Man cannot represent mere humanity before God, since his physical head symbolizes Christ. Therefore, man is not permitted to use a headcovering in worship. He may not cover Christ (his head) in God's presence.

Woman in worship stands in a different relation before God. Because of her origination from man, she is fully qualified to represent the essence of complete, uncompounded humanhood before God. Her physical head emblemizes man as a reminder of her derivation from him. Therefore, she is humanity twice recognized, first for herself and again for man, represented by her physical head as her life-source. As such, she reflects the full "glory of man."

This dual representation is what enables woman to pray and prophesy in the congregation and to wear the headcovering that befits both humans and angels in the presence of God. For Paul, a woman's disposition to wear the headcovering was the sign of her willingness to represent the glory of full (male and female) humanhood before God.

Verses 8–9. If these two verses were interpreted as a teaching from Paul on female subordination by virtue of man's primacy in creation, consistency would require that Paul forbid women to exercise leadership in prophesying. As defined in the New Testament, prophecy represented the second-ranking authoritative ministry in the apostolic church. It was a role hardly fit for the subordinate members of a congregation.

The fact that Paul makes no such restriction indicates that subordination is not the issue in this passage. The point of the passage is not gender roles but worship protocol. The application Paul draws from these two verses does not concern relations between male and female but their relation to God. Paul addresses these arguments to support his contention that woman is better qualified to represent humanity before God since her head emblemizes man.

The "for" that begins verse 8 indicates that these sentences provide an explanation for woman being the "glory of man." Paul cites two privileges of woman that were denied to man at creation: she received the double advantage of being made from man and for man. She thus qualifies by both origination (from man) and purpose (for man) to represent male and female in worship (herself and man as her head). This is an honor to which man cannot lay claim, since "he was not made from woman" nor was he "created for woman" (RSV). He did not have a human antecedent. Woman has an entitlement to humanity that man did not receive in creation. He was the prototype of humankind; woman was its confirmation.[21]

Verse 10. The literal rendering of this verse is, "Therefore, the woman ought to have authority on the head because of the angels."

This much-debated and often-mistranslated text ("veil" instead of "authority" in the Revised Standard Version!) is introduced with the word *Therefore*, indicating that a conclusion is drawn from what precedes. In verses 7–9 Paul demonstrated the privileged status of women in worship. This verse is the clincher. It signifies that woman has the authority upon her (thanks to her head, which emblemizes man as her life-source) to stand in worship with angels in God's presence, as the embodiment of the fullness of humanity, both male and female.[22]

No doubt, this command was given to oppose the misinformed zeal of Judaic misogynists who, as we shall discover in our study of 1 Corinthians 14, were trying to impose repressive rules designed to restrict female participation in the life of the church.

Lesson: The climactic position of verses 11 and 12 in Paul's argumentation and the commanding tone of the statement give it the force of a summation. In the Greek text, this thought unit begins with a Greek word (usually translated as "nevertheless") that indicates a sharper focus on what precedes it. In the previous verses, Paul's argumentation had caused him to establish comparisons between the relative positions of man and woman before God. But he realizes that this is a potentially dangerous venture, since it could result in grievous misunderstandings if such comparisons were carried over into areas of life other than decorum in worship, which is the exclusive topic of this passage.[23] Consequently, in order to dispel any possible misunderstanding of his previous statements, Paul makes a sweeping disclaimer intended to put such speculations to rest forever.

It is also possible that the men who opposed female participation in the worship and leadership of the Corinthian church were building their case on the chronological primacy of man in the Genesis account. For whatever reason, Paul gives his ultimate teaching on the significance for the Christian church of the man-first/woman-second order of Genesis 2. His teaching is that "in the Lord" the sequence of male/female creation has no significance. His words in verses 11–12 may be paraphrased:

> Regardless of what may have been said or taught prior to this, in the Lord, that is, within the unity that exists among Christians, woman may not be viewed apart from man, nor man from woman. For just as woman was originally made

from man, now man is made with the mediation of woman. So, it all evens out.

There is only one who has original primacy, and that one is God, the real source of all things (including both man and woman).

There could hardly be any clearer statement than these two verses to the effect that—whatever implications may have been drawn in the past from the male/female sequence in creation—such implications have been rendered obsolete in Christ. The leveling and unitive power of the cross has made all Christians interdependent (v. 11), which interdependency is deeply rooted in the fact that man and woman are also interdependent by virtue of their reciprocal origination (v. 12). Woman cannot take pride in her representational advantage in worship, because men and women are interdependent in Christ (v. 11). Man should not exploit to rulership advantage his creational primacy, since he is dependent on woman for his very life (v. 12). But both man and woman may ascribe primacy and rulership to God, who alone is the originator of all things.[24]

To rob God of the original primacy that belongs to Him alone as Creator of all things, and to attribute it to man by claiming male privilege because Adam preceded Eve in creation, is an idolatrous offense that is prohibited by this text. Paul affirms that the issue of man's original primacy is irrelevant for Christians.

Singing Males and Silent Women— 1 Corinthians 14:31-40

This passage of 1 Corinthians contains the most surprising statement of the whole Epistle:

. . . As in all the churches of the saints, the women should keep silence in the churches. For they are not permitted to

speak, but should be subordinate, as even the law says. If there
is anything they desire to know, let them ask their husbands at
home. For it is shameful for a woman to speak in church (1 Cor.
14:33–35, RSV).

Without any warning, Paul serves his readers with this abrupt, unqualified, unmitigated statement of prohibition. With
a few categorical sentences, each reinforcing the previous one,
women are reduced to absolute silence within the church. The
reference to "all the churches" allows no exception and no contradiction. To leave no doubt regarding the meaning of the
command for women to "keep silence in the churches," it is
also stated in the form of its negative corollary, "they are not
permitted to speak." The twice-repeated use of the basic verb
for oral communication *to speak* extends the range of the prohibition to any form of articulate expression. It applies to all
manners of speech such as prayer, prophecy, tongues, interpretation, evaluation, teaching, and even to the whisper of women
who might be tempted to ask their husbands a question during
the congregational worship. The rationale given for this sweeping prohibition is that women who speak in church break the
law by committing a "shameful" act of insubordination.

The comprehensive character of this proscription emphasizes its shocking brutality. It is reminiscent more of practices
in ancient Judaic synagogues than the Christian churches established by Paul, where women could pray and prophesy on
an equal standing with men (11:4–5). This statement creates
such a massive contradiction within the Epistle itself, it is so
much out of character with Paul, it so blatantly revokes clear
statements of egalitarian participation that a multitude of attempts have been made to resolve the scandal it provokes.[25]

In particular, the juxtaposition of Paul's approval of women
prophesying (11:5) with this absolute command for women
not to speak in church and to remain silent as a sign of their

subordination constitutes such a monumental contradiction
that only a state of mental dissociation could explain an authorial inconsistency of such proportions. But Paul was no
schizophrenic. All the evidence indicates that he was in perfect
control of his mind and that he was consciously relying on
divine guidance as he wrote instructions to the Corinthian
church (2:4, 7, 10, 12–13, 16; 4:1, 17; 5:3–4; 7:10, 40; and so
on). Obviously, the prohibition statement needs to be examined
minutely, both in its content and from the perspective of the
historical situation in Corinth—in order to determine Paul's
intent in writing it down, and whether the passage reflects his
own thinking or a deviant teaching quoted by Paul
disapprovingly.

As we shall see, it is not necessary to engage in hermeneutical contortions to discover how this passage fits with the rest
of the Epistle. There is a natural explanation that provides a
key for its understanding. But to find it we need to examine
closely both the context and the content of this statement.

The Context

The prohibition is surrounded by two sets of parallel statements that provide a double frame for it.

Frame one consists of verses 31 and 39. In both of those
verses there is a concern for broad congregational participation
in worship. Apparently, Paul had received reports about the
obstructionist activities of domineering leaders who monopo-
lized for themselves the worship exercises of the Corinthian
church. To break their control over corporate worship, Paul
lays down a set of rules intended to provide widespread participation to all members of the congregation. When they gather
for worship, he wants each one to come ready to make a presentation for the edification of the group (v. 26). He establishes
the necessity of interpretation (v. 28) and of evaluation (v. 29),
which will require the involvement of large segments of the

congregation and deter the filibustering strategies of the mo-
nopolizers. He sets a time limit on individual participation and
requires deference toward other participants (v. 30). But most
of all, the apostle insists on the right of *all* believers to make
their contribution to worship (v. 31) and to "earnestly desire"
to take part (v. 39, RSV). Thus, Paul curbs the assertiveness of
the bold and facilitates the involvement of the meek.

Frame two consists of verses 33 and 40, which convey Paul's
concern for "peace" and "order" during the worship services
of the Corinthian church. The competition and the power plays
of the leaders, vying for visibility in ostentatious forms of ministry, produced tumults and confusion instead of peace (v. 33).
The tensions created by such tactics resulted in conflicts that
were too easily dismissed as the by-product of spiritual eu-
phoria. Against such disorders, Paul teaches the Corinthians
that worshipers should always be in control of their actions
(v. 32) and that tumults are not of divine origin (v. 33).

We conclude from this survey of the context of the prohibition statement that Paul was facing a church situation where
arrogant members were competing for conspicuous ministries,
thus excluding less-sanguine believers from bringing their active participation to congregational worship. As we shall discover in our study of the content of the prohibition statement,
they had devised a scheme to shut off women from participation, thus reducing the competition by half. Since women
were already at the bottom of the pecking order in ambiant
society, they became the easy victims of ecclesiastical intolerance.

The Content

The statement of prohibition contains several clues that indicate a non-Pauline authorship and point to a restrictive Judaic
origin.

Verse 33. The practice of keeping women silent is presented
as a model coming from "all the churches of the saints." This

designation of "churches of the saints" appears only once in the New Testament. Its peculiarity resides in its redundancy. A reference to "all the churches" would have been sufficient. The added qualification of "saints" suggests a particular group of churches whose practice is presented as normative for all churches.

In the early years of the Christian movement, the term *saints* designated exclusively the Jewish Christians of Jerusalem and Palestine (Acts 9:13, 32, 41; 26:10). When churches were established in the Gentile world, the Jewish Christians of Jerusalem continued to be called "the saints" (1 Cor. 16:1, *cf.* v. 3; 2 Cor. 8:4; 9:12; Rom. 15:25, 26, 31). Later, the designation of "saints" was extended to all Christians (1 Cor. 1:2), but it also remained a consecrated name for the Jerusalem Christians (1 Cor. 16:1, *cf.* v. 3). Therefore, there is good reason to believe that it is the practice of the original, Palestine-based Christian communities that is presented as being paradigmatic for the Gentile churches.

Verse 34. Whenever the apostle Paul gives instructions that apply to all the churches, he makes it clear that he is the author of the regulations ("This is my rule in all the churches" [7:17]; ". . . we recognize no other practice, nor do the churches of God" [11:16]; ". . . as I directed the churches" [16:1]). In this text, the prohibition is never endorsed as his own. The sanction for the authority is established practice rather than apostolic directive ("the women *should* keep silence in churches").

The same indefiniteness is reflected in the restatement of the prohibition ("they are not permitted to speak"), where Paul would normally assume personal responsibility for making such a prohibition ("I permit no woman to teach" [1 Tim. 2:12]). The authors of the prohibition appeal to the practice of "the churches of the saints" instead of affirming their own authority—because they have none. But realizing the weakness of this approach, they attempt to strengthen their argument by appealing also to "the law." This appeal to the Old Testament constitutes in itself sufficient proof that Paul is not the author of this statement. An appeal to the old-covenant law to justify Christian practice was a Judaizing legalism·that was violently opposed by Paul throughout his ministry. For him the law was either fulfilled allegorically in the new covenant (1 Cor. 9:9–10; 14:21) or superseded by the gospel (Rom. 7:6; Gal. 3:23–25). Paul is reluctant to establish Christian practice on the law. In any case, should he have been tempted to do so, he would have found no ordinance in the Old Testament prescribing women to be silent because they were subordinate. There is not the slightest hint of a regulation in the Old Testament that can be interpreted in this manner.[26] It is more likely that the authors of the prohibition invoked "the law" deviously to claim divine support for the arbitrariness of their own ruling. The stratagem was so obvious that Paul simply countered it by invoking the "command of the Lord" (v. 37).

Verse 35. The literal translation of this amazing sentence is: "If they wish to learn anything, let them ask their own husbands at home." There are several elements in this injunction that reveal its Judaic origin.[27]

1. The fact that women were not even qualified to be learners in the assembly is verified in Talmudic literature. Their presence was tolerated but they remained unobtrusively silent.

2. The fact that a woman might wish to come out of her passivity in order to learn something is viewed as an exceptional occurrence rendered by the conjunction *if.* This is a far cry from women praying and prophesying, according to 11:5.

3. The assumption that women in attendance would all be married (no alternative is given for single women) points to a Judaic background where all women were expected to be married. Paul's preference for Christian women to remain single for the purpose of ministry is not taken into account (7:34).

4. Husbands are presented as their wives' sole resource for

obtaining information. It is assumed that husbands are sufficiently knowledgeable to answer their wives' questions. This
reflects a Judaic setting where only males received religious
education.

5. Women are to ask questions of their husbands in the
seclusion of their homes, not in church or even on the street.
This absolute segregation of the sexes is redolent of ancient
Judaic domestic life.

According to these proscriptions, the silence of women in
church gatherings should have been absolute to the extent that
they were forbidden to ask questions even of their own husbands, while male worshipers would come up with hymns
(presumably sung by men only, while women remained silent),
lessons, revelations, tongues, interpretations (v. 26), prophecies, and evaluations (v. 29). Such conditions better describe
the ancient synagogue, where it was "shameful for a woman
to speak."

The contents of the prohibition statement rule out Pauline
origin. We can be certain that the statement reflects neither his
words nor his views. The appeal to the practice of the "churches
of the saints," the unwarranted adducement of "the law," and
the unyielding comprehensiveness of the injunction to silence
indicate that Paul is quoting derisively the words of his Judeo-
Christian opponents, who often troubled the churches he had
established in Gentile territory. In this prohibition statement
Paul is giving them back one of their own slogans.

One of the leading women of the congregation had alerted
Paul regarding the disorders that were taking place within the
church of Corinth (1:11). No doubt she would have been especially sensitive to efforts exerted by alien elements to subvert
Paul's ministry under the guise of allegedly purist legalistic
concerns. She would have communicated to Paul a summary
of their teaching and some of their choice dicta. By citing them
in this Epistle, Paul was sure that the Corinthians would rec-

ognize the teachings of the troublemakers, especially since they are quoted in the context of Paul's concern for universal participation (vv. 31, 39), and of "peace" and "order" (vv. 33, 40) in congregational worship. The Corinthians would not have failed to perceive the relevance of those two concerns of Paul to the disruptive effects of the false teaching he cited.

In this Epistle more than in any other, Paul is in the habit of quoting the words of the opposition.[28] Such occurrences are not readily recognizable today, because punctuation and quotation marks were not used in the original language. However, the context and content of such statements make them discernable, especially when they stand in contrast with Paul's own views, as is the case with the prohibition statement.

The Rebuke

Verses 36–38 provide additional support to the view that the prohibition statement is cited disapprovingly by Paul as a quote from false teachers.

Verse 36. The grammatical structure of this verse indicates a sharp break with the preceding statement. The Revised Standard Version has caught the progression of Paul's thought as it translates, "What! Did the word of God originate with you, or are you the only ones it has reached?"

Recent scholarship has called attention to the disjunctive force of the particle *ē* that introduces verse 36.[29] It has the impact of an emphatic repudiation of what precedes it. A colloquial equivalent such as "Bunk!" instead of "What!" would come close to rendering the effect of dissociation between the prohibition statement (vv. 33–35) and Paul's response to it in verse 36.

Moreover, the abrupt shift from the third-person pronoun ("they," the women) in the prohibition statement to an emphatic second-person masculine in verse 36 (*monous:* "just you men") indicates that Paul is now taking to task a male element in the Corinthian church, rather than rebuking women for getting out of line.

Paul's reaction to the prohibition statement is couched in the form of an apostrophe with sarcastic overtones. It is an outburst directed at male Corinthians to reproach them for entertaining alien ideas, thus calling in question his own apostolic teaching. The two clauses of verse 36 may be paraphrased:

> Since when have you become the source of divine revelation so that you make your own rules? Or are you the exclusive recipients of a divine revelation that the rest of us should know about?

The rebuke is for their willingness to replace his standards regarding male/female roles with the anti-women proscriptions of the Judaizing teaching.

Verse 37. In this verse Paul narrows down the focus of his wrath upon the ringleaders of the misogynist faction who had laid claim to privileged status ("prophet," "spiritual") in order to disseminate their deviant views in Corinth. They were probably the same sort of people as those who created "dissensions," "quarreling" (1:10, 11, 13) and "divisions" (11:17–19), and who, as a result, were "destroying God's temple," the church (3:16–17). From Paul's description of them we get the impression of arrogant, factious, obstructionist loudmouths competing for positions of power (4:18–19). Paul opposes their perverted teaching with his own views, based on the standards laid by Christ Himself. The Judaizers claim "the law" as authority. Paul claims the "command of the Lord" as his authority. This contrast provides the explanation for the irreducible differences between Paul's views on female roles and those reflected in the Judaizers' prohibition statement.

Verse 38. The matter is serious enough for Paul to threaten divine rejection of the proponents of male dominance for noncompliance to the "command of the Lord." In the light of such a rebuke, it behooves contemporary Christians to align their church life on the command of Christ and the teachings of Paul rather than to proof-text out of its context the Judaizers' prohibition statement and to fall into similar perversions by making it the basis of their practice.

Mutual Submission—Ephesians 5:21–33

Two concepts provide the thought structure of this passage: submission and headship. Before proceeding with the study of this passage, we will endeavor to establish the meaning of those concepts on the basis of the biblical text itself.

Submission

The verb "to be subject" or "to be submitted" appears in verse 21. This sentence serves as a hinge between two different sections. The first section consists of verses 18–20, and the second of verses 22–33, with verse 21 providing the connection between the two. This structure can be pictured as the two flaps of an open folder, with verse 21 constituting the crease.

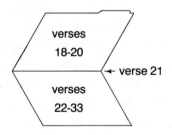

The relation of verse 21 to the bottom section is our main concern, and it will be considered later. Prior to that, it is necessary to discuss the upper side. With verse 21 as part of the upper side, the passage would read:

    . . . be filled with the Spirit, addressing one another in psalms

and hymns and spiritual songs, singing and making melody in
your hearts, always and for everything giving thanks in the
name of our Lord Jesus Christ to God the Father, being submitted to one another out of reverence for Christ. . . .

This passage consists of a series of exhortations addressed
to all Christians regardless of sex or rank. As the result of being
"filled with the Spirit," believers communicate with each other
and with the Lord in the languages of Christian love and they
submit to one another, literally "in the fear of Christ."

The word used for "submit" in this sentence is the same as
the one used in reference to Christians making themselves "subject" to the governing authorities (Rom. 13:1, 5) and to God
(James 4:7). Therefore, "submit" means to make oneself subordinate to the authority of a higher power, to be dependent
for direction on the desires and orders of a superior in rank or
position, to yield to rulership.

This is the natural meaning of "submit" wherever the word
appears in the New Testament, except where its meaning is
deliberately changed by a modifier such as in verse 21 of our
text. The addition to "being submitted" of the reciprocal pronoun "to each other" changes its meaning entirely. "Being subject to one another" is a very different relationship from "being
subject to the other."[30] For instance, two soldiers may be told
by their officer to be subject to one another and to help each
other in their assignment by making themselves available to
each other. But the officer is not subject to the soldiers. By
definition, mutual submission rules out hierarchical differences. Being subject to one another is only possible among
equals. It is a mutual (two-way) process that excludes the
unilateral (one-way) subordination implicit in the concept of
subjection without the reciprocal pronoun. Mutual subjection
is a horizontal relationship among equals. Subjection is a ver-
tical relationship between ruler and subject.

To continue to speak of positions of individual authority where no one by himself exercises authority, because everybody yields to each other, is to talk nonsense. Whenever an individual wields authority over another, we have a case of subjection, not of *mutual* subjection. But when that individual sets aside the authority role and relates to others as an equal, mutual subjection becomes possible.[31]

In the military, should the officer yield to the footsoldier in mutual subjection, there would remain no army. In business, should the boss yield to the workman in mutual subjection, the place would go bankrupt. In government, should the tax collector yield to the taxpayer in mutual subjection, the state would go broke. It is precisely because the church is not the army, nor a business corporation, nor a political empire, that mutual subjection is enjoined by the Word of God as the normal pattern of relationship among Christians. The church thrives on mutual subjection. In a Spirit-led church, the elders submit to the congregation in being accountable for their watch-care, and the congregation submits to the elders in accepting their guidance.[32] Indeed, the church ceases to be the church and collapses spiritually when there is no mutual submission among its members. What, then, is mutual submission and how does it work?

The command for mutual subjection is not given in a vacuum. It requires a spiritual context that begins with the fullness of the Spirit (v. 18), continues with a consistent attitude of thankfulness to the Father (v. 20), and culminates with reverence for Christ (v. 21). The prior condition for the success of mutual subjection is subjection to the Triune God. This is made especially clear in verse 21, which is translated almost identically in most versions: "Be subject to one another out of reverence for Christ." Interpersonal subjection among believers is possible only because of the common acknowledgment of the supremacy of Christ. He alone is Lord among them, and He alone is to be revered (literally "feared") among them. Again, we find here the leveling power of the cross at work in the Christian community. Christ is the authority before whom all Christians bow.

In this perspective, mutual subjection is a very precious reality of corporate Christian life. It takes the full involvement of the Trinity to make it possible. As the hallowed hallmark of Christian communities, both church and family, mutual submission should be worked out in "the fear of Christ" and jealously protected from hierarchical encroachments that might be imported among believers from the world and not from Christ.

In everyday life, mutual submission requires that Christians, regardless of status, function, sex, or rank, "through love be servants [literally "slaves"] of one another" (Gal. 5:13). When Christians love one another to the extent of serving each other as slaves, there remains no justification for distinctions among them of ruler and subordinate. They all become subordinate to each other.[33] Then the dynamics of community life spring from a shared desire to serve others, to give of oneself, and to make a primary concern the interests and the welfare of fellow believers. Although they may continue to exist, the distinctions of rank and hierarchy become insignificant as they are transcended by the higher principle of mutual submission. The quality of community life described in Ephesians 4:31—5:2 and Philippians 2:3–5 is the result of mutual submission, not the product of coercion by persons in authority exerting executive power over their subordinates.

We conclude that mutual subjection as defined on the basis of Ephesians 5:18–21 refers to relationships of reciprocal servanthood under the sole lordship of Christ, and that the reciprocity of such relationships renders hierarchical distinctions irrelevant within the Christian communities of church and family.

Headship

As we dealt with the concept of headship in relation to 1 Corinthians 11:3, we discovered how important it is not to impose current meaning on ancient vocabulary. In approaching this passage (Eph. 5:21–33), we face again the challenge of finding in the biblical text itself the meaning of the word *head*. It would be easy for us to simply assume that *head* in Ephesians 5:23 means "authority," as it does in the English language. But having already been exposed to the hazards of making such facile equations while studying the Corinthian text, we realize the need to conduct a careful word study and to determine the meaning of this word from the text itself. The passages relevant to such a study are contained in two related Epistles: Ephesians (1:22; 4:15; 5:23) and Colossians (1:18; 2:18, 19). Whatever definition is yielded for *head* in those six verses, it should become our definition.

Ephesians 1:22—The most natural translation of this verse is "He [God] subjected all things under His feet and gave Him as head, above all things, to the church."[34] This verse contains two metaphors. The first one has to do with feet. Christ has assumed a position of universal transcendence in His post-resurrection exaltation, as all things were placed under His feet. The second concerns His headship to the church, described in the next verse as His body. Christ is head to the church that is His only body. He is not head to all things or head over all things, since all things are already under His feet and since He has only one body, His church. Above all things, He is head to the church. His supreme role is in relation to the church.

In verse 23, additional insight is given into the purpose of Christ's headship to the church. Christ as head supplies the body with its "fullness." He provides the church with the nurturance that is necessary for growth and completion. In His headship, He is the source of life and increase for the church.

In this passage, there is no reference to headship as assumption of authority over the church.

Ephesians 4:15–16—The same concept of the head as provider of fullness and growth is developed in this passage. Believers "grow up in every way in him who is the head" (RSV). He provides what is necessary for the joining and the knitting together of the body, and He is the source of its growth. The function of the head, according to this passage, is to provide life, cohesion, and growth. There is no authority or rulership significance attached to headship.

Ephesians 5:23—This passage offers a succinct, formula-like definition that goes to the heart of the matter: "Christ is the head of the church." To help his readers understand properly the significance of this statement, Paul adds this explanation: "He is himself the Savior of the body." The emphatic pronoun rendered here by "himself" indicates that Paul makes a point of the fact that saviorhood pertains to Christ's headship. This servant-ministry of the Savior receives further elaboration in verse 25: "Christ loved the church and gave himself up for her," and in verse 29: "For no man ever hates his own flesh, but nourishes it and cherishes it, as Christ does the church" (RSV). The motif of Christ as the source of nurture appears again in this passage.

In this development on the meaning of headship, there is nothing in the text to suggest that *head* might have implications of rulership or authority. Had this been the case, Paul would have more appropriately stated, "Christ is the head of the church. He is himself the Lord of the body" instead of "the Savior of the body." However, the terminology of authority is not used in reference to Christ and His headship. To the contrary, His headship is clearly defined in terms of saviorhood, servanthood, and nurturance. Again, *head* designates the source of life ("Savior"), of servanthood ("gave himself up"), and of growth ("nourishes it").

At first sight, it might seem strange that Paul uses the servant role of Christ as an argument for wifely submission as indicated by the conjunction *For* at the beginning of verse 23. As will be shown later at greater length, the point made by Paul is that submission is the proper response to servanthood. This is the very meaning of mutual submission (v. 21). The church is submitted to Christ in reciprocation of Christ's servanthood to her. In the same manner, wives submit to their husbands to reciprocate, in mutual submission, their husbands' self-sacrificing love for their wives (vv. 24–25).

Colossians 1:18—The statement about headship is almost identical to the one in Ephesians 5:23. "He is the head of the body, the church." Again, the immediate context provides a definition for headship. Christ is the source of the church's cohesion as in Him "all things hold together" (v. 17), and He is the source of the church's life since He "is the beginning" (v. 18).

The reference to the headship of Christ on behalf of the church occupies the central position in this great christological statement (vv. 15–20), which deals essentially with the creation activity of the pre-existent Christ (vv. 15–17) and His servant-ministry in death and resurrection (vv. 18–20).

There is no reference in this text to Christ's rank, authority, or rulership relative to His headship. The mention of Christ as having first place (*proteuo*) in all things (v. 18) has a chronological significance since it is brought up as the explanation for His being the "beginning" and the "first-born from the dead," which both give a time indication. The term of itself does not convey the meaning of rulership. It declares Christ's preeminence as originator of the church (He is "the head of the body"), the creator of all things (He is "the beginning"), and the initiator of the universal resurrection ("the first-born from the dead"). All three functions describe Him as the source of new realities.

Colossians 2:10—Christ is "the head of all power and authority" because He is the source of their existence. Indeed, Paul has stated earlier in this Epistle that in Him "all things were created," including "powers and authorities" (1:16). Christ's headship of "powers and authorities" is not a role of subjugation but of origination. Again, He is head as provider of life to forces that might have become part of His body, the church. However, He had to defeat them because of their rebellion (2:15).[35]

Paul draws a headship parallel to the church in our text as he emphasizes also the generative and nurturing function of Christ in relation to believers. He states that "you have come to fullness of life in him." As we discovered previously, providing "fullness" is a headship function of Christ. The reason for the mention of headship in this verse is to emphasize the life-giving function of Christ. Just as the church is dependent on Him for "fullness of life," in like manner the "powers and authorities" derive their existence from Christ. This text, like the others, is also devoid of any mention or connotation of rulership in reference to the headship of Christ.

Colossians 2:19—". . . the Head, from whom the whole body, nourished and knit together through its joints and ligaments, grows with a growth that is from God" (RSV). Although the grammatical reconstruction of this verse in translation is open to debate, its meaning is clear. The body draws from the head the vitalities that make cohesion and growth possible. Again headship is described in terms that evoke solicitous servant-hood and sustained provision of life resources. There is no trace in this passage of "head" as signifying anything that might suggest authority or rulership.

As we conclude this survey, it should be parenthetically noted that "head" is also used figuratively in Paul's parable of the members of the body, illustrating the interdependency of believers within the church (1 Cor. 12:14–25). The head is just one of the parts that is mentioned on a par with hand, foot, ear, eye, and less presentable parts that are treated with greater modesty. There is no mention made in that passage of the head's enjoying a privileged position or of its exercising authority over the rest of the body.

The use of "head" within the contexts where it is found in 1 Corinthians, Ephesians, and Colossians forces on us the conclusion that the concept of headship in the New Testament refers to the function of Christ as the fountainhead of life and growth and to His servant role of provider and sustainer.[36] The New Testament contains no text where Christ's headship to the church connotes a relationship of authority. Likewise, the New Testament contains no text where a husband's headship to his wife connotes a relationship of authority.

The meaning of the head-body duality is not authority but reciprocity. *Because* Christ is the wellspring of the church's life and provides it with existence and sustenance, *in return* the church serves Him in loving dependency and in recognition of Him as the source of its life. In a similar manner, the head-body metaphor applied to the husband-and-wife relationships serves to emphasize their essential unity, deriving from creation. *Because* man as the fountainhead of the woman's existence was originally used to supply her with her very life, and because he continues to love her sacrificially as his own body in marriage, *in return* a Christian wife binds herself to her husband in a similar relationship of servant submission that expresses their oneness. The imposition of an authority structure upon this exquisite balance of reciprocity would paganize the marriage relationship and make the Christ/church paradigm irrelevant to it.

As noted previously, such definitions have been drawn from the biblical text itself. They are also confirmed by the best lexical research available to date on extra-biblical usage contemporary to the authors of the New Testament. Owing to the pressure exerted upon Bible versions by the meaning of the word *head* as "authority" in the English language, it would be preferable to substitute the terminology *fountainhead* for the word *head* in the passages discussed above.

Wives and Husbands

As we began our consideration of the role played by verse 21 (our hinge verse) in relation to the two sides of our open folder, we discovered that its relation to the upper side (vv. 18–20) concerned the practice of mutual subjection by believers in their relationship within the church. We still need to discover how verse 21 relates to the bottom side (vv. 22–33).

We called verse 21 a hinge verse because it belongs grammatically to both sides of our imaginary folder. It fits with the

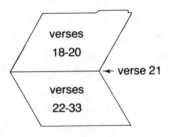

upper side in that it is the last of a series of injunctions deriving from the command to be filled with the Spirit (addressing . . . , singing . . . , making melody . . . , giving thanks . . . , being submitted . . .). But it also belongs with the bottom side. If verse 21 is separated from verse 22—as some versions do through faulty paragraphing (the New International Version provides a prime example)—verse 22 becomes meaningless, since the sentence is devoid of a verb in the original text. Literally, verse 22 reads "wives to their own husbands as to the Lord." Verse 22 derives its verb from verse 21.[37] Thus, verse 21 serves as a conclusion to the top side of our two-part development and also as an introduction to the bottom side. Verse 21 introduces the topic of husband-wife relationships under the title of mutual submission. The pivotal role played by verse 21 between its two contexts might be brought out by this literal rendering of the Greek text:

Verse 20 . . . always and for everything giving thanks in the name of our Lord Jesus Christ to God the Father,

Verse 21 being submitted to one another out of reverence for Christ,

Verse 22 wives, to your husbands as to the Lord. . . .

Thematically, the hinge function of verse 21 means that mutual submission is the proper attitude of believers toward one another within the church (upper portion, vv. 18–20) and also within the home (lower portion, vv. 22–23).[38] Since mutual submission is the rule for *all* believers, it also applies to all husbands and to all wives who are believers. This is why Paul can easily shift from the application of the principle of mutual submission among believers within the church (vv. 18–20) to its application between husbands and wives within the home (vv. 22–33).

With verse 21 functioning as a title and as an introduction for the whole section in verses 22–23, the conclusion for this passage is drawn from the creation text in Genesis 2:24 (vv. 31–32). Thus, verse 21 at the top and this climactic statement from Genesis at the bottom form together an appropriate thematic frame around the discussion of mutual subjection in married life. Paul states in verses 31–32:

"For this reason a man shall leave his father and mother and be joined to his wife, and the two shall become one." This is a great mystery, and I take it to mean Christ and the church (RSV).

In this concluding statement, Paul shows the continuity of purpose that exists between the union of man and woman in creation, the union of Christ and the church in redemption, and the union of husband and wife in marriage. The consistent link between those three sets of relationships is the principle of mutual self-expenditure—that is to say, the subordination of oneself to the interests of the other. In creation, man gives up his father and mother and joins himself to his wife to become one body with her (v. 31), and vice versa for the wife. Likewise, in redemption, Christ gave Himself up in order to bring the church in union to Himself (v. 25). The church reciprocates by subordinating herself to Him in everything (v. 24). Similarly, in marriage, the husband gives himself up for his wife as Christ did for the church (v. 25), and the wife reciprocates by subordinating herself to her husband (v. 23).

In order to justify such a revolutionary concept of marital relations, the apostle Paul invokes a "mystery," which in his language means a now-revealed truth that discloses a reality that had previously remained hidden. In this case, the revelation lies in the fact that mutual submission is much more than an ethical novelty or a convenient solution to the war of the sexes. Mutual submission pertains to the very nature of Christ and His ministry. It reaches deeply into the creation work of God. It provides the archetypal paradigm of God's dealings with mankind through Christ. For Paul, the marriage relationship is the environment where the deeper meaning of Christ's sacrificial love for the church can be exhibited through the practice of mutual subjection by both husband and wife. Therefore, we should not regard the concept of mutual submission as being relegated to verse 21. It permeates the entire development concerning husband/wife relations in verses 21 through 33.

The Meaning of Mutual Submission for Wives—Ephesians 5:21–24. There are different definitions of "submission," deriving from a variety of situations and motivations.

For instance, there is a calculating kind of submission that is manipulative, parasitic, and self-serving. Its aim is to obtain advantages by ingratiation. Within recent years, several female authors have written books for Christian wives that advocate this kind of calculating submission, intended to obtain the fulfillment of secret desires through the practice of "feminine wiles."

Another form of submission is that which results from the self-depreciation of persons who have been socialized to view themselves as inferior in rank or ability. It is the servility of the "loser," the fawning of the vanquished, the surrender of self-esteem by the powerless and the oppressed.

Then there is the submission of conciliation, which is extended out of a desire to placate petulance and irascibility. It yields to appease. It concedes in compliance for the sake of peace. It gives in rather than fight.

Finally, there is the submission of resignation to bitter necessity—the resentful, begrudging, foot-dragging recognition of the inevitable; the reluctant bowing to power, be it the power of the laws of men or the decrees of inscrutable destiny.

When the apostle Paul enjoins wives to be submitted to their husbands, he rejects all worldly patterns of submission and substitutes for them a new definition. This new definition of submission is based on the following considerations:

Verse 22. When wives are instructed to be subject to their husbands "as to the Lord," it does not mean that a wife suddenly acquires two lords or that her commitment to her husband has the unconditional ultimacy of their commitment to Christ. This would be an idolatrous substitution. Christian wives have only one Lord, who will cede His place to no other. However, "as to the Lord" means that a wife's commitment in submission to her husband should be of a quality similar to her devotion to the Lord. The parallel text in Colossians 3:18 makes this even more explicit as it states, "Wives, be subject to your husbands, as is fitting in the Lord." A wife's submission to the Lord, like any other believer's, is the response of love to the Savior, the fountainhead of the life of the church and, therefore, of every believer (v. 23). The proper response to the Savior's servant love is reciprocal servant love. Therefore, "as to the Lord" means that a wife submits to her husband in the same kind of loving service that she renders to the Savior. She submits to the Lord not in servility but in servanthood. Likewise, a wife submits to her husband not in servility but in servanthood. Wives submit not because they have to (obedience), but because they want to (servanthood). They submit not because they knuckle down under authority, but because they respond to love with love.[39]

Verse 23. The explanation provided in this verse ("For") expands on the rationale for a wife's submission by rooting the principle of mutual submission in creation and redemption. The husband or the man (the Greek word may mean either) is the fountainhead of a wife or a woman (the Greek word may mean either), in that woman was made out of man. A marriage relationship is an ever-present sign of the goodness of God in creation. It emblemizes creation by pointing to God as the source of all blessing, the very God who used man as the source of woman's life (Gen. 2). We have discovered in 1 Corinthians 11:8–9 how important this reminder was for the life of the church. It is also important in the life of the couple. As Adam submitted to a sort of death to become the fountainhead of a woman's life, in the same manner and in reciprocality, a wife dies to herself in order to live for her husband.

The reference to creation is further enriched with an appeal to redemption. The same goodness of God that was active in the creation of man and woman became instrumental in causing Christ to be the fountainhead of the life of the church. In His role of Savior/Servant, Jesus generated the church, His body, as Adam had been used to generate the woman with whom he became "one flesh," one body. Both Christ and man are "head" or "source of life" to their respective brides, the church for One and the woman for the other.[40] The proper response to the gift of self is the reciprocal gift of self. Therefore, the church submits to Christ and the wife to her husband. This is mutual submission.

Verse 24. Viewed from the perspective of nineteen turbulent centuries of church history, this verse could be interpreted as an invitation to domestic sedition. However, the context makes it clear that the apostle is referring here to the church as Christ sees it, "presented before Him in splendor, without spot or wrinkle or any such thing," "holy and without blemish" (v. 27). Paul is saying here that the submission of the church to Christ and of the wife to husband is something more demanding than and different from obedience to codes, or conformity to authority, or acceptance of rulership. It is the disposition of one's whole being for another's sake, the espousing of total servanthood in every dimension of shared lives, a life orientation of service joyfully assumed in response to love.

This kind of submission is not motivated by considerations of self-interest, self-depreciation, compromise, or resignation, but by deliberate self-surrender in recognition of God's ennobling initiatives on behalf of women in creation and redemption. Wives are to surrender themselves to their husbands in celebration of their God-given unity as a couple, by virtue of their having been created "one flesh," and of their belonging together in the body of Christ in redemption.

Such surrender is worlds away from mere obedience to authority. Indeed, Christians are required to be subject to governing authorities in order to receive the ruler's approval, because "he does not bear the sword in vain" (Rom. 13:1–4), and he is established to "punish those who do wrong and to praise those who do right" (1 Peter 2:14). But such authority-based submission holds nothing in common with the interpersonal dynamics of a Christian couple. The word *authority* is never used in the New Testament to describe any aspect of the husband/wife relationship (except in 1 Corinthians 7:4). Husbands are never instructed to exercise authority over their wives. Wives are never commanded to obey their husbands or to submit to the authority of their husbands, and no threat ever accompanies the injunction for wives to submit to their husbands.

The reason for such seemingly glaring omissions is obvious: the surrender required by the principle of mutual submission is so radical in its demands and so comprehensive in its scope that it causes "obedience to authority" to pale into insignificance and reduces it to the babblings of a child. Any pagan wife can submit to the authority of a husband. Only a Christian woman can submit to her husband in servanthood "as to the Lord."

The Meaning of Mutual Submission for Husbands—Ephesians 5:25–33. In the previous section, had Paul's purpose been to enjoin wives to submit in obedience to the authority of their husbands, the next step for him would have been to instruct husbands on the proper use of authority and on the Christian manner of keeping their wives in subjection. However, it is exactly the opposite approach that is taken in this passage. The only role prescribed for husbands is one of love-motivated self-surrender that is willing to subject itself to death for the sake of their wives. The requirements laid here on husbands demand of them a surrender infinitely more stringent and exhaustive than the submission expected of wives. Indeed, although it is possible to submit without love, it is impossible to love without submitting.

Verse 25. The husbands' love for their wives is defined according to the standard set by Christ at the cross when He took the form of a servant, humbled Himself, and became obedient unto death, even death on a cross. In this perspective, any claim to rulership or any assertion of authority would make a mockery of the cross where Christ gave Himself up for the church. In the same manner, husbands are expected to give themselves up for their wives. Whenever Christ is upheld as the model for husbands to follow, it is not His power, His lordship, and His authority that are presented as the traits to emulate but His humility, His abnegation, and His servant-behavior.

Verse 26. Christ's sacrifice on behalf of the church was effected for the sake of a transformation that continues with the "washing of water by the word." This is probably a reference to baptism as a constituting rite of the church, with a possible allusion to the servant-ministry of Christ when He washed His disciples' feet (John 13:5–8). In the same manner, Christian husbands are to enhance and rehabilitate their wives by becoming servants to them. It hardly needs to be observed that this program called for a radical reversal of practices pertaining to marital life within Paul's contemporary culture.

Verse 27. The purpose of the preparation described in the preceding verse was the presentation of the church before Christ. The head/body metaphor is changed to the groom/bride relation, which provides a closer analogy for application to marital life. The same imagery is also present in 2 Corinthians 11:2. The application for husbands is that their God-appointed ministry in regard to their wives is to confer upon them the dignity that God has intended for them and to remove the constraints that might hinder them from achieving the fullness of their God-given personhood. According to this verse, this is Christ's present ministry on behalf of the church. In the same vein, Peter will require husbands to "bestow honor" on their wives (1 Pet. 3:7).

Verse 28. In actual practice, such a teaching means that husbands should grant their wives the same consideration that they might expect for themselves, since they should treat their wives as their own persons. Wives should not be treated as servants or subordinate persons by their husbands but as equals, as if they were their own bodies. Wives should receive from their husbands the same rights and privileges that husbands would expect for themselves. Verse 31 of this passage shows the practical implications of the "one flesh" union of Genesis 2:24. It calls for total reciprocity, which also happens to be the essential principle that underlies the concept of mutual submission.

Verses 29–30. The supportive, nurturing, caring role of the husband for his wife requires Paul to make a shift back to the head/body analogy. The head fulfills the servant role of provider and sustainer to the body, exactly as Christ nourishes and cherishes the church. To deprecate, to humiliate, or to dominate one's wife is a denial of the principle of mutual submission. Therefore, a man should view his wife as he views himself, as an equal.

Verses 31–32. The union between Christ and the church is similar to the creation definition of the marital bond. The reciprocal-servant relationship that exists between a man and a woman pertains to the eternal order of things, since it reflects the nature of Christ's relationship to the church. The principle of mutual submission reveals a deep reality within the person of God. It may not be dismissed lightly.

Verse 33. This sentence of summation brings to a close Paul's exhortation, with a final word of advice for both husband and wife that is designed to enable them to work out the doctrine of mutual submission in their lives. The comparatively heavier demand made on husbands in this sentence corresponds to the disproportionate lengths of Paul's instructions to husbands (vv. 25–30: ninety-two Greek words) and to wives (vv. 22–23: forty Greek words). Paul makes it clear that the submission of their wives (which was taken for granted in his day and therefore needed no special elaboration) should not be exploited by Christian husbands as an opportunity to claim authority rights over them. The proper Christian response to wifely submission is the reciprocal submission of husbands, which submission is best expressed in husbands loving their wives as themselves.

At the fall, the divine institution of the family had been commandeered by Satan, who transformed family units into strongholds of his evil kingdom. The subversive power of the gospel of Christ was designed to penetrate within them in order to explode the satanic structures that had kept God's creation in bondage, and to convert them into communities of the Spirit where male and female are mutually submitted in a living exemplification of the servant-love that exists between Christ and the church.[41]

Obedient Children—Ephesians 6:1–4

> Children, obey your parents in the Lord, for this is right. "Honor your father and mother" (this is the first command-ment with a promise) "that it may be well with you and that you may live long on the earth." Fathers, do not provoke your children to anger, but bring them up in the discipline and in-struction of the Lord (RSV).

Although this passage primarily concerns children, it has several implications for female roles within the family.

Lesson: The first observation that needs to be made con-cerns the difference in the terminology that is used for spouses on one hand, and children on the other. Whereas husbands were instructed to love their wives, and wives to submit to husbands, children are told to "obey" their parents. In the New Testament, the command to "obey" is given to children and slaves (Eph. 6:5; Col. 3:20, 22), never to husbands or wives. Obviously, the word *obey* does not belong in the dynamics of mutual subjection. To be mutually obedient to each other is a logical absurdity. Obedience pertains to the language of au-thority, whereas mutual subjection eludes it. The apostle Paul uses the language of authority for parental relations but avoids it for marital relationships.

Lesson: This mutuality in equality is reflected in the fact that both husband and wife have a responsibility of leadership in the home. Had it been different, Paul might have written: "Children, obey your mother who obeys your father," or "Children, obey your parents as your mother obeys your father," or "Children and mother, obey father." But Paul establishes no such hierarchy between husband and wife. Children are made accountable to both parents.

This shared responsibility presupposes a harmonious relationship between parents. Obviously, children would not be able to follow parental guidance if the leadership provided by one spouse were antithetical to the other's. This shared responsibility requires a relationship of mutual subservience between husband and wife in order for it to be credible to the children. A husband and a wife locked in a power struggle will have no more credibility as leaders to their children than a mother who demands obedience from her children while she is herself treated as a child by being required to obey their father. The appropriate climate for parents to raise children is one where husband and wife are submitted to each other in the spirit of Ephesians 5:21–33.

Lesson: Since the raising of children has traditionally fallen within the purview of mothers, Paul addresses a special corrective to fathers in order to redress the imbalance (v. 4). Apparently, Paul's concern is that fathers also become involved in the leadership needed by their children. But since the fathers' relationship with their children is not tempered by mutual submission, their attitude may be overbearing and arbitrary. In order to prevent such conduct, Paul offers fathers some negative advice by warning them against the abusive recourse to authority that elicits rebellion. Instead, fathers are to nurture their children in a responsible manner, worthy of "the Lord."

Obviously, children remain in an obedience relationship to their parents while they are still being "brought up." When they become independent adults, the provisions of the fifth commandment govern their relationship with their parents (vv. 2–3).

The special mention of fathers in verse 4 is not intended to exclude mothers from bringing up children in discipline (behavioral structure) and instruction (cognitive structure), but to include fathers, with the provision that they will not antagonize their children with needlessly authoritarian leadership.[42]

Women Teachers—1 Timothy 2:11–15

A woman should learn in quietness and full submission. I do not permit a woman to teach or to have authority over a man; she must be silent. For Adam was formed first, then Eve; and Adam was not the one deceived; it was the woman who was deceived and became a sinner. But women will be saved through childbirth, if they continue in faith, love and holiness with propriety.

The sentence that stands out in this text is the command stated under the full weight of Paul's apostolic authority: "I do not permit a woman to teach or to have authority over a man; she must be silent." These are Paul's own words. He is not quoting any opponents. The statement is unequivocal in its clarity and absoluteness. As God's inspired messenger writing to Timothy, the pastor of the church in Ephesus (1:3), Paul lays down an ordinance that has the character of a universal norm for all Christians in all ages. The ban on teaching by women is made all the more binding by the corroboration adduced from the Genesis creation account.

Unfortunately, this ideal scenario is very superficial. Once the contents of this passage are considered at close range and its larger context is made to bear upon it, a host of difficulties crop up and clamor for resolution. We shall now consider some of them under the designation of "problems" rather than "difficulties" or "contradictions" because, as we shall discover, they are all susceptible to receiving a solution.

Problems

Problem 1: There is continuing disagreement among New Testament scholars on what it is exactly that Paul prohibits in this passage. Some believe that Paul excludes women from only one activity. Others view the statement as proscribing two different activities. The first claim that the second clause of the prohibition reenforces the former in that women are forbidden to teach men, which would be tantamount to their assuming a position of authority over men. According to these scholars, women may teach anyone except men, and they are not to hold positions of authority above men. For the other school of thought, the statement is a clear prohibition for any woman to engage in any teaching of anyone (which is precisely what the text says), and for any woman to hold a position of authority over men.[43]

The problem is complicated by the fact that Paul does not use the common, time-honored Greek word for "authority." Instead, he has recourse to a verb that is never used anywhere else in the New Testament and on the meaning of which there remains a great deal of scholarly discussion—some interpreting it as meaning "authority," others as "usurpation," and still others as anything in between.

Obviously, depending on the positions taken on those variables, Paul's prohibition can be made to mean different things. However, regardless of the details, the conclusion is inescapable that as a lowest common denominator to this diversity of views, Paul places a restraint on the didactic ministry of women in the church.

Problem 2: This being the case, we are encountering in this text the first infraction to the principle of mutuality in equality that characterizes the relationship of the sexes in the economy of redemption. The inaugural texts of the church, one penned by Paul himself, emphatically declared the church to be a community where distinctions of race, class, rank, and sex were irrelevant. We further discovered that Paul jealously protected this egalitarian principle against the encroachments of Judaizing legalists who were trying to impose synagogual practices on the church. Moreover, Paul carefully spelled out the meaning of mutual submission as complete reciprocity within the church and within a Christian couple's married life. In the light of Paul's track record on female-role issues, this prohibition sounds oddly discordant with the rest of his teaching.

Problem 3: Not only is the statement discordant, but it also stands out by its singularity. That women should be systematically excluded from a significant phase of the ministry of the church is big news. It is a restriction that affects the life of every church at a deep level. If the prohibition needs to be mentioned in one Epistle, it is worth being repeated in several others, especially in those Epistles that deal with matters of propriety in the exercise of ministries in the churches. References to the churches' teaching ministry are found in Romans 12, 1 Corinthians 12, and Ephesians 4, but in none of those passages is there any expression resembling an exclusion concerning women, although it is clear that women participated in the ministries. The gifts of the Spirit to the church are never differentiated on the basis of sex in the New Testament, except in this one sentence of eight Greek words.

Problem 4: As a matter of fact, there are some texts that deliberately open up the teaching ministry to all qualified believers, women included. In the Epistle to the Colossians, Paul describes his ministry as "admonishing and teaching everyone with all wisdom" (1:28, NIV). Later, in a section where he lists a number of rules designed to foster unity and mutuality in the life of the Colossian church, Paul confers upon the whole community the marks of his own apostolic ministry as he tells them: "Let the word of Christ dwell in you richly as you teach and admonish one another in all wisdom . . ." (3:16). Some observations are in order:

1. The word *teach* which describes both Paul's individual ministry and the shared reciprocal ministry of the Colossians is the same as in 1 Timothy 2:12, which forbids women to teach.

2. The subject matter of this teaching is the highest form of revelation available, the "word of Christ."

3. According to the context, the teaching ministry (Col. 3:16) is made accessible for unrestricted participation, on the same basis as the other Christian duties listed in the text and the musical ministry of the church. If it is absurd to assume that mutual compassion and kindness (v. 12), mutual forgiveness (v. 13), mutual love (v. 14), and mutual admonishment (v. 16) were to be restricted to people of one sex, then the same must be true of the shared teaching (v. 16).

4. In the same context, when there is a need to specify instructions on the basis of sex differences, it is done explicitly (vv. 18–19).

5. If a ban on women teachers was an important issue for all churches, some reminder of it in conjunction with this general invitation for mutual sharing of basic Christian teaching would have been in order. The complete absence of such an expression creates a tension between this text and the prohibition in 1 Timothy 2:12.

The same is true of a text in Titus 2:3 where older women in the churches of Crete are "to teach what is good. Then they can train the younger women . . ." (NIV). The composite Greek word for these women "teachers of what is good" is a construct similar to the term for "teachers of the law." It suggests specialists who are recognized in the community as formally appointed teachers. The fact that one of the attributions of these women teachers was the training of younger women does not limit their teaching to women only. A seminary teacher whose main task is the training of candidates for the ministry may also teach in other environments. Likewise, there is no limitation set for these women not to teach persons other than young matrons, including children, young people, and men in need of instruction. Whatever the case may be, the existence of authorized women teachers in the Cretan churches must influence the interpretation of the prohibition in 1 Timothy 2:12.

Problem 5: Such an interpretation must also take into account Paul's evaluation of the ministry of teaching according to its relative importance in the life of the church. According to him, the most authoritative ministries are those of apostles and prophets, second only to that of Jesus Christ. To describe the importance of those two ministries for the church, Paul uses the imagery of a structure established on the foundation provided by the teaching of apostles and prophets, Christ Himself being the "chief cornerstone" (Eph. 2:20). Moreover, both apostles and prophets are agents of revelation in the church (Eph. 3:5).

In every catalogue of ecclesiastical gifts found in Paul's writings in Romans 12, 1 Corinthians 12, and Ephesians 4, the ministry of teaching is ranked subsequent to the ministry of prophecy, more pointedly so in the numerically graded list of 1 Corinthians 12:28, where teachers appear in third position, after apostles and prophets. Because women were allowed to prophesy (1 Cor. 11:5), the comparative value of prophecy and teaching in terms of their authority-intensiveness has momentous implications for the interpretation of the prohibition in 1 Timothy 2:12. Since apostles and prophets provide the foundation of the church, their ministry is by necessity more authoritative than the third-ranked teachers whose ministry is not described as being foundational to the church or revelatory as is that of the prophets.

The problem results from the fact that in 1 Timothy women are forbidden to teach or to exercise authority over men, while they otherwise have access to the most authoritative ministry in the church after that of the apostles. A modern equivalent might be to prohibit women in the military to accede to the lesser rank of captain, while allowing them to be promoted to the superior rank of colonel.

Problem 6: The meaning of the concluding sentence of the passage (v. 15) is difficult to ascertain. The reference to having a child or children does not seem to have any direct relevance to the teaching ministry in the church. Moreover, according to the rest of Scripture, salvation is to be obtained by grace through faith, not by having babies. That Paul was referring here to salvation from sin is made plain by the mention of transgressor in the preceding verse, and also from the outworkings of salvation listed as faith, love, sanctification, and circumspect conduct.

This list of some of the difficulties surrounding the interpretation of 1 Timothy 2:12 should be regarded as an invitation to exercise great care in the use of this text by the church. Other equally important and seemingly divergent teachings can be easily pushed aside when this verse is used as a proof-text in isolation from its biblical context. The difficulties we have encountered also call us to probe further into the meaning and the intent of this passage.

Solution

As we search in the biblical text itself for solutions to the problems enumerated above, we shall discover four explanations, all pointing to the same answer as to the meaning of Paul's prohibition.

First explanation: A glance at the immediate context of the statement shows that it is surrounded by two references to silence (vv. 11 and 12). From previous experience, we have learned to recognize the importance of such occurrences, and we called them a "frame" for the text under consideration. In this case, the frame provides a situational context for when women are not "to teach or to have authority over a man." In the life of the Ephesian church, there were teachers and there was time set aside for instruction (perhaps remotely equivalent to adult Sunday school classes). During those sessions, the women were required by Paul to become quiet and submissive learners instead of struggling to assert themselves as teachers. The silence twice enjoined here is not the mute passivity of women in the synagogue (required of Corinthian women by the Judaizers in 1 Corinthians 14:34, where in the Greek text a stronger word is used for "silence"). It is the silence of the docile disciple who receives instruction eagerly and without contradiction or self-assertion (the word for "silence" is the same as in 1 Timothy 2:2, where it denotes "quietness"). Such persons who were still in the learning stages could obviously not be permitted to become teachers. They first had to earn their credentials.

Second explanation: The distinction between men and women reflected in this passage may appear strange, especially in view of the fact that in other church contexts Paul allowed women to perform the higher-ranked and more authoritative ministry of prophecy (Acts 21:9 and 1 Cor. 11:5). Verses 13–14 provide the explanation for this anomaly. As he often does elsewhere, Paul has recourse to an illustration to make a point. He often cites an episode from the Old Testament, especially from the Book of Genesis and the early history of Israel, to illustrate a teaching (1 Cor. 9:9; 10:1–11; 15:45; 2 Cor. 3:3, 7, 12–15; 8:15; Gal. 4:22–30; Eph. 5:31; and so on). In this case, he draws the illustration from the Genesis account of creation and the fall.

In the fateful story of the fall, it was Eve, the lesser-qualified person, who initiated a mistaken course of action and who led herself into error. Eve was not created first or at the same time as Adam. She was the late-comer on the scene. Of the two, she was the one bereft of the firsthand experience of God's giving the prohibition relative to the tree. She should have deferred the matter to Adam, who was better qualified to deal with it since he had received the command directly from God. Regarding God's word, Adam had been teacher to Eve, and Eve the learner. Yet, when the crisis arrived, she acted as the teacher and fell into the devil's trap. Her mistake was to exercise an authoritative function for which she was not qualified.[44]

Likewise, there were ignorant but assertive women in Ephesus who had created considerable trouble because of their unenlightened exuberance. Paul deplores the excesses of such women who would go from house to house gossiping, speaking the wrong things (1 Tim. 5:13). Some, in fact, had already strayed away to follow Satan (v. 15), just as Eve had done at the fall. Paul brings a decisive solution to this problem: while they are still in the learning stage, women should not attempt to become teachers or aspire to teach their own male teachers. Scholars have already pointed out that the present tense of Paul's "I do not permit . . ." has the force of "I do not permit *now* a woman to teach." But when these women will have learned sufficiently by sitting quietly and receptively under authorized teachers and when they "continue in faith, love, sanctification and discretion," there would remain no hindrance for them to serve as teachers, just as other women served as prophets in other churches.

Sometimes, attempts are made to relativize this Pauline prohibition regarding women teachers by making it appear as culturally conditioned and irrelevant to the modern church. Such efforts are to be resisted. Paul's teaching in this passage has an absolute and universal relevance. The principle he lays down to protect the teaching ministry and the exercise-of-authority functions from incompetent persons is valid for all times and for all churches.[45] Christian communities should always remain watchful to authorize in positions of leadership only those persons who have received adequate training and whose lives are characterized by faith, love, sanctification, and circumspection. In the very next paragraph of his Epistle, the apostle fleshes out this principle in the life of the Ephesian church, as he minutely catalogues the qualifications required of leaders in order to prevent the church from being deceived and from falling into transgression (1 Tim. 3:1–13). Like their female counterparts who were still in need of training, male leaders should not be recent converts—from fear that, like Eve in the garden, they might "fall into disgrace and into the devil's trap" (3:7, NIV). According to Paul's principle, neither men nor women should be appointed to positions of leadership in the church until they can show evidence of maturity and competency.

Third explanation: The restriction placed on female teachers in Ephesus by the apostle Paul receives additional illumination when the prohibition text is viewed from the perspective of the specific historical conjunction in the life of that church at the time of writing. There is overwhelming evidence in the New Testament that the church in Ephesus was the site of an acute crisis created by a massive influx of false teaching and cultic intrusions.

The gospel had been planted in Ephesus in the midst of a flurry of confrontations with superstitious, occult practices and with the pagan religious establishment (Acts 19:9, 13, 18–19, 27). During his subsequent visit with the Ephesian elders, Paul warned them that fierce wolves would come among them, not sparing the flock, and that from among their own selves would arise men speaking perverse things, to draw away the disciples after them (Acts 20:29–30). In the Epistle to the

Ephesians, he exhorts them not to be "tossed to and fro and carried about with every wind of doctrine, by the cunning of men, by their craftiness in deceitful wiles" (4:14, RSV). However, Paul's worst fears became realized as the church reeled under the impact of false teaching of various kinds that resulted in the defection of several segments of its constituency.[46] Eventually, the church countered such assaults successfully but not without suffering from spiritual fatigue and loss of fervor (Rev. 2:2–4).

Undoubtedly, the restrictive measures prescribed by the apostle Paul in the two Epistles to Timothy played a decisive part in the doctrinal survival of the Ephesian church. The principal instrument of Paul's counteroffensive was his disciple Timothy who was specifically commissioned by Paul to enact a series of measures designed to defeat the cultic onslaughts on the Ephesian church.[47] At the core of Paul's strategy was the elimination of all unqualified or deviant would-be teachers, both male and female, so that the church's teaching ministry would be carried out exclusively by a small retinue of approved "faithful men" who would be able to take from Timothy the teaching he had himself received from Paul and transmit it to others (2 Tim. 2:2). Thus, neither women nor all men could teach in Ephesus, but only a group of trained and carefully selected individuals. The restrictions placed on women applied also to most male members of the Ephesian church in the spirit of James 3:1: "Let not many of you become teachers, my brethren."

Fourth explanation: Viewed from this holistic perspective, the statement in verse 15, which may seem baffling at first, begins to make sense. Even in Ephesus, the ban on women teachers or on women occupying authority-intensive positions is not final. At the same time that Eve became a transgressor, she received the promise of redemption both through her divine seed (Gen. 3:15) and as perpetuator of the human race through childbearing (3:16, 20). From the perspective of the fall, although the woman became transgressor, *yet* she will be saved from the effects of that transgression through her childbearing function. She is the mother of both the human race and of the Savior who will achieve its redemption. She holds within her the means for the salvation of the world and of herself.

The second part of the verse moves from consideration of Eve's destiny to a practical application for the Ephesian women. The singular "woman [she] will be saved" becomes the abruptly plural "if *they* continue." A rehabilitation similar to Eve's is also possible for the Ephesian women, provided they are properly discipled by learning in quietness and submission— so that they grow in faith, love, sanctification, and good judgment. Naturally, the prohibition on teaching would no longer apply to women who exhibited those virtues, since they would have achieved qualifications also required of male teachers (1 Tim. 3:2–5).

The exclusion of the Ephesian women from teaching positions is not final. Just like the fall, which was not a terminally disqualifying transgression for the woman, so the necessity for the Ephesian women to learn in silence is a temporary restriction that will lead to avenues of service, once their training has resulted in the maturing of their faith, love, sanctification, and sound judgment.

The solution for the proper understanding of this passage is to follow its development to the letter: women in Ephesus should first become learners (v. 11), and quit acting as teachers or assuming the authority of recognized teachers (v. 12). Just as Eve rather than Adam was deceived into error, unqualified persons will get themselves and the church in trouble (vv. 13–14). Yet, as Eve became the means and the first beneficiary of promised salvation, so Ephesian women will legitimately aspire to maturity and competency and to positions of service in the church (v. 15).

In the manner of a *postscriptum* to this discussion, we should add that the role of a teacher (either male or female) in our day has a significance entirely different from the ministry of teaching in apostolic times. Prior to the writing and the canonization of the books of the New Testament, teachers were the dispensers of Christian truth. Their authority was absolute and normative, provided that they were duly trained and authorized. With the formation of the New Testament canon, the locus of authority was displaced from the teacher to the teaching enscripturated in the New Testament. As a result, a current-day teacher has no personal authority other than his or her competency. The authority resides in the text of the Bible and not in the person teaching the Bible. A teacher today is only a person *sharing* knowledge and insights from Scripture. A sexless teaching machine may do as much without making any authority claims. In our day, restrictions to the teaching ministry of the church on the basis of sex are necessarily made with the tacit implication that the authority resides in the teacher rather than in Scripture. Such a priestly/pontifical concept of Christian ministry cannot be reconciled with evangelical adherence to Scripture as the only authority for the church.

Women Elders—1 Timothy 3:1–13

In the verses that immediately precede chapter 3 of 1 Timothy, Paul emphasized the importance of competency for the teaching ministry of the church. In this passage, he continues to express concern for the proper qualifications of church leaders as he discusses the functions of bishops and deacons. Since mention is made of male and female personnel, a rapid examination of this passage is relevant to our study. Only two observations need to be made.

1. The division of leadership responsibilities among bishops and deacons seems to present a classic case of ecclesiastical

organization in New Testament churches, one that may be safely duplicated in present-day churches. Such simple transposition would be very desirable. Unfortunately, it founders on several obstacles.

The patterns of church leadership seem to have been very fluid in New Testament times. The evidence shows that there were significant differences from one congregation to another in office titles, recognized ministries, and methods of governance. There is general concurrence among scholars that "elder" and "bishop" (meaning "overseer") are equivalent terms on the basis of their interchangeable use in Acts 20:17, (*cf.* 18) and Titus 1:5, (*cf.* 7). But the agreement stops here.

Elders and deacons are mentioned together only once more, in Philippians 1:1. The designation of "elder" does not appear in the ecclesiastical lists of Romans 12, 1 Corinthians 12, and Ephesians 4, although some attributions that fall under the responsibility of elders in 1 Timothy—such as teaching (3:2) and leading (5:17)—are mentioned as independent ministries not visibly related to the eldership in the ecclesiastical lists. Moreover, some leadership functions that should normally fall under the jurisdiction of the elders (such as administrators or governors [1 Cor. 12:28]; pastors [Eph. 4:11]) are mentioned independently of any elder supervision and apart from the statement concerning elders and deacons in 1 Timothy 3. To further complicate the matter, in his discussion of elders and deacons in 1 Timothy 3, Paul is more concerned with listing qualifications than with the assignment of responsibilities. Amazingly, there is no job description accompanying either list of qualifications, except for the mention of aptitude as a teacher for elders (v. 2) and the obvious necessity for both to care and serve the church.

If we try to determine the respective tasks of elders and deacons from their activities within the churches, the picture becomes even more confusing. In a church such as Philippi's

where there were elders (Phil. 1:1), Paul does not submit to
their care a case involving inimicality between two of its leaders, but he himself entreats the aggrieved parties to seek reconciliation and requests the assistance of one other individual
to help them settle their differences (Phil. 4:2–3).[48]

It is equally difficult to define with precision the responsibilities of deacons. In response to the crisis created by the Hel-
lenists' discontentment in the Jerusalem church, seven men
were chosen by the congregation (not imposed by the apostles)
to serve at tables (Acts 6). Although none of them is ever described serving at tables, one of them, presumably their leader,
is said to be "full of grace and power" (v. 8). He is presented
as doing "great wonders and signs among the people" (which
is a christological and apostolic prerogative, as in Acts 2:22,
43; 4:30; 5:12, and so on), teaching crowds with "wisdom and
the Spirit," delivering before the Sanhedrin the largest discourse
recorded in the Book of Acts, and dying a martyr's death, modeled in many respects on the death of Christ (Acts 7). Obviously,
the task of those seven men was not limited to serving at tables.
Stephen, their leader, and possibly the others with him were
involved in performing "great wonders and signs among the
people" on a par with the apostles themselves, in speaking
publicly as leaders of the church and in teaching with authority
in defense of the gospel, both among the people and before the
foremost rulers of the land. It cannot be said that deacons
served only physical needs or that they could not preach with
authority and serve the spiritual interests of the congregation.[49]

It is obviously unwise to draw rigid definitions of the actual
functions that devolved to elders and deacons in various communities. It is equally difficult to determine how those two
offices interrelated, and how together they combined with the
score of other church ministries that derived from spiritual
gifts, including some with leadership functions that overlapped
with elders and deacons—such as teachers (Rom. 12:7), lead-

ers (v. 8), governors or administrators (1 Cor. 12:28), and pastors or shepherds (Eph. 4:11).

The evidence that may be garnered from the Book of Acts and the Epistles suggests that the organizational structure of the churches was flexible, and that it was adapted locally to the corporate personality and the specific needs of each community. That there was a plurality of elders appointed in every church is undeniable, but the definition of the eldership and its relation to the diaconate and to other offices seems to have varied from church to church. Consequently, there is little justification for isolating and elevating the Ephesian church experience, reflected in Paul's discussion of it in 1 Timothy 3, as if it alone were normative for all times and all places. Church communities are as diverse today as they were in apostolic times, and the Holy Spirit is as willing to conform to such diversity in the munificence of His Creator-versatility as He was in New Testament times. The provisions of 1 Timothy 3:1–13 offer excellent guidelines for the qualifications-definition of only two of the church's multiple ministries, provided that relevant data found elsewhere in the New Testament are also incorporated in such definitions.

2. The critical need for conducting this process of collation across the New Testament will now become evident as we consider the requirement Paul makes of both elders and deacons that they be "husband of one wife" (vv. 2, 12). At first sight, this twice-repeated formula may be viewed as a requirement for all elders and all deacons to be male and married.[50] However, such a reading cannot be maintained when the following facts are taken into consideration:

First, Paul's preference for the marital status of believers committed to ministry is that they remain single (1 Cor. 7:32–35). If celibacy is a desirable qualification for someone "caring for the things of the Lord," and if elders and deacons represent the most responsible positions in "caring for the things of the Lord," then it stands to reason that Paul does not exclude qualified single men from the eldership or the diaconate. In his instructions to Timothy for the Ephesian church, Paul requests that leaders be married men, because of specific circumstances proper to the Ephesian church at that particular stage of its history. But those peculiar requirements dictated by local needs cannot be absolutized for all churches of all times. Should marriage be made a universal requirement for Christian leadership, all single men would become disqualified, in contradiction to Paul's explicit instructions in 1 Corinthians 7:32–35.

Second, and in the same vein, Jesus Christ—since He was single—would have been unqualified to exercise leadership among the people He taught before and after the resurrection. Paul and Barnabas, who both served as missionaries and leaders of local churches (Acts 13:1), would have been violating Paul's marriage requirement since they were both working as single persons (1 Cor. 9:5).

Finally, should this requirement to the Ephesian church be absolutized, men who accept Jesus' radical challenge to celibacy for the sake of the kingdom of God (Matt. 19:12), thus exemplifying obedience to His call to deny themselves, take up their cross, and follow Him (16:24)—the very men who should be upheld as exemplars of commitment before the Christian community—would be systematically and universally rejected from the most visible positions in church leadership. The personal sacrifice they would have made for the very purpose of serving the community with total dedication would be held against them as an impediment to such service.

The absurdity of such conclusions shows how necessary it is to interpret all related teachings on a given subject comprehensively rather than to proof-text one passage as if it were the sole teaching on the subject. In this case, it becomes obvious that the requirements set down in 1 Timothy 3 are not exhaustive. They neither include consideration of single men and of women as elders and deacons, nor do they forbid it.[51]

Again, Mutual Submission—1 Peter 3:1–8

Peter's domestic code and Paul's statement in Ephesians are similar in that the motif of submission runs through both of them, but dissimilar in the order of their components. In Ephesians, Paul moves from wives, to husbands, and then to slaves. Peter begins with servants, goes on to wives, and finishes with husbands. In 1 Peter, the whole section is dominated by the christological example cited as the proper Christian response to oppression (2:21–25). Servants suffering unjustly at the hands of overbearing masters must submit to them in patience and with their hope set upon God. Neither vengeful confrontation nor bitter resignation are appropriate options for oppressed Christians. But patient and confident submission will receive God's approval (2:19–20).

The transition from slaves to wives is made with the important word translated "in the same manner." The servant attitude modeled by Christ and required of slaves is also the example for wives.

Christian wives are cautioned against committing themselves to patterns of behavior that would be counterproductive. Peter identifies three such responses, and proposes their appropriate corrective:

1. The natural reaction to oppression is revolt. However, on the domestic scene, aggressive and confrontational behavior will only invite more repression, which would turn against both slaves and women since they cannot contend from a position of strength. For wives, to harbor hostility and rancor or to exhibit antagonistic attitudes would be self-defeating. As an alternate behavior, Peter advises the kind of submission that

will so affect unbelieving husbands that "they will be won over without talk" (v. 1, NIV).

Both the example of Christ cited in the same context and the eventual conversion of husbands help define the nature of this submission. A submission that is mere obedience or required conformity to authority will cause nobody's conversion. It is simply assumed or taken for granted as a fact of life. However, the voluntary submission in servanthood of a believer bent on conforming to Christ's example and on following in His steps (2:21) is likely to elicit reflection. This is the servant submission that walks the extra mile and turns the other cheek. The motivations for such submission have nothing in common with submission defined as obedience to authority. It is the submission of a "gentle and quiet spirit, which in God's sight is very precious" (3:4, RSV). Any pagan wife can submit in obedience, but only a Christian woman can submit in servanthood so as to demonstrate the power of the gospel without saying a word and thus win her unbelieving husband. Mere submission to authority has no power to demonstrate the gospel. Only the element of sacrifice present in submission as servanthood can point to Christ. The persuasive power of the submission enjoined by Peter makes submission as compliance to patriarchal authority pale into insignificance. It is a dynamic, redemptive self-disposition patterned after the servant-ministry of Christ.

2. Another predictable response to power is obsequious ingratiation, the truckling of the weak, the cunning charm of the cheated, the fawning smile of the vanquished. Peter warns women against the cosmetic vanity that may be used to seduce and curry favors by "the outward adorning with braiding of hair, decoration of gold, and wearing of robes" (v. 3, RSV), all the accouterments and mannerisms which in our day are advertised as constituting the indispensable secret arsenal of total womanhood. Against these he proposes "reverent and chaste

behavior" (v. 2) and qualities of the inner self (literally, "the hidden man of the heart" [v. 4]).

3. Finally, Peter reminds us that the lives of subservient people can be dominated by fear. It is a frightful thing to be at the mercy of the unmerciful powerful. Peter forbids Christian wives to submit out of fear. His last word to them is "let nothing terrify you" (literally, "fearing no terror" v. 6). The remedy is twofold. First, wives place their confidence in God as did the "holy women who hoped in God" (v. 5). Second, they "do what is right" (v. 6), which in this context means to be submissive to their husbands.

The example of wifely submission cited by Peter is Sarah, who "obeyed Abraham, calling him lord" (v. 6). The use of Sarah as an example of obedience shows that Peter was not devoid of a sense of humor. In Genesis, Abraham is shown as obeying Sarah as often as Sarah obeyed Abraham—once at God's behest as he was told, "Whatever Sarah says to you, do as she tells you" (Gen. 16:2, 6; 21:11–12). Moreover, Sarah referred to Abraham as "lord" in a monologue to herself, when he was out of earshot (18:12 "lord" or "master" in the Hebrew text). If the designation of "lord" was intended as a compliment, Sarah's assessment of Abraham in the same verse was hardly calculated to boost his self-confidence. More likely, the point of Peter's reference to Sarah is that wives in the new covenant can learn from their spiritual ancestress ("you are now her children" [v. 6])—who lived in the "dark side" of the old-covenant compromise, when she had to "obey" her husband. If Sarah submitted in obedience, the least her spiritual daughters can do is to submit in servanthood. Sarah obeyed Abraham, but Christian wives, her spiritual daughters, are never told to "obey" their husbands neither here nor anywhere else in the Bible. Instead, they are asked to "do what is good." Sarah called Abraham "lord," but Christian wives are never told to call their husbands "lord" anywhere in the Bible. Instead, they are told to "let nothing terrify you" (v. 6).[52] "There is no fear in love, but perfect love casts out fear ..." (1 John 4:18).

The transition from wives to husbands is made with the important word translated "in the same manner." The servant attitude modeled by Christ and required of slaves and wives is also the example for husbands (v. 7).

In this one sentence, the apostle Peter subjects husbands to a traumatic role reversal. Under the patriarchal system, it was the duty of wives "to live considerately" with their husbands, "bestowing honor" on the husband as the stronger sex, to regard husbands as the supreme heirs to the blessings of life, thanks to their privileged position—and for those in the Judaic tradition to hear their husbands thank God daily in prayer that they had not been created a slave or a woman. But the gospel of Jesus Christ turned this convenient little world upside down on its head, shattering each one of those patriarchal presuppositions.

Although Sarah called Abraham "lord," now it is husbands who must show consideration for their wives and bestow honor upon them, much like a servant to his master. Women may be considered the "weaker sex," especially since their subjection to male rulership at the fall, but now, in the new creation, they become "joint heirs" with their husbands.[53] Both husband and wife have become equal recipients of the grace that is the source of their new life. And should husbands default in any of those areas by reverting to carnal, self-assertive ways, they might as well cease praying. By acting like masters to their wives instead of like servants, they create a spiritual obstruction that makes them and therefore their prayers unacceptable to God.

Peter's final word for all of them, including wives and husbands, is to live in harmony with one another; to be in tune with each other's feelings; to practice love, compassion, and humility toward each other (v. 8). A shared life energized by such dynamics of reciprocity cannot but make efforts to maintain differences of rank, hierarchy, authority, and rulership between Christian husband and wife seem repulsive.

To summarize in plain language: The teachings of the apostolic church are in full accord with the inaugural statements of the church. Husband and wife are to enjoy a relationship of mutuality in equality within the home. Men and women have equal access to positions of leadership in the church, provided they are properly qualified.

The Practice of the New Community

As important as they may seem at the moment when they are uttered, inaugural speeches soon become forgotten. The grandiose programs they announce rarely materialize. Likewise for theoretical teaching. It may look impressive on paper or echo vibrantly through the ivory towers of abstractions, but its conversion into the practicalities of everyday life is another matter. As we have discovered in this study, the apostolic church propounded lofty ideals for male/female integration in the new community both in its inaugural statements and in its teaching. But was it able to implement them in real life?

During its period of infancy, the church had to overcome formidable obstacles to practice what it preached concerning social structures. On one hand, the church was to realize the new community where there would be no Jew nor Greek, no slave nor free, no male nor female. But on the other hand, the church could not afford to segregate itself from the world, since its mission was to penetrate society and make disciples from all nations. The logic of its inner life required radical adherence to Christ's vision and, therefore, repudiation of the worldly status quo. But the exigencies of its mission called for continued openness to society and the ability to relate to it positively in order to speak to its needs. The choice was not easy. The church could become a radical, other-worldly sect and cut itself off from the mainstream of life, or it could temporize its ideals for the sake of outreach and lose its distinctiveness.

History shows that—under the guidance of the Holy Spirit and more specifically through the instrumentality of the apostle Paul as the unsurpassed genius of missionary strategy that he was—the church was able to steer clear of both extremes. Within the sanctuary of its fellowship, it lived out the radical demands of the gospel. But at the cutting edge of communication with society, it offered no offense other than that of preaching Christ crucified and risen, while endeavoring to become all things to all people. Thus balanced, the church continued its irresistible advance, infiltrating culture at its critical nerve centers, wary of projecting the image of a movement of social and political subversion. Without compromising its convictions, it elaborated an approach of strategic accommodation that became jeopardized only once the church was overpowered by the forces of secular imperialism in the fourth century, when it quickly degenerated from a movement of God's future into an establishment dedicated to the proliferation of despotic institutions and to the perpetuation of traditions extraneous to its origins.

This being the case, we would not expect the texts of the early church to be replete with resounding, militant manifestos denouncing the evils of racism, slavery, and sexism. Those scourges were successfully defeated within the communities of believers. But in its outward manifestations, the church maintained the winsome posture of a new creation in Christ made available by God to the world. And yet, despite this element of restraint, there are clear indications in the New Testament that the church was able to implement in its life the deep convictions relative to the divine gift of nondiscrimination among Jewish and Greek believers, enslaved and free believers, male and female believers.

In the pages that follow, we shall confine ourselves to a brief survey of the evidence in the Book of Acts and the Epistles, substantiating the claim that the church practiced in its life what it taught on male/female equality. As we consider those texts, it should be noted that none of them was designed to make a statement for the benefit of posterity or to prove a point in a debate. They all have an incidental character as they appear fortuitously in task-oriented documents. The ideological innocence of such information enhances its unpremeditated authentication with compelling power.

To conduct our survey, we shall first consider the contribution of women converts to the initial phase of the gospel's implantation in local communities. Then we shall again have recourse to Paul's list of the ministries of the church found in 1 Corinthians 12:28 to determine whether women had indeed access to the various levels of leadership present in early Christian communities.

Women Converts

The presence of women among the believers gathered in Jerusalem after the ascension of Jesus causes no surprise, but their being highlighted in a separate mention of the church records does startle the alert reader (Acts 1:14). During His ministry, Jesus had expended Himself in discipling women to become His followers. And indeed some of those women had followed Him from Galilee, had stood by Him during the crucifixion (Luke 23:49, 55), and had become the first witnesses of the resurrection (24:10). Undoubtedly, several of those women were present among the small band of believers, numbering a hundred and twenty, who were destined to become the nucleus of the Jerusalem church on the day of Pentecost (Acts 1:15).

The identity of the hundred and twenty remains unknown except for three groups of people: the eleven apostles, the women (including the mother of Jesus), and the brothers of Jesus. Since there were four brothers (Mark 6:3) and eleven disciples, the only people who are identified from the remaining hundred and five are the women. One suspects that they receive mention as a separate group because they enjoyed an independent status comparable to that of the apostles. They were converts of Jesus who had banded together to minister to Him during the days of His itinerant mission (Luke 8:3). Now they were ministering to His body, the church.

With the advent of Pentecost, the number of those women increased phenomenally as "believers were added to the Lord, multitudes of both men and women" (Acts 5:14, RSV). Like their predecessors at Pentecost, these new female converts were able to make their distinctive contribution to the life and ministry of the church. Their involvement and their visibility were such that when persecution became inevitable the female Christians who had followed the leadership of Stephen became the victims of repression along with their male fellow believers (8:3), not only in Jerusalem but in other places as well (9:2). While the apostles received immunity from persecution because of their tacit acceptance of the Judaic status quo (8:1), these women and their male companions were committed to prison and exiled to foreign lands. However, this wave of persecution proved to be beneficial to the gospel since the scattered Christians launched the beginnings of the missionary movement (8:4).

The progress of the missionary movement was itself dependent to a large extent upon the conversion of influential women in strategic locations. The first convert to the gospel on European soil was a businesswoman named Lydia who offered her

home as the headquarters for the establishment of the gospel
(16:13–15) and as the place of meeting for the fledgling church
at Philippi, with herself as one of the teachers (v. 40). As Paul
and Silas pressed on with their mission, they discovered that
the conversion of some prominent women along with male
proselytes became the basis for the establishment of the church
in Thessalonica (17:4). The same phenomenon took place in
Beroea where "many Greek women of high social standing and
many men" became converts and formed the core of a new
church in Gentile territory (17:12). And when the gospel reached
Athens, the world capital of learning and of the arts, several
converts joined Paul. Two of them are identified by name,
obviously because their renown would have elicited recognition
from the original readers of the Book of Acts. The man was
Dionysius and the woman Damaris (17:34).

Although they are incidental to the chronicles of the church,
such references remind us that it was thanks to the involvement
of women converts that the Christian movement spread as
successfully as it did during the early stages of its outreach.

Women Apostles

The term *apostles* designates three different groups of people. Initially, only the original disciples (meaning "students,
learners") of Jesus were called apostles (meaning "those sent
forth with a mission"). Later, the name was given to missionaries involved in church planting who were also eyewitnesses
of Christ's resurrection, such as Paul himself (1 Cor. 9:1–2) and
a group of Jesus' followers other than the Twelve (1 Cor. 15:5,
7). Finally, the designation was extended to people who had
never seen Christ but who were involved with apostles in pioneer missionary efforts—Apollos (1 Cor. 4:6, 9); Epaphroditus
(Phil. 2:25); Silvanus and Timothy (1 Thess. 1:1, *cf.* 2:6). The
definition of "apostles" as one of the three higher gifts to be

desired bears evidence to the continued accessibility to this ministry for qualified individuals (1 Cor. 12:28, *cf.* 31). Corinthian Christians could aspire to become apostles, prophets, or teachers. The term *apostle* was still used in this broad sense in the post-apostolic writing of the Didache.

In his writings, the apostle Paul also refers to some of his associates as his "co-workers" or his "fellow workers." Under his pen, this term seems to have become a technical label to designate people who identified closely with him in his church-planting efforts as front-line, pioneer missionaries. Interestingly, the same people whom Paul calls "apostles" are also referred to as his "co-workers"—Barnabas (1 Cor. 9:5–6, *cf.* Acts 14:14; Col. 4:10–11), Epaphroditus (Phil. 2:25), Timothy (Rom. 16:21). In 2 Corinthians 8:23, Titus is a co-worker and his lesser companions are apostles. We can therefore deduce that there exists some interchangeability between the terms *apostles* and *co-workers*.

As we search Paul's writings, we discover that he gives the name "co-worker" to several women—Priscilla (Rom. 16:3); Euodia and Syntiche (Phil. 4:2–3). Since there existed some equivalency between the terms *co-worker* ("fellow worker") and *apostle*, we might wonder if Paul would call a woman leader an "apostle." The biblical text suggests a positive answer to this query, as Paul sends greetings in Rome to Andronicus and Junias, probably a husband-and-wife team of veteran missionaries, who are told to be "outstanding among the apostles" (Rom. 16:7).[54]

The significance of this designation lies in the fact that the term *apostle* connoted the highest level of leadership and authority in the early church (1 Cor. 12:28; Eph. 2:20; 3:5). Even in its broader, more general use, it was an appellation of the highest distinction. Apparently, the openness of the early church to women in positions of leadership was such that their identification as "apostles" was received without difficulty.

Women Prophets

In Paul's graded scale of the "greater gifts" and of their corresponding ministries, prophecy is given second place after
apostles (1 Cor. 12:28). According to Paul's teaching, both men
and women had access to this ministry in the early church
(1 Cor. 11:4–5).

The Book of Acts provides evidence that what the church
taught in this regard, it also practiced. On his way to Jerusalem,
the apostle Paul stopped in the city of Caesarea and enjoyed
the hospitality of Philip the evangelist (21:8–14). Philip was
one of the seven men who had been chosen with Stephen to
represent that segment of the Jerusalem church that had become dissatisfied with the leadership of the Twelve (6:5). He
had suffered persecution at the hand of Paul when he and the
Hellenistic segment of the church had been driven away from
Jerusalem. Philip had gone to Samaria, from where he carried
a successful evangelistic ministry that reached all the way to
Africa (8:5–8, 26–40). While he ministered in Samaria, the
apostles Peter and John had visited him from Jerusalem in
order to help integrate the Samaritan church into the main
body of believers (8:14–17).

As the author of Acts describes Paul's visit in Caesarea, he
mentions the fact that Philip "had four virgin daughters who
prophesied," and that Paul remained there for several days
(21:9–10). It is very likely that this reference to four women
who had remained single for the sake of ministry was intended
to emphasize the congeniality of Philip's situation for Paul during a critical period of his life (1 Cor. 7:34). These four women
had benefited from an exceptional wealth of experiences, as
they had participated in the miraculous development of the
church in Jerusalem, the persecution and the exile from Jerusalem, the implantation of the gospel in Samaria, and more
recently the ministry in Caesarea. One can easily imagine the

lively discussions and the long sessions of mutual sharing and instruction that took place between the evangelist, the four prophetesses, and the apostle.

It was probably during one of those sessions that a prophet specially commissioned from Jerusalem with ominous news of potential persecution in Jerusalem came to the house of Philip. The content of this message agreed with the sentiments of Paul's hosts, but Paul decided to follow his own intuition and, taking leave of his friends, he proceeded toward Jerusalem to fulfill his destiny. However, during one of the most somber periods of his life, Philip and the four female prophets had been able to provide Paul for a time with the comfort and refreshing support of kindred spirits. Neither Paul nor Luke, the companion and chronicler of Paul, had any objection to the four women exercising the ministry of prophecy. Luke's reference to the daughters' prophetic ministry flows as naturally as the mention of the fact that their father was an evangelist.

Women Teachers

The third-ranking gift to the church was that of teachers (1 Cor. 12:28). According to the Epistles, women were appointed to teach, provided they were properly qualified. There is no restriction mentioned in the numerous references to teachers and teaching in the Epistles except in 1 Timothy 2:12, where it is required that learning precede teaching.

The classical example of a woman teacher in early church circles is the celebrated missionary, pastor, co-worker of Paul, grand lady Priscilla. Except for the time she and her husband are introduced for the first time in the Book of Acts, and the one instance when they both send formal greetings to the Corinthian church, their names as a couple are consistently inverted, in defiance of "proper usage" (Acts 18:2; 1 Cor. 16:19).

The most surprising aspect of this reversal of traditional roles is its widespread acceptance in the churches where the couple was known. The Epistle to the Romans was intended to have been read to the congregation(s) in Rome, obviously in the presence of Aquila and Priscilla and of the home-church that met in their house and which they co-pastored. Yet the apostle Paul, who is always sensitive to individual susceptibilities and to matters of protocol, does not hesitate to address them as "Prisca and Aquila" (Prisca is the real name; Priscilla was a friendly diminutive. This coincidence of formality and unconventional usage is startling [Rom. 16:3–5]). The same is true of the last greeting ever penned by Paul in his extant writings (2 Tim. 4:19). Luke, the author of Acts, takes it for granted that his readership knows and accepts the prominence of Priscilla as the leading member of the pair (Acts 18:18, 26).

At the end of his second missionary journey, Paul left Priscilla and Aquila in Ephesus to minister to the newly formed church. During that time, they became acquainted with young Apollos, a disciple of the early days whose understanding of the faith did not include Pentecost and the church. Apollos was speaking boldly in the synagogue when Priscilla and Aquila discovered him. They befriended him and taught him the Christian faith as "they explained the way of God more accurately." Eventually, Apollos left them to become an important part of Paul's strategy in church development. He went to Corinth to help "those who through grace had believed" and he "powerfully confuted the Jews in public, showing by the scriptures that the Christ was Jesus" (Acts 18:24–28, RSV). Later, Paul was to describe Apollos's ministry as equal to his own: "I planted, Apollos watered, but God gave the growth. . . . He who plants and he who waters are equal" (1 Cor. 3:6, 8, RSV).

Under the instruction of Priscilla and Aquila, Apollos became an able pastor to whom Paul could entrust one of the most critical church situations at the time. For all practical purposes, Priscilla and Aquila acted as a seminary faculty for a promising male pastoral student. They taught him those redemptive events of the life of Christ about which he had been left uninformed along with their theological significance, and they gave him the overview of Christian doctrine that is suggested by the expression "the way of God" (Acts 18:26). Paul and the churches reaped the benefits of their teachings through the ministry of Apollos.[55]

That a woman should have been permitted to play such a determinant role in the training of a key leader of the apostolic church has not always been easy to accept. In order to avoid divulging such a scandal, the translators of the King James Version discreetly inverted the names of Priscilla and Aquila in Acts 18:26, thus preferring to commit violence on the text of Scripture rather than face the fact that God calls qualified women to be teachers.

Women Helpers

Among the unnumbered gifts listed in 1 Corinthians 12:28, there is the mention of "helps" (KJV). In the original text, this is an old Greek word that appears often in religious writings other than the Bible, but is found only once in the New Testament. However, its meaning is clear. It refers to the assistance that the church is to bring to basic human needs, both within and outside the Christian community. The command of Christ for His followers to expend themselves in feeding the hungry, helping the needy, receiving the poor, and visiting the sick and the prisoner (Matt. 25:31–46) had been incorporated in the teaching of the church (2 Cor. 9:6–15; 1 Tim. 6:17–19; James 2:14–17; 1 John 3:16–18). It was also practiced in its daily life, most notably during the early days of the church in Jerusalem when corporate funds were used to help the needy (Acts 2:44–45; 4:34–35) and provide for widows (6:1). Eventually, the Jerusalem church became itself the beneficiary of such a relief program, as the Gentile churches pooled their resources to help in a time of need (Rom. 15:25–26; 1 Cor. 16:1–4; and so on).

The task of administering this welfare program of the church had originally fallen on the apostles. The direct involvement of the Twelve in this aspect of the ministry of the church suggests the high level of priority it had for the community. Later, seven other men were appointed to carry out this responsibility (Acts 6:3–6). However, the records of the church also indicate that the administration of the welfare program of the church did not remain the exclusive prerogative of male believers.

In the beautiful seaside harbor city of Joppa there was a lively community of Christians. When one of their numbers died, a woman with the evocative name of Tabitha, which means "gazelle," they refused to believe that she was gone. As a leader in the community (she is called a "disciple" in Acts 9:36), she had become indispensable to its life. Those Christians knew that death was inevitable and even the best leaders must go. But when Tabitha died, the grief of the community was so intense that instead of burying her body immediately as was the custom, they sent two men to another city twelve miles away to press the apostle Peter to return with them. It is very unlikely that the Joppean Christians were expecting a resurrection. No one had come back from the dead since the resurrection of Lazarus and of Christ, many long years ago. Most likely, they were looking for comfort in their distress, for someone important to give significance to the funeral, for an apostle to tell them of eternal life in Jesus.

Tabitha had been a person who "was always doing good and helping the poor." When Peter arrived, her bereaved friends showed him the coats and garments she had made for the needy. Peter, in his wisdom, could have quieted the people and explained to them that Tabitha had left them a great example to follow, that they would themselves have to rise to the occasion and assume the ministries that she had fulfilled. But, instead, something strange happened. While listening to the mourners, Peter became convinced that at that point of time in the life of that community, Tabitha had become indispensable and irreplaceable. She was fulfilling such an important dimension of leadership that even God would not want her to be gone. So Peter went in and, following closely the method he had seen Jesus employ for another woman (Mark 5:35–43), he restored Tabitha to life and gave her back to her loved ones (Acts 9:40–41).

That the beneficiary of this unprecedented event in the life of the church was a female leader should give us reason to pause. Her leadership was important enough to the church for it to send two men on a mission to fetch Peter, for Peter to interrupt a successful evangelistic campaign (v. 35) and return with them for the funeral of a woman he did not know, and for Peter to decide that the only solution to the crisis created by her death was to bring her back to life. Some leader she must have been, Tabitha.

Women Administrators

Among the unnumbered gifts of 1 Corinthians 12:28, there is also one literally called "governings," better rendered in most versions as "administrators." Again, it is difficult to define the exact relation of this ministry to other policy-making-level positions in the church, such as leadership in Romans 12:8, or shepherding in Ephesians 4:11, or elders and deacons in 1 Timothy 3. The specific job descriptions attached to these titles probably varied from church to church according to local needs. But it does seem that the gift of administration was exercised by people who had the ability to motivate others and to coordinate human efforts toward the attainment of specific goals. In her own area of expertise, Tabitha performed such a ministry. But certainly another outstanding female leader who qualified for the title was Phoebe of Cenchreae (Rom. 16:1–2).

Most commentators agree that the occasion for Paul to write the Epistle to the Romans was Phoebe's trip to Rome, and that Paul gave her the Epistle to take with her to the Roman Christians. As her titles indicate, Phoebe was an impressive person. Paul refers to her as "a deaconess of the church at Cenchreae,"[56] and as a "helper" of many and of himself as well. The word translated "helper" appears only in this passage in the New Testament and it is not a religious appellation. In the Roman world, it designated a legal person who spoke for the rights of aliens. There is no evidence to the effect that this word could constitute a title of leadership within the church. But outside the church, it definitely described a person of influence who could intervene with clout on behalf of people in precarious situations. Phoebe had apparently been able to use her good offices to protect or deliver a number of Christian leaders in critical circumstances, including Paul himself. As such, she rightfully deserved the consideration of Roman Christians.

But more than her titles, it is Phoebe's mission that gives us an insight into her leadership responsibilities. Paul gives the Romans two sets of instructions relative to her visit. The first concerns their attitude toward Phoebe herself. The Roman believers are to "receive her in the Lord as befits the saints." Paul wants them to know that Phoebe is no ordinary person. She is to be treated with the same deference and respect as any of the male leaders who traveled among churches, as one of the "saints." Although the word could designate all believers, when "saints" was used as an honorific term, it primarily referred to the Jerusalem Christians and to their leaders as representatives of the mother church. Paul instructs the Romans not just to welcome Phoebe but to welcome her as a recognized leader sent on an important mission. They are to pull out the red carpet for her, not just the welcome mat.

The second instruction of Paul to the Romans is for them to make themselves available to assist Phoebe in whatever she may request of them. Phoebe is coming to Rome commissioned to organize a specific project. For all practical purposes, Paul secures for her full requisition rights over Roman believers. It is very likely that Phoebe is to organize a fund-raising campaign in Rome to obtain support for Paul's projected missionary travel in Spain. Indeed, Paul seems to be eager to create a sense of ownership among the Roman believers toward the forthcoming outreach effort in Spain (15:24–38). Whatever the case may have been, the evidence shows that a female church leader was recommended by Paul to the Roman church with a mandate that gave her authority to request their collaboration in fulfilling a mission of strategic importance for the progress of God's word. Obviously, Paul called on Phoebe to carry out this delicate mission because she had previously demonstrated her ability to function as a capable administrator.

To summarize in plain language: The lofty ideals for male/female integration among Christians as enunciated in the church's inaugural statements and in its teaching were also practiced in the life of the church. The evidence indicates that women participated in roles of leadership at the highest levels. Such continuity between faith and practice was achieved against pressures to conform to partriarchal norms in ambient culture.

Since the writings of the New Testament were action documents produced in a patriarchal setting, the number of references to women they contain was normally affected by this factor. The positive evidence available in the New Testament for male/female integration may, like the proverbial tip of the iceberg, represent only a fraction of the radical changes effected in the practice of the new community under the impact of the ministry of Jesus. However, as relatively sparse as it may be, the evidence is conclusive. The apostolic church conformed its practices to its teaching: "There is neither male nor female for you are all one in Christ Jesus" (Gal. 3:28).

Conclusion

The purpose of this study was to place the teachings of the Bible on male/female relationships in a comprehensive perspective that would show God's design in creation and its restoration in redemption. Many Christians will find here a scriptural confirmation for their God-honoring practices of nondiscrimination in church and family life. Others will realize that their attitudes and practices need to be reevaluated in the light of the holistic teaching of Scripture. The following remarks are presented for such believers who are desirous of complying with the dictates of the Word of God.

The Scriptures repeatedly warn believers against the subtle danger of uncritically adopting prevalent cultural concepts and worldly practices. Christians are commanded to examine their assumptions in the light of God's Word and, should they do so, they are given the promise that they will be able to discover His divine will. "Do not be conformed to this world but be transformed by the renewal of your mind. Then you will be able to test and verify what God's will is, His good, pleasing, and perfect will" (Rom. 12:2).

Perhaps no other area of corporate Christian life requires as critical a reappraisal of its basic presuppositions as that which concerns the relationships of believers among themselves. Faulty relationships among Christians have paralyzing effects on the vitality and the effectiveness of their corporate witness. Discriminatory and divisive practices grieve the Holy Spirit and hinder the growth and outreach of Christian communities.

The transforming power of the gospel needs to be applied to individual lives *and* to the way Christians relate among themselves. Fragmentation and divisions constitute massively successful weapons in Satan's arsenal directed against the people of God. Where God wants to create unity and cohesion, the enemy seeks to cause alienation and separation. From the moment of our birth, a fallen society presses us into compartments and niches that become our private prisons for life. The concept of sex roles is one of those bondages from which the gospel can set us free. Nowhere does the Scripture command us to develop our sex-role awareness as males or females. It calls us—both men and women—to acquire the mind of Christ and to be transformed in His image (Gal. 3:27; Eph. 4:13; Phil. 2:5; and so on). Both men and women are called to develop their "inner man," which means their basic personhood in cooperation with the Holy Spirit. The "fruit of the Spirit," or the result of the Holy Spirit's impact on human personality, is a character that exhibits "love, joy, peace, patience, kindness, goodness, faithfulness, gentleness, self-control" (Gal. 5:22–23).

Biblically, such qualities pertain neither to masculinity nor femininity. They are the reflection of the person of Christ Himself. In order to attain this ideal, some men may indeed have to repudiate the traits that a pagan culture portrays as true masculinity. They will have to surrender toughness for love, ambition for joy, aggressiveness for peace, expeditiousness for patience, forcefulness for kindness, competition for gentleness, and assertiveness for self-control. If the "fruit of the Spirit" requires the cultivation of traits traditionally associated with femininity, so be it. Genuine Christian spirituality is located beyond the entrapments of sex roles. Men should learn to temper the masculinity instilled into them by the world with the authentic humanity produced by the Holy Spirit. In this manner, they will truly reflect the character of Christ, who embodied to perfection the "fruit of the Spirit." In order to do so, men may have to relinquish their bogus masculinity as they "crucify the flesh with its passions and desires." This is the *sine qua non* condition for "belonging to Christ Jesus" (Gal. 5:24).

Reminding the Colossian Christians of their high status as the elect people of God, Paul enjoins them to adopt new modes of behavior with the same eagerness that they might display in discarding an old outfit for a new one:

> Therefore, as God's chosen people, holy and dearly loved, clothe yourselves with compassion, kindness, humility, gentleness, and patience. Bear with each other and forgive whatever grievances you may have against one another. Forgive as the Lord forgave you. And over all these virtues put on love, which binds them all together in perfect unity (Col. 3:12–14, NIV).

Again, the essential traits characteristic of the people of God are qualities that would be popularly considered as feminine: compassion, kindness, humility, gentleness, patience, a forgiving spirit, and—supremely—love. Such traits are not cited by Paul at random. This is how he describes the new nature which is renewed in Christ Jesus (v. 10). Both men and women are to acquire such characteristics because they are the manifestations in human life of the image of God. Men who continue to assume superior attitudes, by claiming exclusive positions of power and dominance prerogatives, and pathetically inflating their macho image at the expense of the very persons whose servants they should be for Christ's sake, need to examine their basic assumptions about the transformation claims of the gospel. The renewal of the Christian mind calls for a merciless eradication of pagan modes of thought and behavior so as to remove the risks of conformity to this world. Conversely, such a metamorphosis requires the radical brokenness and pliability that will enable the Creator to replace pride, arrogance, and the urge to rule others with compassion, kindness, humility, gentleness, patience, forgiveness, and love.

This transformation calls not only for a change of the "inner man" but also for a change of attitudes toward the other sex. Whereas both the biblical account of creation and the New Testament emphasize those elements of the identity that exists between men and women, fallen society overwhelms us from a very tender age with the physiological and symbolic differences that exist between the sexes. This process of socialization is so thorough and so pervasive that it becomes second nature for us to regard the opposite sex as *opposite*. As members of the community where "there is neither male nor female for you are all one in Christ Jesus," we should strive to exhibit to the world our "sameness" in Christ. But too often it is the world that succeeds in inculcating among Christians its notions of the "otherness" of the members of the other sex. The sanctification of our attitudes toward the other sex will require nothing less than a systematic effort of deprogramming, designed to purge the Christian mind of abusive interpretations of portions of Scripture that should have been left alone when not understood, and of the vulgar popular stereotypes that such misinterpretations have reinforced.

Normally, changed attitudes should result in changed behavior. The Bible places on men the onus for the rehabilitation of women in the new community as they are exhorted to "bestow honor on the woman" (1 Peter 3:7). Female efforts to obtain equal treatment meet with increased oppression unless men are sensitized to respond humanely. It is the responsibility of Christian men to realize that women do not derive their identity from men but from having been created in God's image and from being new persons in Christ. Efforts to keep women under male tutelage work against both men and women. By maintaining women in dependency relationships, men guarantee the infantilization of their female companions. They deprive themselves of the God-given opportunity to enjoy partnership and collegiality with their female counterparts in facing the challenges and the tasks of life shoulder to shoulder. Even more seriously, they become perpetrators of the satanic scheme, devised at the fall, of socializing women to live with guilt about the fact that they are women. Only as men learn to encourage women to stand strong, courageous, and free can they both discover the magnificent complementarity for which the sexes were created.

Secular socializations regarding sex roles have become so institutionalized in some segments of religious life that nothing short of deliberate programs of depatriarchalization can begin to identify them and, hopefully, to overcome them. Such a movement should begin with a courageous but repentant submission to the teaching of the Word of God, and a total abdication of vested interests and personal advantage to the lordship of Christ.

Obedience to Scripture regarding male/female relationships within the church will release undreamed-of vitalities and potentialities for the work of the gospel. Sterile definitions of leadership in terms of rigid authority lines and restrictive power structures will then give way to integrated and flexible organizational models within which spiritual gifts and human resources can be pooled together in an effervescent fellowship of mutual solicitude and servant ministries.

In family life, such obedience will stem the tide of dead or broken marriages as husbands and wives learn to share together the responsibilities of leadership in their homes.[1] Inevitably, the question arises as to the resolution of the decision-making impasses that occur when opinions differ. Consistently placing the responsibility for the final word on the husband is the least God-honoring method for resolving such deadlocks. This puts an unrealistic burden on the husband to make always the right decision, and it promotes a cop-out mentality for the wife, who then resigns herself to the status of permanent loser or of devious manipulator of the power-wielding male. The following are some alternate suggestions for honorably and peaceably settling split decisions.

1. Defer to each other, give the other person the advantage, strive to please the other person, give in to the preferences of the spouse. Create opportunities for the other person to have his or her way. Try to please the other person rather than yourself. This is the meaning of servanthood and mutual subjection (Phil. 2:3–4). Some couples may need to learn deferring by taking turns in giving in to the other's preference. Deliberate stalemates cannot persist between two spouses who are bound together in a shared desire to please one another, to give each other the advantage, to be servants to each other, and to anticipate and fulfill each other's needs, desires, and pleasure. Defer when you differ. Yearn to yield. Submit as servant. If the commands to submit (Eph. 5:21) and to be servants of one another (Gal. 5:13) do not apply primarily to your own subjection to the person closest to you, wife or husband, who else should they apply to? Like charity, submission begins at home.

2. Exercise the spiritual gifts for the outcome of problematic decisions (Rom. 12:3–6; 1 Cor. 12:4–7). Divide responsibilities for decision making on the basis of competencies, experience, and expertise. Such areas of service can be predetermined by prior agreement so that each spouse is designated to render final decisions in specific areas of proficiency.

3. Compromise. Seeking a middle ground is a biblically sound

procedure (Luke 14:31–32; Acts 6:1–6; 15:37–40). Most couples need training in successful negotiation and conflict resolution. Taking a course together in methods of conflict
management could help many couples in transforming tensions into positive gains and in saving their marriages.

4. Define the biblical principles involved in the debated issue
(if needed, with a paper-and-pencil drill of the pros and cons)
and make decisions on the basis of such evaluations.

5. Pray together for guidance and wait for it. Postpone the
decision to gain the perspective of time. God uses both prayer
and time to resolve differences and conflicts.

6. Allow God to provide guidance through circumstances.
History has a way of reducing alternative options to one obvious
course of action that a knock-down-drag-out contest of the
wills cannot bring about.

7. Whenever a decision affects one spouse more than the
other, the spouse who has more at stake in the decision should
have more say in it. This is the meaning of partnership. For
example, a husband wants to have more children because he
likes babies, but his wife knows that she is teetering on the
verge of a nervous collapse under the burden of her present
household. She should have the determinant voice in their decision—unless, of course, he is willing to stay home and raise
the children.

8. Initiate joint research projects on the debated issue. Read,
attend conferences, take courses, to develop a basis for sound
judgment (Eph. 5:17; James 1:5–6). For instance, the use of
physical discipline on children is a sensitive issue that can become a grievous matter of contention for young couples. Rather
than acting on emotional impulses or relying on past socializations, the couple should reach a consensus by researching
both sides of the issue.

9. Decide to refer the matter to a trusted and objective third

party, after agreeing to abide by his or her determination (1 Cor. 6:5).

10. Engage in role reversals. Both spouses can take turns in articulating their respective positions as clearly as possible. Then they assume the position of the other spouse for a period of time in order to identify with his or her thinking process. The empathy generated by this exchange will generally break the deadlock.

Under the guidance of the Holy Spirit, other creative methods can also be found to resolve differences without resorting to the repulsive pagan practice whereby one spouse exercises power over the other. According to the "one flesh" principle, the more directive and authoritarian you act toward your spouse, the more you damage your marriage and impoverish your own life. Conversely, according to the same "one flesh" principle, the more you affirm and build up your spouse and encourage his or her independent growth, the more you enhance your marriage and enrich your own life—to say nothing of simple obedience to God, who wants none of His children to fall under a yoke of bondage (Eph. 5:28).

The words of the apostle Paul ring out today with compelling actuality: "It is for freedom that Christ has set us free. Stand firm, then, and do not let yourselves be burdened again by a yoke of slavery" (Gal. 5:1, NIV). Every generation of Christians needs to examine its beliefs and practices under the microscope of Scripture to identify and purge away those worldly accretions that easily beset us, and to protect jealously the freedom dearly acquired for us—both men and women—on the hill of Calvary.

Notes

Chapter 1: God's Creation Design

1. In Hebrew, the word for man (*adam*) used with the article is a common noun. Without the article it becomes a proper name (similar to "the guy," and "Guy" as a first name). The latter occurs in Genesis 3:17; 4:25; and 5:1a (". . . account of Adam's line"). In 5:1b ("When God created man") and in 5:2, the word *adam* is used with the article as a common name.

2. Hurley correctly states, "Genesis says that both men and women are the image of God" (p. 172).

3. The poetic structure of Genesis 1:27 suggests an explanation for the nature of the image of God or *imago Dei*. The parallelism of lines one and two is resolved in the formal synthesis of line three. The third line provides a definition of the *imago* as male and female. Although sexuality does not exhaust the meaning of the *imago*, it expresses an essential trait of the divine nature. In other words, the difference between male and female in human life is similar to the distinctions between the persons of the Trinity within the being of God. The *imago* concept justifies this analogy while allowing for unity, equality, and complementarity within the plurality of persons in the divine mode of existence as well as in human life. The fact that the Trinity is imaged by a duality in human life instead of a human "trinity" indicates

215

that the intent of the *imago* is not to create miniature duplicates of divinity. There can be only one God.

4. The use of sexual symbology in Scripture and of male imagery for divinity continues to be discussed in biblical scholarship, especially in the context of research pertaining to inclusive language translations. For alternative views, see Mary Daly, *Beyond God the Father* (Beacon Press, 1973), Donald Bloesch, *Is The Bible Sexist?* (Good News, 1982), and Paul Jewett, *The Ordination of Women* (Eerdmans, 1980).

5. Hurley discusses the authority structure of Genesis 1 in a short paragraph (pp. 205–206) that contains several errors:

(a) He states that God "established a variety of realms with creatures to rule over them (day: sun; night: moon; sea: fish; air: birds; etc.)."

Critique: God did not command the fish to rule the sea, nor the birds to rule the air. He simply ordered them to proliferate and populate the elements (v. 22).

(b) According to Hurley, mankind has "dominion over *all* of the realms and the rulers."

Critique: God did not give mankind dominion over the sun, the moon, the day and the night (vv. 26, 28).

(c) In order to account for the absence of any mention of authority structure between man and woman in Genesis 1, Hurley states that "the chapter does not bring relationships within species into view. It does not comment on headship among animals, although there are clear dominant and subordinate roles among them."

Critique: Besides the inappropriate parallel drawn from "headship among animals" to humans, Hurley assumes gratuitously that "dominant and subordinate roles" existed among animals prior to the fall. Nothing in the text warrants such an assumption. The concept of idyllic conditions devoid of dominance/subservience patterns is not foreign to the Old Testament (Isa. 11:6–7).

Genesis 1 is a taxonomic statement that conspicuously exempts the male/female relationship of internal hierarchical constraints. Maleness and femaleness are presented as divine gifts reflecting diversity within the *imago Dei*. The text does not permit their exploitation to support hierarchical dichotomies that might justify predetermined role distinctions.

6. *See* Matthew 19:10–12; 1 Corinthians 7:25–35.

7. Hurley's sentimental statement that God created the woman "to end the loneliness of man" (p. 32 and again p. 209) misses the point altogether. Beyond concern for the emotional welfare of Adam, the creation of the woman stemmed from ontological necessities rooted in the very nature of God. Femaleness was also an aspect of the *imago Dei*.

8. Hurley states correctly that Eve was formed from Adam "to join him in ruling the earth to the glory of God" (p. 32).

9. The Hebrew word for "helper" in Genesis 2:18 and 20 (*ezer*) appears about twenty times in the Old Testament in references such as Exodus 18:4; Deuteronomy 33:7, 26, 29; Psalm 33:20; etc. The Hebrew language has four other words for "helper" that denote subordination. None of those words is used in reference to woman in Genesis 2.

Hurley acknowledges the strength of the biblical evidence and concludes, "Woman's role as 'appropriate helper,' therefore, does not carry with it an implication of subordination" (p. 209).

10. Hurley attempts to develop into a major argument the practice of primogeniture (a legal provision that entitled the eldest son in a family to inherit twice the amount of the estate received by his brothers). He states, "Paul's appeal [in 1 Timothy 2:8–15] to the prior formation of Adam is an assertion that Adam's status as the oldest carried with it the leadership appropriate to a first-born son" (p. 207). The fallacies contained in this approach must be pointed out.

Critique: The only legislation contained in the Bible relative to primogeniture was enacted a considerable time after creation, since it is found in the Mosaic Law (Deut. 21:15–17). The only instance of the practice of the birthright contained in the Bible also occurs much later, in the story of Esau and Jacob (Gen. 27:19). Generations upon generations of families with multiple children are mentioned in the early chapters of Genesis with no hint of the existence of primogeniture regulations (Cain, Abel, and Seth in 4:1–2, 25; the sons and daughters of Lamech in 4:20–22; the sons and daughters of Seth's descendants in 5:7, 10, 12, 16, 19, 22, 30; Noah's three sons in 5:32; the sons of Noah's descendants in 10). It is therefore unjustifiable to project retroactively into the creation story a practice that receives no sanction in the creation account.

Critique: Ironically, in addition to the case of Esau and Jacob, the one other mention in the Bible of an instance of first-born rights refers to their loss by Reuben (1 Chron. 5:1–2). This reduces the concept of primogeniture in the Bible to two or three incidental references—hardly sufficient grounds to exploit the concept of primogeniture as a device controlling the meaning of Genesis 1 and 2.

Critique: By Hurley's own admission, the principle of primogeniture applies to male siblings ("The inheritance laws of Israel . . . pass property through the male line" [p. 37]. "The first son inherited . . . twice what his brothers received" [p. 207]). Consequently, Hurley's attempt to apply the primogeniture model to the relationship of Adam and Eve (who were male and female and also husband and wife—not brothers!) puts a strain on the definition of primogeniture and makes it irrelevant to the relationship of Adam and Eve.

Critique: The biblical legislation on primogeniture concerned exclusively property rights. Despite Hurley's claim in the passage cited above, primogen-

iture did not accord rights of "leadership." Although older, Ishmael did not
rule over Isaac (Gen. 21:12–13); Manesseh did not rule over Ephraim (Gen.
48:19); Judah, fourth in line among Jacob's twelve sons, was given the promise
that his brothers would bow down before him (Gen. 49:8); although the
youngest among eight brothers, David was made king over all of them (1 Sam.
16:11); Solomon ruled over his older brother Adonijah (1 Kings 1:53); and
Shimri, although not the eldest, was chief over his brothers (1 Chron.
26:10–11). These few instances taken at random testify to the fact that the
practice of primogeniture was observed loosely, and that rights of leadership
were not intrinsic to the legislation. Hurley's claim that "Adam's status as the
oldest carried with it the leadership appropriate to a first-born son" is an
invention not supported by biblical data. The creation text of Genesis 1 and
2 does not present man as the leader of woman, either explicitly or by
implication.

Critique: The appeal to primogeniture as an argument for male rights of
leadership over women contains its own contradictions. When enforced, primogeniture concerned primacy rights among male siblings. Should primogeniture considerations be now extended to apply to the status of women,
consistency would require that primogeniture regulations be also and primarily enforced among male relations, since this was their original intent.
If primogeniture should affect the status of women in church and family, it
affects *a fortiori* the status of men in church and family.

The honest application of primogeniture would require that no males
except first-born sons hold positions of leadership over their brethren in the
church. In the family, the same rigor that demands the subservience of wives
to husbands should obtain the subservience of all males to the oldest surviving
male relative, be he father or brother. Inheritance practices should also be
made to conform to the requirements of primogeniture with the oldest son
receiving most of the estate. Such practices should be legislated in churches
with even more enthusiasm than the subservience of women since they allegedly constitute the original points of application of primogeniture. As a
result, the very men who prohibit women from acceding to positions of
leadership on the basis of primogeniture considerations would, by the force
of their own argument, rule themselves out of church leadership positions
and forfeit the right to speak on the issue—unless they happen to be first-
born sons. Since this is unlikely to happen, one may rightfully be suspicious
of a mentality that is willing to exonerate men of compliance to restrictive
structures that pertain to them while imposing the same on women.

11. Hurley conflates disparate teachings from Ephesians 1:22–23; 5:22–23;
and Colossians 1:15–18, noting "the cryptic imagery of this complex passage,"
and yet he goes on to draw the following conclusion: "Christ's authority, the
model for husbands, is tied with his being the 'first-born.' We should not be

surprised that Paul saw Adam's being 'first-formed' as implying authority!" (p. 208). Surprised we are indeed, and we make the following points:

Critique: Contrary to Hurley's assertion, Christ's authority is never cited as a model for husbands in the New Testament, nor are husbands ever charged to wield authority over their wives.

Critique: Hurley's use of "first-born" betrays a misunderstanding of the title's christological application. The title refers to the eternal generation of the Son and to His primordial preexistence. It is a title denoting dignity, not a description of origin. To draw a parallel between Christ as "first-born" and Adam as "first-formed" smacks of subordinationism, a heresy condemned by the church long ago. Neither the title nor its implications apply to Adam. In the Bible it is never bestowed on Adam, although, of all humans, he alone might have qualified for the designation of "first-born" in its generative sense.

Critique: Paul's use of the title "first-born" does not emphasize the principle of authority. It describes Christ as originator and inheritor of the church (Rom. 8:29–30) and *of* (not "over" as Hurley has it despite the genitive case) all creation (Col. 1:15–20).

The christological title "first-born" has no relation to the fact that Adam was formed before Eve. To try to force a correspondence between those two independent facts entails the risk of christological confusion.

12. See the discussion of 1 Corinthians 11:2–16 and 1 Timothy 2:11–15, p. 134-44 and p. 173-84.

13. Animals are described as enjoying a high status before the fall. They were not to be consumed as food by humans (Gen. 1:29). They were "formed" in the same manner and of the same material as Adam was (Gen. 2:1, 19a). Both Adam and animals received the identical designation of "living being" (Gen. 2:7, 19b). There existed sufficient correspondence between animals and Adam to suggest their suitability as plausible company for him. The affinity between pre-fall animals and Adam was such that God deemed it a worthwhile experiment to parade the cattle, the birds of the air, and every beast of the field before Adam for the purpose of selecting a "helper suitable for him" (Gen. 2:19–20). The dignity of animals was such that one of them, the serpent, being the most "subtle" or "crafty," was presumably able to stand upright before the curse, to communicate verbally as a matter of course with humans, and to lead them astray by imposing its will upon them (Gen. 3:1–6). If chronological primacy of itself confers rank, the animals were actually Adam's superiors since they were created before him. Some commentators believe that the possibility of an animal takeover was so real that God had to preempt such an eventuality by entrusting rulership over them to humans (Gen. 1:26, 28). Others argue that what they consider to be the rightful superiority of animals over man by order of temporal primacy was negated by the fact that the man, not animals, was made in God's image, and that the image took precedence over the principle of original primacy.

The answer to this sophism is obvious. The woman was also made in the image of God. If the image takes precedence over the principle of original primacy, man may not claim superiority rights over woman.

This line of argumentation throws Hurley into a dilemma. He maintains as dogma the notion of rulership based on priority of formation. At the same time, he also admits that the argument which "makes mankind subordinate to the animals which were made before him needs to be explored" (p. 209). But he does not explore it. He hurriedly dismisses the argument in one paragraph consisting of a hodgepodge of Pauline teachings taken out of context and injected into the creation story (pp. 208–209). The lesson to be drawn from God's subordination of animals to humans is evident: priority of origination does not confer hierarchical superiority, either to animals over humans, or to man over woman.

14. The expression "mutuality in equality" may need to be defined. Of itself, mutuality does not imply parity. A relationship of mutuality may indeed exist between master and slave, father and son, colonel and corporal. But this does not make them equal in function or rank. Equality exists among persons who make decisions conjointly and who apportion tasks among themselves on the basis of gifts and qualifications rather than rank or sex.

15. For the meaning of "woman" see note 16, the sixth critique, point (c).

16. With several other exponents of male dominance, Hurley attempts to find a basis for it in verse 23, which he interprets as Adam's naming of the woman. Astoundingly, he discusses this matter under the title, "Naming the Animals" pp. 210–212. He states that Adam's reaction to the newly formed woman in verse 23 "stresses his role over her in that he assigns her a name" (p. 212).

Critique: Hurley draws a parallel between the naming of the animals by Adam, assuming it to be "his exercise of authority" over them, and the naming of the woman "that reflected his role [of headship] with respect to her" (p. 220).

The text of Genesis 2 does not justify drawing such a comparison. In verse 19, it is clearly stated that the purpose of the animals' being brought to man was for him to give each one its own name. No such mandate is given Adam in regard to the woman. In verses 22–23, there is no indication that a naming process was a necessary part of the woman's presentation to Adam.

Critique: Hurley posits that Adam's "rule is expressed in his naming of the animals" (p. 210). This view contradicts the stated purpose for the naming of the animals in verses 19–20. The presentation of the animals to Adam was intended to find "a helper suitable for him." This phrase constitutes a frame for the whole episode of the naming of the animals as its introduction (v. 18b) and conclusion (v. 20b). In this light, the naming process serves to determine the nature of the relationship between Adam and the animals as potential partners. This requires no determination of authority roles, especially in view of the fact that by Hurley's own admission, a "helper" means an equal with no "implication of subordination" (*see* note 9). Hurley does not seem to be aware of the contradiction he creates for himself with the concept of Adam allegedly exercising rulership over creatures through the action of naming them, which action was divinely initiated to find him a partner that would be his equal!

Critique: According to Hurley, Adam's naming of the animals "demonstrates his control" over them (p. 211). However, Hurley does not reveal who is intended to benefit from this exhibition of power. Actually, such a demonstration of control would have been unnecessary since God had already placed the animal kingdom under human dominion as per His decree twice repeated in chapter one (Gen. 1:26, 28). A rebellious uprising might have justified a show of strength to remind the animals of who their boss was. But the text gives no hint of such a movement. Calling the serpent some appropriate names when it approached the forbidden tree would have been an infinitely more felicitous demonstration of control than browbeating unsuspecting animals when they were doing nothing wrong. All they wanted was to become "helpers," not tempters.

Critique: Should it be assumed for a moment that the naming of the animals was indeed an act of authority over them, there is nothing in the text to indicate that the naming of the woman was intended to fulfill the same function. In the Old Testament, the naming process serves a variety of purposes. Hurley does not consider those distinctions. Yet, the Genesis text requires that Adam's encounter with the animals be treated differently than his encounter with the woman. Not only was the man dealing with two different categories of being, but as the outcome demonstrates, God had a different purpose for each. One resulted in the self-definition of the man vis-à-vis the animal world and in their disqualification as "helper." The other led to his recognition of God's design and to human fulfillment. The text itself calls for this distinction. That the man "gave names" to the animals is specifically stated in the first case (v. 20). No mention of "giving a name" is made in reference to the woman in verse 23.

Critique: Hurley's insistence that giving a name constitutes an affirmation of authority is affected by the consideration that in the Old Testament, mothers named children more often than fathers did. There are twenty-five instances of women naming children for only twenty by men (*cf.* Otwell, *And Sarah Laughed*, p. 112). According to Hurley's premises, if giving a name signified assumption of authority ("the power to assign or to change a name was connected with control" [Hurley, p. 211]), mothers wielded authority in a most important area of family life more often than their husbands. This biblical fact is detrimental to Hurley's theory that man was ordained to rule over woman from their first encounter as a couple.

Critique: Hurley's contention that Adam gave the woman a name in Genesis 2:23 is unfounded.

(a) The designation "woman" was already attributed to the newly formed female prior to their encounter. The previous verse states that God had made the rib "into a *woman*" (v. 22). In his own statement, Adam does nothing more than acknowledge God's prior designation and appropriate it for himself. He does not invent a new name for the woman. He accepts God's definition. Adam's statement is an expression of obedience, not an arrogation of rulership.

(b) In the Bible, the word *woman* is not a name but a common noun. The term *woman* is no more a proper name for the female than *man* is for the male. They are both generic designations used in acknowledgment of the sexual differentiation among humans. There is no attribution of a name in Adam's statement. The intent of his words is similar to Eve's exclamation at the birth of Cain: "With the help of the Lord, I have brought forth a man" (Gen. 4:1). In both cases, the stress is on the awed recognition of God's handiwork.

(c) In Hebrew, the words used in Adam's statement for "woman" and for "man" have a similarity of sound comparable to their English equivalents: wo/man (*ishshah*) is simply the feminine form of man (*ish*). This near-homonym serves to stress the continuity that exists between man and woman. It completes the first part of Adam's statement in this manner:

> bone / of my bones
> flesh / of my flesh
> woman / out of man.

Adam's calling the woman by an extended form of his own self-designation expresses his wonderment at God's method of creating her. The plants came "out of the ground" (2:9), the animals were formed "out of the ground" (2:19), Adam was made "of dust from the ground" (2:8). But the woman was formed of the same substance as the man. In his statement Adam does not call the woman by a name. He exclaims at the sameness that exists between the two of them.

(d) The particular word used for man (*ish*) in Genesis 2:23 appears for the first time at this point in the biblical text. So far he had been referred to as "the man" (*adam*). The word *ish* is an entirely new designation.

If Adam's calling the woman *ishshah* is to be construed as an act of naming, then necessarily and by the same token, Adam is also giving himself a new name (*ish*); even more so for Adam since the word *ishshah* had been used previously for the woman (v. 22), whereas the word *ish* appears for the first time in Adam's statement. This being the case, whatever implications are read into Adam's "naming" of the woman, they should apply to himself as well.

Critique: Hurley makes a reference to the real instance of Adam's naming Eve (Gen. 3:20); but he confuses the issue by stating that Adam "assigns the woman a new name" to fulfill his "responsibility to act as God's subordinate ruler" (p. 212).

(a) Eve is not a *new* name for the woman, or an additional name. It is the *only* name she has been given. The name "Eve" is a proper name, not a generic designation like the common noun "woman."

(b) The contrast between Genesis 2:23 and 3:20 bears out the fact that there was no act of naming in the first instance. When Eve actually receives her *name*, the text uses that very word, "The man called his wife's *name* Eve." This is consistent with the *naming* of animals (2:19–20), but not with the text in 2:23.

(c) Hurley's statement—according to which the naming of Eve in Genesis 3:20 was the implementation of a God-given responsibility for Adam to be His subordinate ruler over the woman—is misleading. Within the creation design, it was not God's intent for Adam to rule over the woman. There was no need for such a thing, and it is not borne out in the text. Adam's rule over Eve began at the fall and as a result of it.

(d) The name given by Adam to the woman in Genesis 3:20 is a mark of honor. In a world that has become permeated with the somber reality of death, Adam recognizes in Eve the only hope for the continuance of life. The name "Eve" (*ḥawwa*) resembles in sound the word for "living" (*ḥayya*); hence, the explanation that Adam called her Eve (*ḥawwa*) "because she would become the mother of all living (*ḥayya*)." The one who had just received the sentence of death for having brought death into the world (Rom. 5:12–14) acknowledges the woman as the perpetuator of life, and therefore as the means of future redemption.

We conclude that there is no support to be found in Genesis 2:23 for the theory of male rulership over woman within the creation model.

17. This crucial text is not discussed in Hurley's book. He only makes two passing references to it in relation to other topics (p. 145, 205). One can only speculate about the reasons for this glaring omission in a work dedicated to the study of male/female relations. Obviously, the content of verse 24 militates against Hurley's interpretation of verse 23. Should the emphasis of verse 23 be seen as the *naming* of the woman, itself understood as Adam's exercise of rulership over her, then our text might have read, "Therefore, a man shall leave his father and mother, and take a wife and she shall become his obedient subordinate."

18. Our text does not even reflect the keena-marriage in which the hus-

band was co-opted by his wife's family (such as Jacob's marriages to Leah and Rachel [Gen. 29]). No reference is made in Genesis 2:24 to her family.

Chapter 2: Sudden Death

1. One gets weary of reading about the alleged susceptibility of Eve because of the emotional, volatile, impressionable, irrational, temperamental, impulsive, compliant, fragile, and passive psychological makeup of women; or that she was the likely candidate to fall since women are incurably devious whereas men are honest, straightforward blokes. With this line of reasoning, the tempter might also have chosen the allegedly wrong time of the month to get Eve to make a bad decision. If such was the plight of Eve, one wonders what was Adam's excuse in making the same bad decision.

2. The dialogue between Eve and the tempter begins with a test of her knowledge of God's prohibition (vv. 1–3). The tempter is obviously aware of the mediated nature of Eve's acquaintanceship with the information. He takes advantage of it.

Satan tries to obfuscate the issue by generalizing God's prohibition in two ways (v. 1). (1) He deviously extends the prohibition to "any tree in the garden." (2) Whereas the prohibition had originally been addressed to Adam in the singular as a personal order, it is now given a broader frame of reference with the use of the plural form (*cf.* 2:16–17).

Eve's retort indicates that she was adequately informed. Yet, her version of the prohibition contains enough variants from the original statement to render it obvious that her information was the product of oral transmission. (1) God had stated both the permission to eat of all the trees (v. 2), and the prohibition to refrain eating from the tree of knowledge (v. 3). Eve cites only the prohibition as God's statement. (2) God had addressed the statement to Adam in the second person singular. Eve cites it in the plural, similarly to the tempter's misquote in the first verse. (3) Eve's version is a condensed rendition of God's original statement to Adam. (4) Eve does not seem to be aware of the fact that there were two designated trees in the middle of the garden (2:9). (5) Eve falsely attributes to God the practical application that had been drawn from the prohibition, "neither shall you touch it."

These variants are not serious inaccuracies, but together they point to the reportorial character of Eve's knowledge. They do not reflect a high degree of internalization of the prohibition. Her knowledge was no doubt satisfactory to help her obey the prohibition under normal circumstances, but it was inadequate for her to face the tempter's attack successfully.

3. The passing of time will ineluctably cause the vividness and the immediacy of powerful experiences fraught with revelatory authentication to dim in the memory of participants and, even more so, of future generations. This phenomenon, eloquently deplored in Psalm 78, is as ancient as history

(*see* Gen. 40:23; Exod. 1:8, *cf.* Acts 7:18; Judg. 2:10; 8:34; etc.) Its occurrence was anticipated by Jesus in reference to the post-resurrection mission as He exclaimed to Thomas, "Blessed are those who have not seen and yet believe" (John 20:29). As I show elsewhere, the Gospel-writing enterprise was motivated by a desire to remove the story of Jesus from the hazards of apostolic ownership in order to commit it to the safety of permanent records. "By committing that story to writing, Mark transferred apostolic authority to his Gospel and rendered the function of 'apostle' superfluous." (*The Liberated Gospel*, pp. 144–145). A similar motif underlies the introduction of Luke's Gospel (1:1–4).

4. I just happened to glance at the "Letters" page of a periodical in which a correspondent states a commonly held opinion. He writes, "Some Scriptural passages say quite pointedly that women are different spiritually—inferior, in fact." To support his gratuitous pontification the letter-writer adduces the following "evidence" as coming from Scriptures: "the curse came through the woman" (*The Other Side*, February 1984, p. 2). This crude illustration cited at random is typical of similar teachings that are propounded through an abundance of preachments and publications that shape the popular Christian mind.

5. The tempter exploited Eve's deficient background regarding the nature of God. He appealed to her intellectual capacities to convince her that she and Adam could become "like God." Satan knew that, by attempting to rival God, the humans would inevitably join him in his alienation from God. The same ambition had caused his own downfall (Isa. 14:14).

6. The ancient Greeks called *hubris* the human proclivity to aspire to dethrone divinity and usurp its powers.

7. The temptation may be summarized in this schematic form:

God spoke to Adam. He heard God's prohibition.
God did not speak to Eve. She did not hear God's prohibition.
Eve was at a disadvantage.

Satan did not speak to Adam to deceive him.
Satan spoke to Eve to deceive her.
Again, Eve was at a disadvantage.

Yet, despite Eve's double jeopardy, Adam "listened to her voice and ate of the tree" (v. 17).

8. Hurley admits that "While it is precarious to build much upon the fact, it is worth noting that it is the man who is addressed and questioned." Yet, Hurley ventures, "It is apparently he who is the family spokesman" (p. 216). Without making any further elaboration of this point, he goes on to declare that "Adam functions as priest" (p. 219), and that "the headship of the man was reflected in his being called upon to answer for the pair" (p. 220). Not only are Hurley's statements false in that Adam was *not* called upon to

"answer for the pair" and Adam was *not* functioning as "priest," but his method of starting with a supposition and then turning it into fact a couple of pages later without citing any evidence is misleading.

9. Hurley's statement, according to which "it is the man who is addressed and questioned," and, as a result, that he is the "family spokesman" is not accurate (p. 216). Eve was also "addressed and questioned."

10. Hurley's speculation that Eve's "curse comes not only for her sin, but also because Adam, the head of mankind, has sinned and those whom he represented suffer as a consequence" (p. 218) contradicts itself. If, indeed, Eve's "curse" had been the first example of Adam's "original sin" as Hurley speculates, there would have been no need for a separate judgment upon her. She would have been covered like all other humans by Adam's sentence. Moreover, to confine the concept of original sin only to Adam's offense can lead to absurdity. According to this view, another human would already have committed sin prior to the existence of *original* sin, since Eve ate of the fruit before Adam did. If anything, the Genesis text emphasizes the solidarity of the original pair rather than functional differences between them, such as the presumed "headship" of Adam over Eve before the fall.

11. Hurley rightly notes that whereas God's curses upon the serpent and the man are prefaced with a description of their offense, no such explanation accompanies that of the woman. He states, "The woman is not told that the curse flows from *her* deed" (p. 218) and he adds, "the headship of the man was reflected . . . possibly in the lack of explanation of the basis of her curse" (p. 220). But Hurley concedes the first point for the wrong reason. Had Eve's sin been the usurpation of male "headship," she should have been rebuked for having unrightfully assumed leadership, and for having broken the alleged hierarchical structure of their relationship. But nowhere in the text is Eve reproved for having taken the initiative. Obviously, there was no crime in her doing so. Eve was judged because she had been deceived, not because she had usurped purported male prerogatives of Adam.

12. The clearest implication of this statement, conferring rulership to Adam as a result of the fall, is that he was not Eve's ruler prior to the fall. In order to overcome this uncontrovertible fact and preserve the theory of a hierarchical structure between Adam and Eve based in creation, Hurley has recourse to an unusual device propounded before him by Susan T. Foh (*Women and the Word of God*, pp. 68–69). According to this approach, God would be telling Eve in Genesis 3:16 that she will now desire to overthrow her husband, but that he will rule over her. This conclusion is obtained by injecting the notion of "overthrow" in Genesis 4:7 (which makes it read, "sin is lying in wait at your door; its desire is to overthrow you, but you must master it"), and then importing the new meaning into Genesis 3:16 because of the presence in both passages of the words *desire* and *rule* (pp. 218–219). The con-

trived nature of this expedient is obvious enough, but some observations need to be made about the theological and exegetical difficulties it creates.

Critique: The propounders of this theory seem to have missed the fact that if Adam had ruled over Eve prior to the fall, there would have been no point to the sentence since it brought no change in her status after the fall—except that she might not have enjoyed his rule as much as before the fall.

Hurley states that Eve's desire to overthrow Adam's rule after the fall is the "painful distortion of an existing relation" that constitutes the curse upon her. However, Eve's violation of the divine order that resulted in the fall provides an evidence *before* the fall of her proclivity to "overthrow" authority. The human desire for self-transcendence did not originate after the fall. It was the reason for the fall. God had warned against it from the beginning by giving the tree as a sign of deterrence. The "desire to overthrow" was nothing new for Adam and Eve; they both tried to overthrow the authority of God by eating of the tree. The new element introduced by the fall was the rule of Adam over Eve, not the "painful distortion" of Eve's enjoying his rulership before the fall but resisting it after the fall. Had Adam been ruler over Eve prior to the fall, and had she enjoyed his rulership, she would obviously not have taken the independent initiative of eating of the tree, and the fall would not have occurred. Male rulership was precipitated by the fall as an element of the curse. There is no evidence of its existence prior to the fall.

Critique: According to this theory, God would be punishing Eve's rebellion by ordaining more rebellion. She would be granted divine sanction to do more of the same, like punishing a petulant child who just smashed an antique vase by providing him with more antique vases to smash. In fact, God would be found ordaining female rebellion as a permanent pattern of behavior for wives, and male repression as the appropriate response of husbands. In other words, God would have decreed that married life would be characterized by a relentless power struggle between husband and wife, an evil competition that would pit them against each other, locked in an insoluble confrontation of mutiny and repression.

Such a warped view of the ordinance of marriage is foreign to both Old and New Testament. Male rulership is announced in the Bible as the result of Satan's work at the fall. It was not a part of God's design for relationships between men and women.

Critique: The elaboration of Foh's and Hurley's theory necessitates a considerable amount of tampering with the biblical text in Genesis 4:7. The verb "to overthrow" is arbitrarily supplied after "desire" where there is no word needed to complete the meaning. The noun "desire" (*šwq* or *shoq*) is treated as if it were a verb ("to desire") waiting for a complementary infinitive to complete its meaning ("to desire to overthrow"). However, the "desire" is a noun, and its meaning is complete in itself. The verbal form does not appear in the Old Testament.

Besides Genesis 3:16 and 4:7, this word—"desire"—is used one more time in the Bible, in a passage where the meaning is emphatically the "one flesh" union of Genesis 2:24, the very opposite of "overthrow" (Song of Sol. 7:10). This fact was not incorporated into Hurley's discussion of *šwq*. Moreover, the mixture of genders in 4:7 ("at the door sin [feminine] is lying [masculine] and toward you his [masculine] desire and you will rule over it") suggests an illicit situation that justifies the translation of the New International Version: "sin is crouching at your door; it desires to have you, but you must master it." The flow of the passage suggests an urge for associative union rather than a plot to overthrow.

Neither this word for "desire" nor the dozen other Hebrew words for "desire" found in the Old Testament are ever used with the idea of "overthrow," "overcome," or "supplant." The author of Genesis knows a specific word for "overcome" as "supplant," and he uses it in 27:36. He does not use it in either 3:16 or 4:7 because that is not his intended meaning. The word *overthrow* is arbitrarily inserted by Hurley in 4:7 where other concepts would fit more naturally: to entice, tempt, lure, deceive, seduce, attract, etc.

Critique: Once exegetical violence has been committed on Genesis 4:7, a second mishandling is allowed to compound the first error. The modified meaning of 4:7 ("its desire is to overthrow you") is transposed to 3:16, and the same interpolation is inflicted on this text so that "the woman is being told that she will come to desire (*šwq*) to overthrow her husband, but that he will rule (*mšl*) [or *mashal*] over her" (p. 219).

This procedure places both texts under unbearable exegetical strain. If the modified meaning of "desire" is transposed to 3:16, the same parallel must be drawn with "rule." In 4:7, the word *rule* has a negative meaning, since God orders Cain to oppose the sin whose desire is for him. This theory would require that Adam treat the woman with the same enmity that Cain was to exhibit toward sin. Far from ordaining man's benevolent rule over woman, as is Hurley's claim, God would be found allowing men to crush women as if they were sin incarnate.

The presence of the words *desire* and *rule* in Genesis 3:16 and 4:7 hardly justifies taking such liberties with the text. In any case, the textual form of the Genesis 4:7 statement is such that its use as a control text for the interpretation of 3:16 is not justified. The textual shape and the clarity of the context in Song of Solomon 7:10 make it a better test case to determine the meaning of *šwq*. To impute the meaning of "overthrow" to "desire" makes no sense in this text, but allowing it to stand as associative desire gives meaning to all three of its usages in the Old Testament. Indeed, there does not seem to exist one single version of the Bible in the English, German, and French languages that shows the "overthrow" translation as a possible reading.

As Carol Caster Howard, Ph.D. candidate at Harvard Divinity School, puts it, "The woman wants a mate and she gets a master; she wants a lover and she gets a lord; she wants a husband and she gets a hierarch. This is the clear meaning of Genesis 3:16."

13. That the fall had profound disruptive consequences on all aspects of life is undeniable. However, the point must be made that the Bible never presents the provisions of the curse as universal norms. Except for the clause of death, there is no further reference in either the Old Testament or the New Testament to a single element of the curse.

The writers of the Old Testament did not draw explicit lines of extrapolation from the curse statements to their own contemporary situations. It was during a later period of the history of Israel, in the flourishing age of rabbinic Judaism, that Genesis 3:16 was given wider applications. Although the writers of the New Testament knew of such interpretations, they did not follow them. My guess is that a study of the history of the interpretation of Genesis 3:16 would show that this text began to be used in a restrictive manner at a much later date in the life of the church, and that it came to be used in ways that are totally foreign to its biblical significance and purpose.

Although at this time I am not ready to venture more than a cautious opinion, it would seem to me, in view of the total absence of further references to this text in the Bible, that its original intent concerned the situation of Adam and Eve at the time of the fall, and that universal applications drawn from it are not valid unless they can be corroborated in other biblical teachings.

Parenthetically, some quick observations may help document my reasons for the comment above. The contents of verse 14 seem to be directed at a specific creature rather than to all serpents. Snakes indeed creep on their bellies, but so do other creatures such as snails, slugs, and worms that cannot be suspected of having been party to the temptation in Eden. Contemporary snakes do not eat dust. The enmity referred to in verse 15 concerns Eve and not all women. Some women are not afraid of snakes. They even keep them as pets. Not all snakes are inimical to humans. Some are so helpful in various ecological systems that they are protected by law. Hurley's comment that the "fall has distorted relations between actual snakes and humanity (real snakes strike people; people crush snakes)" (p. 217) is more applicable to mosquitoes. These are remorselessly swatted to death by humans, and their sting propagates deadly infectious diseases such as malaria and encephalitis. Not all snakes are venomous, and snakebites are not contagious. Likewise for verse 16, whatever situation may have prevailed between Adam and Eve, most women do not seem to desire men as much as men desire women. Many women do not suffer in childbearing or childbirth. In matriarchal societies and families, women do a pretty good job of ruling men. The ground cursed in verse 17 may not be taken as a reference to the whole earth, since in many regions the soil is fertile and productive. Adam was told he would work hard for survival, and many people do likewise. But many work nine-to-five jobs in comfortable environments, while some don't work at all. The only part of the curse that became an inescapable universal reality is the prediction of death in verse 19. It may be significant that it is also the only part of the curse that has been picked up in the remainder of the Bible (Rom. 5:12; 1 Cor. 15:22).

My fear is that the uncritical and abusive universalization of Genesis 3:16 may have erroneously legitimized male dominance and caused it to become so thoroughly ingrained into the social consciousness of our Judeo-Christian culture that an alternative mode of male/female relations has become inconceivable for most Western men and women.

14. When Hurley states concerning Adam, "He is cursed because he listened (i.e., yielded) to the voice of his wife" (p. 217), he distorts the meaning of Scripture by deleting from the text the complementary clause "and have eaten of the tree." Adam's crime was eating of the forbidden fruit. Listening to his wife only provided the occasion for the sin. At no time had God commanded Adam, "You shall not listen to the voice of your wife, for in the day that you listen to her you shall die."

15. Hurley's treatment of the fall is controlled by his insistence on grounding the male/female authority structure in creation and not in the fall. He tries to prove that for Adam and Eve the fall did not result in "the establishment of a new marital hierarchy, but [in] the painful distortion of an already existing hierarchical relationship" (p. 219).

In order to do so, he attempts to force a similar format of disruption of an existing order of relationship upon the serpent and on the man. But this attempt to reduce the consequences of the fall to mere disruption of existing relationships leads Hurley to unfortunate conclusions with serious theological implications.

In the case of Satan, Hurley has to assume that friendly relations existed between humans and Satan prior to the fall. He states, "The fall has distorted relations between . . . Satan and humanity (Satan seeks to destroy the race)" (p. 217). The biblical fact is that the fall did not distort any relations between Satan and humans. Such relations did not exist. The fall itself was the result of the intrusion of Satan on the human scene; and this intrusion brought death to humans, not a mere disruption of alleged relations between humans and Satan. Satan did not seek to destroy humans *because* his relation with them went sour. He came in the garden seeking to destroy God's creation.

Likewise, Hurley reduces the curse upon Adam to the appearance of painful labor that will cause him to drop from his toil as a result of God's judgment for his sin. According to Hurley, man "had previously ruled over [the ground] and it had yielded its fruit peaceably. The new element introduced by the fall is the conflict and the pain" (p. 218). Hurley leaves out the sentence of death upon Adam as the main element of the curse. It does not fit his model of a mere disruption of a preestablished order. So, "the conflict and the pain," not death itself, become "the new element introduced by the fall."

If it were true that the fall merely distorted previously existing relations, God's warning to Adam (2:17) should have been: "In the day you eat of it you shall experience conflict and pain," or "In the day you eat of it your wife will begin to resist your authority," or "In the day you eat of it Satan will begin to seek to destroy you." But the warning concerned an evil infinitely more pervasive and terrifying than disrupted human relationships. It was God's attempt to protect humans from sudden death, from the destruction of life, not just from disruptions. Indeed, once the fall was consummated, Adam heard the terminal sentence, "Dust you are and to dust you shall return." Any attempt to minimize the catastrophic dimensions of the fall will result in the trivialization of sin and death, which is a heresy called Pelagianism. It has been repudiated by the church long ago.

Hurley's mishandling of this text (3:14–19) illustrates the subtle dangers inherent in the practice of interpreting Scripture from the perspective of predetermined models such as a hypothetical authority/subordination construct for male/female relations in Eden. Instead of Scripture being allowed to control our teaching, it is our teaching that eventually controls Scripture and produces deviant interpretations.

16. The author of Genesis provides a rapid glimpse into the personality of Lamech and the life of his *ménage à trois*. In 4:23, this unsavory character is described as gathering his wives and staging a concert to boast to them of his macho attributes. The lyrics of his braggadocio consist of a recital of his murderous accomplishments. It can be rendered, "I don't care who he is; somebody just touches me, I waste him. If you think Cain was trouble, you ain't seen nothin' yet. This honcho here's gonna make Cain look like an altar boy."

As the author of such lyrics, Lamech receives the additional distinction of having been first to glorify violence as an acceptable transaction among humans. By claiming the right to dispose of human life, he committed the ultimate act of arrogation against the sovereignty of the Creator, who alone may give and take life. Thus, Lamech can claim the dubious honor of having introduced on the human scene both the degradation of the "one flesh" relationship and the consecration of violence as a problem solver. The fact that the sons of this degenerate became leaders in the areas of animal husbandry, the musical arts, the metal crafts gives a measure of God's uncommon "common grace" in a sinful world.

Chapter 3: The Old Covenant Compromise

1. Curiously, while Hurley devotes twenty-six pages to a survey of "Women in Israelite Culture," including a section on "Family Structures and Marriage

Laws," he omits any reference in his book to the problem of the breakdown of monogamous marriage after the fall. The subject index shows no entry under "bigamy" or "polygamy."

2. Hurley's remark in connection with this text obfuscates the issue. He states, "Parallels to this sort of authority structure are found in many present-day business situations in which delegated authority is subject to review" (p. 44). Obviously, women whose commitments were revoked by their husbands had not "delegated" them to do so. The discriminatory system was imposed upon them. The parallel drawn by Hurley between modern corporate business procedures and interpersonal relations in family life does not reflect a high view of the family.

3. A male Israelite's property rights included his share of the national patrimony that assured his participation in the promised eschatological inheritance. When causing conception with someone else's wife, the violating interloper was robbing the husband of his portion of the covenant by substituting his own progeny for the wronged husband's descendants. Hence, the necessity of capital punishment to prevent this potential substitution from materializing.

4. Hurley acknowledges the existence of prophetesses in a section of his book entitled "Women in Social Life," but he excludes any reference to them in the next section on "Women in Religious Life." He defines the role of prophets as pertaining to civil rather than religious activities without offering a rationale for such a startling classification (p. 47). The concept of women as occupying positions of authority over men in the religious sphere does not fit his model of female subservience. However, he admits the legitimacy of female authority exercised in civil life. Therefore, he conveniently but erroneously categorizes prophecy as a civil rather than a religious function!

5. This point is contested by Hurley as he writes of women placed in high official capacities: "These roles were outside the family structure as the women were in no way their husband's legal agents when they spoke for the Lord or rendered judgment by the law" (p. 56). Hurley's contention that ruling women were not "their husband's [sic] legal agents" is meaningless in view of the fact that such women had been commissioned by God and did not need to be delegated by their husbands. Having been appointed by a higher authority, they could dispense with their husbands' delegation as "legal agents" (whatever this is supposed to mean). Although such husbands had no say about their wives' privileged status, there is no indication that they disapproved of their wives' calling or that they did not submit to it.

6. Referring to the story of Nabal and to a similar instance in the life of Moses when his wife assumed authority that he himself had failed to exercise (Exod. 4:24–26), Hurley states: "Despite their failure and the wise actions of their wives, Moses and Nabal retained the responsibilities and authority which were theirs as husbands" (p. 45). It is very difficult to understand how Hurley

can affirm that Nabal retained the responsibilities and authority which were his as husband when every statement in the story argues against it. Abigail was the one who assumed responsibility and authority by overruling her husband's decisions, and God blessed her for doing so.

7. "Subordinate authorities" is used several times by Hurley in his book as a designation for wives. It is probably intended as a euphemism for women under the rulership of their husbands.

8. The Hebrew word for "peace" plays a significant part in the Song of Songs. According to 1:1, it is authored by Solomon which means "peaceable." The woman is the Shulamite, a name that has the word for "peace" as its root (6:13). Moreover, the whole poem is framed between two subtle puns that provide variations on *shalom*. The first occurs in 1:3 where the "name" (*shem*) for Solomon (*shelomo*) is like fragrant oil (*shemen*). In the second (8:10), she is the one who finds (and perhaps brings) *shalom*. Her lover is the peaceable one, and she becomes the peaceful one.

9. We know that this piece is a poem because it is written in Hebrew verse on an alphabetical acrostic pattern. Hurley erroneously states that the woman described in Proverbs 31 is "admittedly seen through the eyes of a man" (p. 55). Actually, the man who wrote down the poem served only as a copyist, transcribing the teaching given by his mother (Prov. 31:1). This portion of the Bible was authored by a woman. It presents a feminine perspective on the life of a married woman.

10. Hurley notes that the woman "is involved in the manufacture of clothing for her family and servants at both the level of purchase and of sewing (31:13–14, 19, 21–22)" (p. 43). He omits any reference to the fact that the strong wife is also manufacturing apparel for business purposes and that she, and not her husband, runs the business. Obviously, the woman's independent career contradicts Hurley's contention that "her husband is legally responsible for her actions" (p. 55), and that "her actions were subject to the review of her husband" (p. 56). There is absolutely no indication of the husband's supervision of or interference with the woman's business. To the contrary, her husband is said to trust her and her ability to make money (v. 11). The woman is described buying and selling without any mention of her husband reviewing her actions. The very point of the poem is that a strong wife does not need rulership. Mutual trust supersedes rulership. Because this poem anticipates the redemption of marital life, it transcends the confinements of the Mosaic Law (Num. 30:3–16). Jesus taught that the law was legitimately superseded by the application of higher principles, even during the old-covenant period (Mark 2:25–26).

11. In opposition to this perspective, Hurley's assessment of the "ideal wife" is determined by the interests of the husband. She is "ideal" because of her productivity for the benefit of her husband. He states, "The ideal woman is capable of prodigious achievements. She is tremendously valuable

to her husband." His "confidence [in her] proves well-founded as she makes a fine profit from her business ventures" and her efforts bring "honour to her husband and to herself" (p. 43). Thus, the primary purpose of the woman is to enhance the life of her husband by bringing him profit and honor. It is the very intent of the poem to invalidate such an androcentric definition of married life for women.

Chapter 4: The New Creation in Christ

1. Because the church is still awaiting the final consummation, its redemption, although sure, is not yet complete. Christians die physically, and they don't go about unclothed as in Eden—because the redemption of their bodies will become fulfilled at the final resurrection (1 Cor. 15:49–50).

2. Hurley offers a good summary of those features (pp. 58–74).

3. It is obvious that discussions of source and redactional influences on the materials surveyed in this chapter are not germane to the point at issue. We assume that whatever impacts the early communities had on the shaping of the tradition, such impacts found their impetus in the person and teaching of Jesus.

4. The verb for "rise" (egeirein) is commonly used in conjunction with the miracles of Jesus. These are to be viewed as predictive signs of the resurrection. The same word became a symbol for the identification of the risen Christ (Matt. 9:25; 16:21; 17:23; etc. See also Acts 3:15; 13:37; 1 Cor. 15:4).

5. On a similar occasion, Jesus told His detractors that the Sabbath had been established to serve human purposes rather than for humans to become slaves of the Sabbath and of its rules (Mark 2:27).

6. "Eschatological" refers to teachings relative to the end times. Although the main events of the end times are still to be fulfilled, the New Testament perspective is that the ministry of Jesus inaugurated the last phase of history, or the "last days" (see Acts 2:16–17; Heb. 1:1–2; etc.). Consequently, both the ministry of Jesus and the church age have eschatological significance.

7. Hurley writes about this text, "The central point being made is that the thought of a man's heart, as well as his deeds, are taken into account by God" (p. 109). This observation is correct only incidentally. It stops short of explaining the significance of Jesus' denunciation of specifically male concupiscence. Moreover, Hurley glosses over the cause of the inequity that permitted a man to look with impunity at a woman as a potential victim for his adulterous designs: the assumed proprietary rights over women of their male rulers.

8. The intent of Jesus' prohibition is to prevent "leapfrog" or serial marriages. A man sees a woman he likes better than his wife. He divorces and remarries, until someone he likes better comes along. The process can be endless. However, it must be admitted with grief and reluctance that there

may be some biblically legitimate reasons for divorce such as "unchastity" (Matt. 5:32), desertion (1 Cor. 7:15a), unresolvable dysfunction (15b).

9. The teaching of the apostle Paul agrees with Jesus' views on celibacy and expands upon them (1 Cor. 7:25–35).

10. See Mark 3:20–21, which sheds light on Mark 3:31–35. Whenever Jesus distanced Himself from His mother, it was for the purpose of protecting His ministry from her triumphalist misconception of His suffering-servant Messiahship. The tension between Jesus and Mary was finally resolved when Jesus fulfilled both His ministry on the cross (John 19:25–27) and Simeon's prediction to Mary (Luke 2:34–35). After the resurrection, Mary identified herself with the followers of Jesus Christ (Acts 1:14) and presumably with the Jerusalem church after Pentecost. The Scriptures contain no reference to Mary after that point. Paradoxically, some religious traditions exclude women from pastoral functions while elevating a woman, Mary, to the role of quasi-mediatrix between God and humans.

11. It is difficult to conceive that Jesus would have identified any of the disciples as His spiritual "mother" if there were no women followers present among them. In this case, the word *brothers* would have sufficed to convey His teaching.

12. A couple of references to kitchens might give the impression that this author holds such institutions in disdain. Perish the thought! He enjoys partaking of what is prepared in kitchens and has acquired skills relevant to such places.

13. No mention is made of the appearance to the women in Paul's account of the resurrection because the witness of a woman was not considered acceptable legal evidence in that day (1 Cor. 15:5). A reference to it would have carried no weight in proving the historicity of the resurrection among Paul's Corinthian correspondents. The disciples of Jesus rejected the women's testimony to the resurrection (Luke 24:11).

14. A question might be raised regarding the all-male constituency of Jesus' pioneer missionary task force, the twelve disciples. If Jesus wanted to give equal visibility to both men and women, why did He not appoint six men and six women instead of an exclusively male apostolate?

To answer this question it is necessary to understand the intended purpose for this group. From "disciples" (learners/followers) they would become "apostles" (messengers/representatives), the ones entrusted with the witness and the teachings that were to be propagated on behalf of Jesus after Pentecost. They were the original authorized message-carriers of Jesus. The program for the dissemination of their witness was Jerusalem, Judea, Samaria, and the Gentile world (Acts 1:8). The universal mission was to start in a Jewish milieu and continue through Samaria and on to the ends of the earth ("to the Jew first and also to the Greek" [Rom. 1:16]). The historical sequence required that the early pioneers establish the gospel in the Jewish Palestinian environment before spreading it in regions beyond.

Because of the cultural constraints present in the Jewish world, the ministry of women apostles, or Samaritan apostles, or Gentile apostles would have been unacceptable. Therefore, the exclusion of women, Samaritans, and Gentiles was inevitable during the first phase of the fulfillment of the Great Commission. At a later date, when the gospel spread beyond the boundaries of Judaism, both men and women, Samaritans and Gentiles, became instrumental in carrying out the gospel mission. Those who suffered and were scattered during the "great persecution" in Jerusalem and who went throughout Judea and Samaria preaching the word included "men and women" although the apostles were not among them. They remained in Jerusalem (Acts 8:1–4). Pragmatic considerations of accommodation determined the composition of the first apostolic group. No role conclusions may be drawn from what was a temporary but necessary expedient. Should women be excluded from positions of leadership because there were none among the twelve disciples, Gentile males should follow the same fate. They, too, were conspicuously absent among the Twelve, despite the fact that the apostles were commissioned to evangelize the Gentiles (Matt. 28:19).

A similar question may be raised regarding the fact that the second person of the Trinity came in human form as a male. The New Testament makes it clear that Christ came to earth primarily as a human and secondarily as a male. The significance of the incarnation lies in the fact that the "Word became flesh," not that the Word became a male. The cultural conjuncture at the "fullness of time" was such that it would have rendered the alternative self-defeating.

15. This point is contested by Hurley who states, "The gospels do not comment on 'office' or 'authority' structures for the followers of Christ either before or after his death" (p. 112). Although Hurley's book is "saturated with the language of authority" (his own phrase describing a Pauline text, p. 146), it contains no reference to any of the New Testament texts surveyed in this section. The highest numbers of entries in Hurley's subject index are listed under "Authority" and "Headship." There is even a separate listing for "Exercise authority." However, "Love" is not listed and he does not discuss Jesus' views on the exercise of authority in his book.

16. A distinction needs to be maintained between biblically defined Christian communities (church and family) and church institutions such as missionary organizations, denominational headquarters, church offices, hospitals, schools, welfare services, publishing houses, etc. These may all be staffed with Christians, but they do not fall in the category of biblically defined communities. They are service institutions and usually structured on corporate business patterns. The teaching of Jesus on authority structures applies to life within Christian communities, not to institutions ancillary to them.

17. The words of Jesus in Matthew 18:18 expand on those addressed to Peter in 16:19. The powers given to Peter ("whatever you [singular] bind on earth . . .") are extended to the whole congregation in 18:18 ("whatever you [plural] bind on earth . . ."). There is nothing in this passage that attributes to Peter a role of rulership over the other apostles. The designation of Peter as "rock" ("You are *Cephas* [rock] and upon this *Cephas* [rock] I will build my church") points to the instrumentality of Peter in the establishment of the new community. That the apostle Peter so understood Jesus' statement is made clear in 1 Peter 2:4–6, where Christ is the foundational rock, and all believers built upon Him form a living temple. The power of the keys to the kingdom refers to the ministry of forgiveness to be brought about by the preaching of the gospel as entrusted to all the disciples (John 20:23).

18. Thrones are not only signs of positions of honor. They also signify power. They symbolized participation of believers in Christ's eschatological rulership in eternity (Matt. 19:28).

19. God's preference for communities free from dominant individual leadership was already expressed in the institutions of the old-covenant people. The purpose of the law was for them to function as a theocracy (God was their sole leader). When He established them as an organized community, God used a team, Moses and Aaron (Ps. 77:20). Individual rulers such as the judges were a palliative necessitated by deviations from God's standard (Judg. 2:16–18). The establishment of the monarchy was a violation of the theocratic principle (1 Sam. 8:7; 10:19; 12:17–19), to which violation God had conceded out of mercy (12:20–25).

Chapter 5: The New Community

1. Rulership of itself need not be dehumanizing. Self-appointed dictators may exercise benevolent rulership, and appointive representative rulership is often benign. Rulership becomes dehumanizing when it is viewed as deriving from the biological process of sex or rank differentiation at conception, which process then becomes invested with mythical connotations of power by divine right.

2. The tongues spoken at Pentecost seem to have been specific languages immediately comprehensible to their hearers (Acts 2:6, 8, 11). This phenomenon was different from the glossalalia practiced in Corinth, which consisted of unintelligible utterances requiring interpretation—not translation (1 Cor. 14:2, 9, 28).

3. In the New Testament, the interval between the ministry of Christ (or Pentecost, since Christ is the One who sends the Holy Spirit [Acts 2:33]) and the "End" is viewed as the last phase of history or the "last days" (see Rom. 13:11–12; 1 Cor. 10:11; Heb. 1:2; James 5:3; 1 Pet. 1:20; 4:7; 1 John 2:18; etc.). Joel had telescoped together in one prediction his vision of Pentecost (Acts

2:17–18) and of the "End" (vv. 19–20). Those two events provide a frame for the period of the "last days." This is the time when salvation is made universally available through the gospel mission (v. 21).

4. This text is not mentioned in Hurley's book except for a passing reference with the dispirited comment, "From its very beginning women played a significant, vocal role in the church" (p. 117). No implications are drawn from this observation.

5. Although this is not the approach followed in this study, it is conceivable that due to the commanding position of this text in the economy of redemption, it should be regarded as the hermeneutical benchmark for the interpretation of other New Testament texts on male/female relationships, so that evidences of subsequent deviations from the norms set in Acts 2:17–18 may be viewed as temporary accommodations to adverse situations.

6. The absence of any reference in the Epistle to the decisions of the Jerusalem Council (Acts 15) is often interpreted as an indication that the Epistle was written from Antioch to the churches established by Paul in South Galatia soon after his return from the first missionary journey in A.D. 49.

7. This inference is drawn from the similarities between Galatians 3:28 and two other Pauline formulas stated in connection with baptism (1 Cor. 12:13; Col. 3:11). Although there is no explicit reference to baptism in the last verse, the context contains baptismal language parallel to Romans 6:1–3.

8. Hurley experiences considerable difficulty in relation to Galatians 3:28. At one point he claims that "Paul was not reflecting upon relations *within* the body of Christ when he had the text penned. He was thinking about the basis of membership in the body of Christ" (p. 127). This is precisely the opposite of the conclusion we drew as the result of our survey of the passage. However, further on in his book Hurley inadvertently contradicts himself and agrees with our findings as he states regarding Galatians 3:28: "In that text Paul stressed the unity of all believers in Christ Jesus" (p. 195). Indeed, this latter conclusion is inescapable.

The pop theory—according to which Galatians 3:28 promises nondiscrimination only to people in the process of entering the church through justification by faith—is grotesque. According to such premises, unbelievers are encouraged to make their commitment on the basis of nondiscriminatory acceptance, only to discover that once they are within the church they are faced with discriminatory distinctions.

According to this theory, Paul was actually writing to the Galatian Christians: "When you were becoming members of the body of Christ through justification by faith, there was neither Jew nor Greek, neither slave nor free, neither male nor female; for you were all one in Christ Jesus. But now that you have come into the church, there are distinctions between Jew and Greek, between slave and free, between male and female; for you are not one in Christ Jesus." Such a theory is a preposterous travesty of Christian truth. It should be vigorously rejected. If the principles of equality and unity apply to people in the process of becoming believers, such principles apply even more *after* people become part of the body of Christ. The apostle Paul would not have given a plug shekel for a justification by faith that did not carry its promise into the lives of believers and of the church.

There are two additional statements in the New Testament that parallel Galatians 3:28. They are found in 1 Corinthians 12:12–13 and Colossians 3:7–11. In both context and substance, those statements (including Galatians 3:28) make it crystal clear that they were intended to provide a basic definition of the church as the human community where categoric distinctions are superseded and where all members receive an equal standing before God and before each other. Galatians 3:28 does not describe the "basis of membership in the body of Christ" (Hurley, p. 127) or the conditions for entering the church. It describes the conditions that should prevail *within* the body of Christ.

9. This statement of Paul is all the more remarkable since it seems to have been structured to correspond to a contemporary synagogual prayer that had the faithful bless God daily for not having created them Gentiles, women, or slaves.

10. There is no reference to this text in Hurley's book.

11. Hurley agrees with this point in a different context as he states, "In Ephesians 5 [Paul] once again draws the parallel between the marital union of husband and wife and the relation of Christ and his church (verses 31–32)" (p. 129).

12. Peter concurs with Paul on the power of the witness of a Christian wife's behavior and her ability to "win" her unbelieving husband by doing right and not allowing opposition to terrify her (1 Pet. 3:1–6).

13. Both in this passage and in our study of Ephesians, Paul's use of the word *head* will be defined from the writings of Paul himself. At the same time, it should be noted that the term for *head* in Hebrew (Old Testament) has the meaning of superior, leader, master, ruler. This is not true of either classical or Koine Greek (New Testament). Some Greek lexicons give a simplistic translation of *kephalē* by imposing their own modern concept on the term and then engaging in a process of circular definition: "*Kephalē* means ruler in the New Testament because it means ruler in these New Testament passages."

In order to understand properly the meaning of "head" as used by the apostle Paul, it is helpful to determine its meaning within the language spoken by Paul. The authors of works such as *A Greek-English Lexicon* by Henry G. Liddell and Robert Scott (Oxford: Clarendon Press, 1968), or *Theological Dictionary of the New Testament*, edited by Gerhard Kittel (Grand Rapids: Wm. B. Eerdmans Publishing Company, 1965, 10 volumes) have thoroughly investigated biblical and contemporary extra-biblical writings and reported that the word *kephalē* was used in secular and religious Greek contemporary to Paul, with the meaning of source, origin, sustainer, and not of ruler. The second-century B.C. translation of the Hebrew text of the Old Testament into Greek provides a case in point. The Hebrew word for head (*rosh*), commonly used for leader, ruler, or supreme is translated in the Septuagint by a Greek word other than "head" (*kephalē*) over 150 times. It was much later that the word *kephalē* began to be used as "authority" under the pressure of Latin usage, as evidenced in the writings of some post-apostolic church fathers. For Paul and his correspondents the use of the word *kephalē* as a synonym for ruler or authority would have been as meaningless as attempting to do the same today with *tête* in French, or *Kopf* in German.

14. Hurley agrees that *head* can mean "source," but he stops short of drawing the full implications of this fact. Regarding the first clause of 1 Corinthians 11:3, he correctly states, "Adam is the source of Eve in that she was physically taken out of him." Regarding the second relationship, he also agrees, "Adam did come into existence through the creative work of Christ. In this sense Christ is the 'source'" (p. 166). But Hurley fails to apply the concept of "source" to the incarnation, despite the teaching of Scriptures that God is "the Father of our Lord Jesus Christ" (2 Cor. 1:3), that Christ was announced as the one who "will be called the Son of the Most High" (Luke 1:32); that we beheld the glory of the Word become flesh, "glory as of the only Son from the Father" (John 1:14); that "as the Father has life in himself, so he has granted the Son also to have life in himself" (John 5:26); that "God sent forth his son, born of woman" (Gal. 4:4); that He "who was descended from David according to the flesh" is the Son of God (Rom. 1:3), etc. As the author of the incarnation, God is the source of Christ's earthly being, no less than Christ was the source of man, and man of woman.

15. Such a hierarchical definition would necessitate rearranging the clauses of verse 3 in a sequence different from the sequence given by the apostle Paul. This is precisely what Hurley does as he writes, "The best conclusion seems to be that in 1 Corinthians 11:3 Paul was teaching that a hierarchy of headship authority exists and that it is ordered: God, Christ as second Adam, man, woman" (p. 167). When the Scriptures do not conform to their preju-dices, some people prefer to rewrite the Bible rather than revising their presuppositions.

16. Making *head* to mean "authority" raises difficulties with the doctrine of the lordship of Christ. In what sense can Christ have authority over man and not over woman at the same time? He is ruler over both men and women, and His lordship extends to all. Christ is never presented as Lord over males to the exclusion of females; neither is He Lord over husbands in any sense that would exclude His lordship over wives. When Christ is cited as a model to husbands, He is presented in His servanthood and saviorhood, never in His lordship (Eph. 5:23, 25). And, in any case, modeling Christ is

not the issue in 1 Corinthians 11:3. Therefore, *head* has a meaning other than "authority" in this passage, and it is a meaning that applies to man and not to woman. The use of *head* as "fountainhead" resolves this difficulty, since Christ can be said to be the source of man's life, as man is the source of woman's life.

When applied to the clause "the head of Christ is God," the definition of *head* as "ruler" becomes most problematic. God and Christ are both persons within the one being of the Trinity. Nowhere in the Bible is there a reference to a chain of command within the Trinity. Such "subordinationist" theories were propounded during the fourth century and were rejected as heretical.

Whenever Christ is said to act in obedience, He fulfills His self-assumed destiny as suffering-servant rather than obey orders (Rom. 5:19). In so doing, He displays an obedience not required of Him, since He was a Son. He did not learn obedience *because* He was a Son but *in spite of* the fact that He was a Son ("*although* he was a Son he learned obedience" [Heb. 5:8–9]). His obedience did not derive from submission in sonship but from "being made perfect" in fulfilling His mission. He accomplished His task by being obedient to it.

Hurley is at pains to discover an evidence of God's "headship" (interpreted as "rulership") over Christ in the New Testament. On two occasions he refers to the text in 1 Corinthians 15:24, infusing it with a concept of "headship" which is totally absent from it. He writes: "Christ will acknowledge God as 'head over' mankind by handing the kingdom over to God . . . ,"—and later again, Christ "will acknowledge the headship of God by handing over the kingdom (1 Cor. 15:24)" (p. 167). Such contrived eisegesis is all the more inappropriate since the eschatological subjection of Christ is predicted in the same context as taking place in the future, *after* the delivery of the kingdom to God the Father (1 Cor. 15:28). The natural interpretation of *head* as "fountainhead" resolves this difficulty, since the incarnation took place through God's initiative as He sent His Son to be born of a woman in the fullness of time (Gal. 4:4).

The Gospel of John provides an explanation for the dialectic between the concepts of the lordship of Christ and of His servant function during the incarnation. On one hand, the lordship and the divinity of Christ are unequivocally affirmed. The eternal Logos is God (1:1). He had come from God and was going to God (13:3; 16:28). He was in the Father and the Father was in Him (10:38; 14:10, 11). The Son and the Father are one (5:18, 10:30). Christ is Lord (13:13) and God (20:28).

On the other hand, during His earthly ministry, Christ took upon Himself to act as servant. He had come to seek and accomplish the will of God who had sent Him (5:30; 6:38; 10:18). The Father had given Him commandment what to say and what to speak (12:49) and, therefore, He was doing nothing on His own authority but was speaking as the Father had taught Him (8:28).

He was doing what the Father had commanded Him, so that the world would know that He loved the Father (14:31). During the time of His humiliation, Christ acknowledged the Father as greater than Himself (14:28).

However, during His earthly passage, when Christ became Servant and made Himself temporarily subordinate to the Father by virtue of His human nature, God the Father reciprocated to the Son by ministering to the Son and by making Himself available to the Son. Christ acknowledged that His Father was still working as He was and that the Father who was dwelling in Him was doing His works (5:17; 14:10). All that the Father had belonged to the Son (16:15) because the Father had given all things into His hands (3:35; 13:3). Even all judgment had been given by the Father to the Son, that all should honor the Son even as they honored the Father (5:22–23). Consequently, the Father was bearing witness to the Son (8:18). He would send the Holy Spirit in Christ's name (14:26), and whatever the disciples would ask in Christ's name, the Father would give it to them (15:16; 16:23). Therefore, the Father would glorify the Son as the Son glorified the Father (17:1).

Even during the days of Christ's humiliation, the same principle of reciprocity that constitutes the essence of all God-instituted relationships characterized the interaction between the Father and the Son. C.S. Lewis describes the relationship of mutuality between Father and Son in this manner, "The Father gives all He is and has to the Son. The Son gives Himself back to the Father, and thus gives the world (in Himself) back to the Father too" (*The Four Loves*, Harcourt, 1980, p. 11).

17. In both 1 Corinthians 12:28 and Ephesians 4:11, "prophets" come in second position after "apostles." In Romans 12:6, with "apostles" excluded, "prophecy" is at the top of the list. The interchangeable use of "prophet" and "prophecy" indicates that no distinction is to be made between the office (formal position) of prophet and the function (actual ministry) of prophecy. Prophets are so designated because they prophesy, and someone who prophesies is a prophet. If the recognized function is not performed by the person occupying the office, the latter becomes redundant. The apostle Paul does not make a distinction between the function of prophet and the exercise of the gift of prophecy. Any one who prophesies (1 Cor. 14:31) and whose message passes the test of corporate evaluation (v. 29) *is* a "prophet" (v. 32).

18. In 1 Corinthians 12:28, Paul lists the spiritual gifts in two categories. The first category is made of the "higher gifts" (v. 31). They are numbered by order of decreasing importance as first, second, and third. Their gradation seems to be determined by relative didactic value to the church. These higher gifts are to be desired because of their superior edification usefulness (14:4–5, 12). Apostles, prophets, and teachers provide the church with the authoritative cognitive body of information that constitutes the foundation and the substance of its doctrine and practice.

The hierarchy of decreasing importance between those three ministries probably finds its explanation in the fact that the apostles were the living repositories of the teaching of Jesus; the prophets acted as the expounders and the expositors of this tradition; and the teachers were its systematizers. Whenever prophecy and teaching are mentioned together, prophecy is listed before teaching (Rom. 12:6–9; 1 Cor. 12:28; 14:6; Eph. 4:11). This taxonomy suggests that the third-ranking gift of teaching was dependent on second-ranking prophecy, which was itself dependent on the first-ranking ministry of the apostles (1 Cor. 12:28). Indeed, whenever apostles and prophets are mentioned together they are listed in this same order (1 Cor. 12:28; Eph. 2:20; 3:5; 4:11), and they are both together designated as the recipients of and therefore the authoritative source of revelation in apostolic times (Eph. 3:4–6). The first-second-third gradation of the didactic ministries of the church reflects increasing levels of dependency on the authority of the prior gift. Prophets are dependent on apostles for their ministry of edification and exhortation, and teachers are dependent on both apostles and prophets for their ministry of teaching.

The designations of apostle, prophet, and teacher do not of themselves guarantee the integrity of those functions. The New Testament contains several references to false apostles (2 Cor. 11:13), false prophets (1 John 4:1), and false teachers (2 Pet. 2:1). Just as the old covenant prophets were to be tested and evaluated (Deut. 13:1–5; 18:20–22), so the ministers of the new covenant are to be proven genuine (1 Cor. 14:29; 1 Thess. 5:20–21; etc.).

19. Hurley's book contains a 22-page discussion on 1 Corinthians 11:2–16 (pp. 162–184). The argumentation is often confusing, but his conclusions are clear. He somehow reaches conclusions diametrically opposite to Paul's. According to Paul, women may exercise leadership by prophesying but must wear a headcovering or its equivalent hairstyle. Hurley says the opposite. He concludes that the passage teaches "a pattern of male leadership in the church," and that "no shawls are needed" (p. 184). Such results are not surprising in view of the fact that in those 22 pages Hurley never deals with the issue of women prophesying except for this single sentence: "His [Paul's] specific discussion related to a situation in which women were praying and prophesying, to some sort [sic] of meeting of the church" (p. 180).

20. In 1 Corinthians 11:2–16, the issue is not lines of authority. The word *authority* is mentioned only once in this whole section, never in connection with man or with headcoverings. It is not used in reference to male/female relations, but in reference to women, "because of the angels" (v. 10).

In 1 Corinthians 11:7–10, the issue is not the comparative status of men and women in terms of rulership and subordination, since both men and women are described exercising the same authoritative ministry in prophesying (vv. 4–5).

The headcovering of women does not concern male authority over woman. It pertains to the relation of men and women to God, not to each other (v. 7).

This passage does not concern female attire in public, in social life, or in the home, but uniquely in congregational worship.

According to verse 15, it is plausible that female hair, styled in a manner appropriate to public worship, was considered equivalent to the wearing of a headcovering. This observation does not affect the interpretation of this passage, since Paul's ruling would apply equally to a distinctive hairstyle considered as an acceptable substitute for the covering itself.

21. The following story may help illustrate this teaching. Harry, who was born in Canada, emigrated to the USA and became naturalized as a United States citizen. Although he is a successful politician, he cannot aspire to become president of the USA since he is Canadian by birth. Legally, he still reflects the "image and the glory" of another nation.

However, his son Harry, Jr., who was born in Boston and who is also a politician, may present his candidacy for the presidency of the USA since his "glory" reflects only the nationality of the USA. Because he was born in the USA, as a first-generation citizen, Harry, Jr., is better qualified than his father to represent the country.

In a similar vein, Eve was a first-generation (so to speak) human since she was derived from Adam. Therefore, the headcovering which is the badge of humanity before God should be worn not by man but by woman. Because of her origination from man, she is the fullness of humanity. She is human on two counts, first in her own self, and second with her head, which symbolizes her origination from man.

22. For Paul, angels are awed participants in redemption history and in the worship of the church (1 Cor. 4:9, 6:3, 13:1, etc.). The abuse suffered by this verse at the hands of some translators may be illustrated by the treatment it receives in *The Living Bible*. Although the literal translation is given in small print marginally, the text itself reads, "So a woman should wear a covering on her head as a sign that she is under man's authority, a fact for all the angels to notice and rejoice in." The concepts of a headcovering, of a sign, of man's authority, and of angels rejoicing are all imported gratuitously in this rendering. According to this extraordinary paraphrase, the same angels who celebrate the repentance of sinners (Luke 15:10) would likewise rejoice over the headdress of women. Actually, their glee would be occasioned by seeing women come under men's authority. This may be true of fallen angels, but there is no evidence in the Bible for attributing such perverted sentiments to the angels in heaven.

23. Hurley provides an instance of such misunderstanding when he states regarding this passage, "Paul taught the Corinthians that the appointive headship of the man applied in worship as well as in the home" (p. 184).

24. Hurley merely cites this important passage (vv. 11–12) without discussing it. He only comments that we find here a "strong counterbalance to check male abuse and disregard of the unity of the sexes," and that "the

husband may not consider himself the ruler of his wife and abuse his authority" (p. 178). Hurley fails to explain what leads him to the astounding conclusions that this text refers to married persons and that it deals with marital abuse.

25. Some view this text as normative and explain away, as illustrations or figures of speech, other statements of Paul that affirm female participation. Other scholars consider this text a corruption of the Epistle as the result of an interpolation intended to correct Paul's latitudinarianism. Many view it as a prohibition of only certain forms of speech, such as women asking questions, or as a prohibition for women to speak in church so that they defer to the authority of their husbands.

Hurley's approach is not more felicitous. According to him, "the intent of this passage is to teach that women ought not to participate in the examination of prophets, an exercise which Paul understood as incompatible with the subordinate role which he considered God had assigned to women in the home and in the church" (p. 193). Hurley does not explain why the evaluation of prophets, which was a corporate rather than individual task (1 Cor. 14:29), should have constituted a greater exercise of authority than prophecy itself, in view of the fact that the gift to "discern between spirits" was ranked after prophecy (12:10) and not even included in Paul's hierarchical listing of the gifts (12:28).

According to this interpretation, Christian women in Corinth would have been prevented, in deference to alleged female submission, from evaluating prophecies freely uttered by their own sisters before the whole congregation! The cause of female subordination (supposing for a moment that such a thing existed in the Corinthian church) would have been better served by forbidding women to prophesy altogether. The absurdity of barring women from discussing prophecy while allowing them to prophesy would have been self-evident.

Moreover, the text of the prohibition itself rules out such an interpretation. The women ordered to remain silent were women who wanted to ask questions out of a desire to "learn" ("But if they desire to learn [*mathein*] anything, let them ask their husbands at home" [v. 35]). This is the approach of an inquiring student, not the position of an examiner. An examiner may indeed ask questions. But the purpose of the examiner's questions is to challenge and probe the examinee's knowledge, not for the examiner *to learn* as a student learns, by asking questions.

In any case, it would have been pointless for a Corinthian woman to wait and ask such examiner-type questions of her own husband at home. Questions raised at home would have become irrelevant to the congregation's evaluation of prophecies that had been uttered during its meetings. One also wonders why a woman would be authorized to assume the position of examiner over her husband in their home and be denied the right to exercise the same function with respect to prophets during congregational gatherings.

If it had been Paul's intent to restrict women from participating in the evaluation of prophecies, why did he not say so in the prohibition statement? In verse 29, he used a specific verb for the ministry of evaluation (*diakrinō*; cf. the gift of *diakriseis* in 12:10). This concept does not appear in the prohibition statement or in its immediate context. The prohibition statement is preceded by a ruling for prophets to yield the floor to each other (v. 30), to take turns in prophesying (v. 31), to exercise control over their utterances (v. 32), because God wants peace to prevail in worship rather than tumult (v. 33). If the command for women to remain silent refers to the immediate context, it would apply more naturally to the exercise of prophecy (vv. 30–33), rather than to the more remote and briefly stated ruling about evaluations of prophecy (v. 29). The statement enjoins absolute silence for women rather than impose selective restrictions on women engaging in prophecy or participating in evaluations.

There is no evidence available in either Old or New Testament to support the theory that the prohibition refers to women evaluating prophecies. A superficial reading of the story of Miriam's punishment for having spoken against Moses (Num. 12) might suggest comparisons with the Corinthian prohibition. Indeed, parallels might be drawn between Miriam's punishment for having judged Moses and the silence imposed on women desirous of evaluating prophets in the Corinthian church.

However, Miriam was not punished for having evaluated Moses as a prophet. In fact, God's anger was kindled against her because she regarded Moses merely as a prophet (v. 2) and not as the one who, according to God, was entrusted with all His house, with whom He spoke mouth to mouth and who beheld the form of the Lord (vv. 7–8). This episode from the life of Miriam does not touch on the issue of the evaluation of prophets as was the case in Corinth. It concerns efforts to undermine legitimate leadership in order to usurp it (vv. 1–2). The fact that Miriam was punished for this act of mutiny—and not her male accomplice Aaron—provides another example of the inequity that resulted from the fall and persisted during the old-covenant period in what we called its "dark side."

The position espoused in this study relative to 1 Corinthians 14:33b–35, according to which this statement was a slogan of Paul's opponents in Corinth and quoted by him disapprovingly, has appeared in the following publications:

Bushnell, Katherine C., *God's Word to Women*. (Oakland, California: K. C. Bushnell, 1930), paragraphs 189–215.

Anderson, John A., *Women's Warfare and Ministry; What Saith the Scriptures?* Stonehaven, Great Britain: David Waldie, 1933), pp. 1-36.

Harper, Joyce, *Women and the Gospel*, (Pinner: Great Britain: C.B. R.F., Publications, 1974), pp. 14–15.

Kaiser, Walter C., Jr., "Paul, Women and the Church." *Worldwide Challenge*, September 1976, pp. 9–12.

Flanagan, Neal M., and Snyder, Edwina H. "Did Paul Put Women Down in 1 Cor. 14:34–36?" *Biblical Theology Bulletin* Vol. XI, January 1981, pp. 10–12.

Odell-Scott, David W., "Let the Women Speak in Church. An Egalitarian Interpretation of 1 Cor. 14:33b–36" *Biblical Theology Bulletin* Vol. XIII (1983), pp. 90–93.

26. Some people try to find a basis for this reference to "the law" in Genesis 3:16: "he shall rule over you." Whatever male rulership may have implied in the old covenant, there is no evidence that it was ever understood as women being silent in worship, or that it was ever interpreted in this manner in the Mosaic legislation. Not only could women participate audibly in the worship of Israel, but prophetesses had a vocal, divinely ratified ministry during its history.

Hurley rightly states, "It is difficult to figure out how it could be said that the Law (i.e. the Old Testament) taught that women should be silent at all times in worship" (p. 191). He attempts to explain the phrase "as even the law says" in this manner, "It is not difficult to see that the Old Testament would support the silence of women in judging the prophets, as its whole structure teaches male headship in the home and in worship" (p. 192). However, he is unable to come up with any Old Testament reference where "the law *says*" such a thing. When the Old Testament deals with the matter of judging prophets, there is no reference made to the exclusion of women (Deut. 18:20–22).

27. The status of women in civil, religious, and home life in the Judaism contemporary to Jesus and Paul has often been the object of careful research, which can be documented from a variety of sources including the Talmud. Hurley devotes a section of his book to such a survey and concludes, "Our discussion of the role of women in Judaism has presented a situation in which the subordinate role within patriarchal and Israelite society has hardened to a considerable degree and in which women have been relegated to a position of inferiority. The rabbis continued many old traditions and produced new ones which they thought would guard their people from sin. Increasingly this meant a separation of the sexes. Perhaps it was this distance which led to suspicion and ignorance, and the ignorance to contempt. As has frequently been noticed, the rabbis spoke most often of women in a depreciating manner. A woman's praise was found in her service in the home; criticism of her centred [sic] around her sexuality and her ignorance" (p. 73).

28. Paul had at least two sources of direct information about the Corinthian situation: the reports from Chloe (1:11, 5:1) and the letter from the Corinthians themselves (7:1). Those sources provided Paul with sufficient data to quote choice excerpts from their false teachings in order to refute them. The following are some of the statements often recognized as Corinthian "slogans" quoted by Paul in 1 Corinthians (since quotation marks were not used in Paul's day, the identification of quotes is a matter of exegetical deduction, and it may vary from version to version):

"I belong to Paul," "I belong to Apollos," "I belong to Cephas," "I belong to Christ" (1:12; 3:4).

"All things are lawful for me" (6:12; 10:23).

"Food is meant for the stomach and the stomach for food—and God will destroy both one and the other" (6:13).

"Every other sin which a man commits is outside the body; but the immoral man sins against his own body" (6:18).

"It is well for a man not to touch a woman" (7:1).

"All of us possess knowledge" (8:1).

"We know that an idol has no real existence, and that there is no God but one" (8:4).

"Food will not commend us to God. We are no worse off if we do not eat, and no better off if we do" (8:8).

It is our contention in this chapter that the best interpretation of the prohibition in 14:33b–35 requires that it be recognized as another Corinthian slogan and that it be placed between quotation marks.

29. For instance, David W. Odell-Scott's "Let the Women Speak in Church. An Egalitarian Interpretation of 1 Cor. 14:33b–36" (*Biblical Theology Bulletin*, July 1983, Vol. X111, pp. 90–93).

It is worth noting that in 1 Corinthians more than in any of his other Epistles, Paul uses the $\bar{e}$ particle to introduce rebuttals to statements preceding it. As a conjunction, $\bar{e}$ appears in Paul's Epistles in a variety of uses. But the list below points to a predilection for a particular use of $\bar{e}$ which is characteristic mainly of 1 Corinthians.

In 6:1–2, Paul challenges the Corinthians for their propensity to go into litigations against each other before pagan courts, rather than to submit their contentions to fellow believers. He counters this situation with "$\bar{e}$ (nonsense!) do you not know that the saints will judge the world?"

In 6:9, having exposed the misbehavior of brethren who wrong and defraud each other, he counters with "$\bar{e}$ (nonsense!) do you not know that the unrighteous will not inherit the kingdom of God?"

In 6:16, having made the absurd supposition that the members of Christ might be surrendered to a prostitute, he reacts with "$\bar{e}$ (nonsense!) do you not know that he who joins himself to a prostitute becomes one body with her?"

To the presumed relatively minimal effect of immorality on its perpetrator Paul retorts, "*ē* (nonsense!) do you not know that your body is a temple of the Holy Spirit within you, which you have from God?" (6:19).

A similar pattern is found in 9:6 where Paul, having made rightful claim to food, drink, and the company of a wife—all of which he has willingly renounced—goes on to protest, "*ē* (nonsense!) is it only I and Barnabas who have no right to refrain from working for support?"

To the supposition that he may be speaking on a merely human level of authority, he retorts, "*ē* (nonsense!) does not the law say the same?" (9:8).

Having quoted the Old Testament text concerning the prohibition to muzzle the ox treading the grain, and having raised a question relative to its narrow application to the ox only, Paul responds with "*ē* (nonsense!) does not he speak entirely for our sakes?" (9:10).

In 10:22, after denouncing the practice of partaking of both the Lord's table and the table of demons, Paul repudiates the inconsistency with "*ē* (nonsense!) shall we provoke the Lord to jealousy?"

In 11:13, Paul asks the rhetorical question as to whether it is proper for a woman to pray with her head uncovered. His emphatic negation in the following verse is "*ē* (nonsense!) does not nature itself teach you that for a man to wear long hair is degrading to him but if a woman has long hair, it is her pride?"

In the same manner, having cited the slogan of the Corinthian Judaizers prohibiting women to speak in church (14:33b–35), Paul signals his rejection of it in 14:36 with "*ē* (nonsense!) did the word of God originate with you? *ē* (nonsense!) are you the exclusive recipients of the word of God?"

Special attention should be given to the use of *ē* in 6:19. Commentators are hard-pressed to make sense of the preceding statement when it is viewed as Paul's own words, since committing sins outside the body requires committing them against others, which should be the more reprehensible offense. Moreover, immorality is never committed in a vacuum. It is difficult to conceive of immorality as not affecting others along with the person committing it. Finally, it is obvious that sins other than immorality (such as some listed in verses 9 and 10) are also committed against one's own body.

However, the statement of 6:18b makes perfect sense once it is viewed as a slogan of the Corinthian libertines quoted here by Paul. They would be saying, "Every other sin which a man commits affects someone else; but with immorality I do not hurt anyone but myself (since the prostitute is admittedly a negligible entity doing her work)." In other words, "What I do with my own body is my own business." Should this be the case, we would have here another Corinthian slogan countered by Paul with the particle *ē*, much like his handling of the prohibition slogan in 14:33b–36.

In each case cited above, the pattern is similar. A proposition is presented in the form of a rhetorical question or a declarative statement containing an element of incongruity. It is followed by the particle *ē* which is used to introduce the counterstatement in the form of a question. As indicated above, the consistent use of *ē* in each of those ten instances could be accurately rendered by substituting for it an indignant "nonsense!" expressing disapproval and rejection of the incongruous proposition. The use of *ē* is not different in 14:36. With this particle used twice in rapid succession as an expletive of disassociation, Paul emphatically debunks the Judaizers' prohibition as nonsense, and rebukes them with biting sarcasm about their invention of a new rule or "word of God" not available to Paul and to the other Gentile churches.

30. There are several words in the New Testament whose meaning is changed by the addition of the reciprocal pronoun *allēlōn*. Thus, the verb for "steal" becomes "deprive" with the addition of the reciprocal pronoun, without any idea of fraud (1 Cor. 7:5). Likewise, the verb for "worry" becomes "care for each other" with the reciprocal pronoun (12:25).

31. Hurley admits that "verse 21 is the culmination of verses 18–20" (p. 140), but he fails to discuss the meaning of mutual submission in reference to this passage.

Instead, he uses a self-contradictory definition of mutual subjection as the umbrella concept for the three pairs of relationships addressed in 5:22–6:9 (husband/wife, parent/child, slave/master). He claims: "The idea of mutual submission is . . . exemplified in these three relationships in which one member must yield to another" (p. 141). We need to point out that human language ceases to convey meaning when a unilateral relationship of authority/subordination, where "one member must yield to another," is described as "mutual submission."

Hurley's dilemma stems from the fact that he refuses to accept the concept of mutual subjection as the scriptural pattern for the husband/wife relationship. As a result, he attempts to impose a pattern of unilateral submission on all three pairs of relationships, whereas the apostle Paul places the husband/wife relation alone under the rubric of mutual submission and separates the two other relationships in a different category. He commands children and slaves to "obey" parents and masters, and that is something entirely different from mutual subjection.

Hurley would have obtained better results had he separated 5:21–33 from 6:1–9, and dealt with them as two different categories of submission relationships. Should it have been necessary to place the three relationships (5:21–6:9) under a single rubric, the text would have been better served by applying to all three of them the concept of mutual submission. In the spirit of 5:21, every Christian—husband, wife, parent, child, master, or slave—has obligations of deference, humility, and servanthood to his or her fellow Christians. Although children are to obey parents, yet fathers are obligated to their children in not being arbitrary and aggravating (6:4). Although slaves are to obey and serve their masters, yet masters are to reciprocate by "rendering slave service" to their own slaves (6:9, *cf.* 7).

32. Nowhere in the New Testament are church leaders instructed to exercise authority over their constituents. Deviant teaching and worldly conduct are to be confronted with authority (Titus 2:5). But leaders are specifically forbidden to "exercise lordship" or "rulership" over congregations. Instead, they are to provide guidance by exemplifying authentic Christian life before them (1 Peter 5:1–4). In return, the congregations submit to their leaders by obeying and accepting their guidance (1 Thess. 5:12–13, Heb. 13:17), while all members, elders included, approach each other in an attitude of humility (1 Peter 5:5). As a case in point, in 1 Corinthians 14:29 the apostle Paul empowered the congregation to exercise final authority over the premier church office, that of prophet. The fact that the ministry of prophets was subject to congregational validation indicates that, even at the highest level of ministry, individual authority was not an inherent part of a church office— except, perhaps, for the apostolate itself.

Against such a model, Hurley adopts a militaristic concept of church leadership as he writes repeatedly about "elders who direct the life and work of the church," "those who rule over" the church, "elders who are involved in the direction of the congregations," and those "directing the outworking of the message in the life of the church" (p. 225).

He achieves such results by rendering the reference to "leaders" in Hebrews 13:7 and 17 as "those who rule over you," against all the current versions of the New Testament that translate the word *hegoumenoi* as "leaders." Interestingly, this is the same word used by Jesus to indicate that leaders are servants (Luke 22:26).

Hurley proceeds in the same manner with the reference to "ruling" elders in 1 Timothy 5:17, which translation he accepts uncritically despite the considerable discussion that surrounds it. The same verb for "rule" is generally translated with the softer "manage" when used in reference to the households of elders in 3:4–5. However, when the elders' responsibility to the church is mentioned in the latter context, they are not to "rule" over it but to "care" for it (v. 5). This word *care* is used only on one other occasion in the New Testament, when the Good Samaritan *cared* for the wounded stranger and instructed the innkeeper to *care* for him (Luke 10:34, 35). It is this servant aspect of the ministry of the so-called "ruling" elders rather than the exercise of power which is brought out in 1 Timothy 5:17–20. The double reward accorded to the elders who serve well is confirmed in Scripture when it rewards the ox as it treads out the grain, and affirmed by Christ who declared that the laborer deserves his wages (Luke 10:7). The service rendered by the elders to the community is to be treated similarly to services rendered by the lowly ox and the unassuming laborer. Moreover, the elders were themselves accountable to the whole congregation and subject to rebuke by it in case of sin. In view of such data, it is preferable to translate "ruling elders" as "the elders who manage well" or "who administer well," thus avoiding the authoritarian connotations of rulership.

The principle of mutual submission does not exclude recourse to authority in the church. However, such authority is charismatic, pluralistic, and pastoral rather than institutional, individualistic, and hierarchical. It derives from gifts and competencies rather than entitlements and position. It provides support and self-sacrificing care rather than function through power and decrees. The model for such leadership is expounded in 1 Peter 5:1–5. Unfortunately, Hurley does not discuss this passage in his book.

33. Hurley rejects this concept with the comment, "God, a husband, a parent, the state, or a master, is never asked to 'submit' to the subordinate" (p. 143). The shallowness of this statement is obvious. In Ephesians 5:21, it is fellow believers who are commanded to submit to each other regardless of their subordination status. Since mutual subjection is to take place "in the fear of Christ" among fellow believers, God is evidently excluded from submitting to believers. He hardly qualifies as a fellow believer. All believers submit to Him. As we shall establish later, a husband *qua* husband does not have a subordinate. He submits to his equal. Although the parent becomes servant to the child in a crib, he does not submit in reciprocity to his offspring until the child becomes an adult and a believer. The state(!) is not a fellow believer and it does not have the fear of Christ. Mutual submission is irrelevant to this relationship. However, masters provide a vivid illustration of mutual submission with their slaves. Contrary to Hurley's statement that "a master is never asked to 'submit' to the subordinate," Paul requires masters to "do the same things toward" their slaves that the slaves have been commanded to do for their masters (Eph. 6:9). In this text, which is totally ignored in Hurley's book, Paul enjoins masters to reciprocate submission in obedience and service to their slaves, since both believing masters and slaves have the same Lord in heaven.

The mutuality referred to in this text revolves around the word for "rendering the service of a slave" (*douleuō*, v. 7), which denotes subordination in terms infinitely stronger and more demanding than "submit" (*hypotassō*). Interestingly, it is this stronger word *douleuō* rather than the weaker "submit" which is used in Galatians 5:13 to describe the interpersonal relationships among all Christians without exceptions made for rank, sex, function, or position.

34. The translations that render "above everything" (*hyper panta*) as "su-

preme" or "supremely" are correct. The New International Version which follows the Revised Standard Version at this point, creates an ambiguity by translating: "head over everything for the church." The meaning of "above everything" (*hyper panta*) in this verse should be consistent with the use of the same construct in the same Epistle where it means "above all things" and not "over all things": in Ephesians 3:20 Paul states, "To the one who is able *above all things* to do superabundantly. . . ." This identical construction of *hyper* and the accusative of *pas* is also found in Philippians 2:9, with the meaning of "supreme" or "supremely," as Christ is given the name which is *above all name(s)*. The translation "above all things" remains consistent with such readings, and it avoids the ambiguity of the translation "head over," which conveys in English a meaning foreign to the original text.

Hurley provides an illustration of the misunderstandings that may result from dependency on ambiguous translations as he states regarding Ephesians 1:22, "Paul parallels his assertion that things are subject to Christ with a declaration that Christ is appointed to be head (*kephalē*) over everything. There can be no escaping the idea of rule and authority" (p. 146). With this statement Hurley creates numerous problems. Some of the most glaring are:

(a) In Hurley's statement, the headship of Christ has shifted from the church to "everything."

(b) Hurley recognizes this problem and resolves it with another anomaly by making the same word *head* in 1:22 mean two different figurative concepts in the same sentence. He states, "Paul draws the rule of Christ and Christ's love for his church together by means of two meanings of the word 'head' (*kephalē*)" (p. 146).

(c) This conflation of the concepts of rule and love in the word *head* is a contradiction nowhere confirmed in the New Testament. As we shall discover, the use of *head* never connotes rulership.

(d) Whereas the fact that God has put all things under Christ's feet receives confirmation in 1 Corinthians 15:27, nowhere does the New Testament confirm that Christ is "head over everything." Such a concept is foreign to the Bible.

(e) As shown above, Hurley's translation of *hyper panta* violates the clear meaning of the identical expression in 3:20, and of a similar one in Philippians 2:9.

(f) Hurley's treatment of "above all things" influences his reading of the context as he states, "The context makes it abundantly clear that Paul means to talk of authority" (p. 146).

On the contrary, the context declares how the power of God that was operative in Christ's resurrection and in His exaltation above all things is the same power at work in the lives of believers. The concern of chapters one and two is not relationships of authority but God's ability to effect the same kind of change in the future destiny of believers as He already has performed in their lives through the ministry of Christ. The supreme expression of that gracious power was God's offering Christ as life-giving head to the church. Christ's exaltation in transcendence does not terminate His concern for the church. He will bring to completion His ministry to the church by insuring its eternal destiny.

The immediate context of Ephesians 1:22 deals with Christ's superlative transcendence "far above" the opposition, in the remote splendor of the "heavenly places," so that "all things" are below Him, or under His feet. In this exalted position He has no need to establish a relationship of authority over anything. He is above it all. There is only one relationship He maintains in His glorified state, as per divine appointment: He continues to be "head to the church," thus bringing her to completion of her intended "fullness."

The apostle Paul views Christ's exercise of universal rulership only as an eschatological fact pertaining to His second advent when He destroys "every power, authority and rule," when He puts "all His enemies under His feet," and "when all things are subjected to Him" (1 Cor. 15:24, 25, 28). However, this rulership over "all things" still lies in the future. From Paul's perspective, it makes no sense to say that Christ is ruler over ("head over" à la Hurley) all things prior to His second coming. He is *above* all things.

The emphatic climax of Paul's development in Ephesians 1:22 is that God "gave Him head, above all things, to the church" rather than Hurley's truncating version, God "appointed him to be head over everything for the church" (p. 146). We dare not tamper with this verse and make Christ's headship shift from the church to "everything," which is a concept confirmed nowhere in the Bible.

Apart from the exegetical critique of Hurley's interpretation of this verse, an objection must also be raised on literary grounds. Paul was too careful a writer to place, in the same sentence, something "under the feet" of Christ while making Him "head" over it. Head and feet are at opposite extremities. The imagery of trampling underfoot (derived from Psalm 110:1) is sufficient in itself to convey the concept of victorious domination. Whereas it appears several times in the New Testament, the use of "head" to illustrate the same concept is totally absent in the Scriptures.

Facile treatments of Ephesians 1:22 run the risk of displacing the headship of Christ from the church, His living body, to "all things" manifestedly not His body. However, when approached with exegetical rigor, this text continues to affirm, above all things, Christ's headship to the church.

35. Colossians 2:10 provides very strong evidence to the effect that "head" means source and not authority. In 2:15, the crucified Christ is described as victorious over the same "powers and authorities" (identical words as in 2:10). In view of this conquest, Paul would have been justified in stating that Christ was "*head over* all power and authority." However, despite Hurley's claim, such a construct did not exist in Greek, and "head" did not have the

meaning of rulership. Therefore, Paul establishes that Christ is "the head *of* all rule and authority" on the basis of His Creator activity (1:16). In 2:10, the genitive of possession invalidates any rendering other than "head *of*." Unaccountably, the New International Version translates it as "head over" without providing a marginal alternative or an explanation.

36. Hurley agrees with our analysis of two of the passages under examination. Regarding Ephesians 4:15 and Colossians 2:19, he writes, "The concept of authority is not introduced in these two passages using head (*kephalē*) in the sense of source" (p. 165).

He also recognizes the meaning of *head* as "source" in one more passage, but not without imposing on it abusively the idea of authority. He writes, " 'Head' (*kephalē*) as 'authority' and 'source' may coalesce with the idea of union as in Colossians 1:15–20, where Christ is the source of all things, the head of his body and supreme over all the things which he has created" (p. 165).

He ignores totally the statement in Colossians 2:10. Regarding the two others, he flatly states that "in Ephesians 1 and 5, 'head' meant 'head over' " (p. 165), and that in these two passages Paul used "the head language to illustrate the marital relationship" (p. 166).

Hurley's last quoted statements are in error on three counts. First, there is no reference to marital relationships in Ephesians 1. Second, "head over" is an idiom of the English language which does not exist in ancient Greek (as well as in several modern languages), and which would have made no sense to Paul's Greek-speaking readers. However, both the internal evidence of the New Testament and the lexical attestation show that they would have understood the use of *head* as "source," "point of origin," or "fountainhead." Third, contrary to Hurley's assertion, "head over" is neither used nor meant in Ephesians 5. Those two words (*kephalē hyper*) appear together only once in the New Testament, in Ephesians 1:22 where their meaning in context is obviously open to debate. Hurley's interpretation of *head* as "authority" is manufactured out of this single text with the excision of the two contiguous Greek words *kephalē hyper*, which are then claimed to be equivalent to the English idiom "head over," so that "head" in Greek is finally made to mean the opposite of what it means in all the references taken separately or together. This is a very shaky foundation for the doctrine of headship as authority. It is always precarious to build a doctrine on a *hapax*, especially when its interpretation is open to question.

Hurley's case for male dominance in church and family is structured to a great extent around the concept of *head* as "authority." The growing awareness in current biblical scholarship of the correct meaning of headship in the New Testament is increasingly threatening such constructs with total collapse.

37. Hurley agrees with our assessment of verse 21 as a hinge verse. He writes, "We must therefore agree that verse 21 is grammatically related to

both the preceding and the following material. It is in fact a transitional verse" (p. 140).

38. For the purpose of paragraph division, if a choice must be made between incorporating verse 21 with the preceding section or with what follows it, obviously it should be attached to verses 22–23. Indeed, verses 18–20 are self-explanatory, and their meaning remains intelligible without verse 21. However, verse 22 and the development that issues from it are meaningless without verse 21. The paragraph should begin: "Be submitted to one another out of reverence for Christ, wives, to your husbands as to the Lord. . . ."

39. The New Testament requires that wives submit to their husbands, not to the *authority* of their husbands. The difference is crucial for the proper understanding of the marital bond. I just sent a check to the Internal Revenue Service to pay taxes not because I love the IRS but because I submitted to the authority of the government. As a matter of fact, I sent the money begrudgingly because I disapprove of some of the uses that is made of tax money. I reluctantly submitted to authority because I had no other alternative. Because submission to authority involves this dimension of coercion, it cannot characterize the marital relationship. It is appropriate for a child to be forced to obey parents, but not a wife to obey her husband. A wife is not a child. She is "one flesh" with her husband. And, hopefully, a husband is not the IRS.

I intensely dislike going through department stores. To me, the abundance and the variety of attractive but superfluous goods they offer epitomizes the consumer mentality which I regard as the worship of god Mammon. Yesterday, my wife suggested I accompany her to one of those monstrous modern temples to Mammon for the purchase of a wedding gift. She could have very well taken care of the matter by herself, and I had no inclination to go. But I concealed my reluctance as best I could and went along. In so doing, I submitted to my wife, not to authority. This is submission, biblically defined, not the IRS kind.

Once in the store, we had a difference of opinion as to the gift to purchase. As we discussed the matter, my wife decided to go along with my suggestion. She submitted to my judgment not because she had to obey or because I coerced her. Had she chosen otherwise, I would have accepted her decision. But she voluntarily chose to defer to me. Again, this is Christian submission, not a yielding to authority as in my paying taxes but a voluntary disposition of oneself for the sake of another. There is no merit in submitting to authority. Pagans do it all the time. But God values that submission which is unenforceable and which flows from a servant heart (Gal. 5:13; Phil. 2:3–5).

40. "Head" is used here in its New Testament meaning of fountainhead, not as "head over," which terminology is never used in this section of Scripture. Had hierarchical considerations been Paul's concern in this development, they would have provided him with a golden opportunity to state: "For

the husband is the head over his wife as Christ is the head over the church. . . ." Obviously, this was not the case.

41. Hurley replaces the biblical mandate for mutual submission out of reverence for Christ with the teaching of wifely submission out of reverence for husband. In his own words, there are situations "*not* involving contradiction of biblical teaching, in which husband and wife, even after discussion, prayer and consultation with others, remain irreconcilably committed to different courses of action and are not prepared to give way for the sake of the other. There need not be many such cases, but in a fallen world there will be some. In them, the responsibility of the husband to lead and of the wife to respect his initiative requires her to yield to his decision" (p. 151).

In this last sentence, Paul's call for a husband to love his wife as Christ loved the church and gave Himself up for her becomes a "responsibility of the husband to lead" so that his wife will "yield to his decision." Hurley calls this form of marital tyranny "sacrificial leadership" (p. 149). However, he never explains how the consistent imposition of a husband's preferences over and against the will of his wife can be viewed as a sacrifice on his part. The husband's model is Christ's giving Himself up for us. This husband is unwilling to sacrifice his personal preferences for the sake of his wife, much less his own life. The only way this program can be viewed as "sacrificial leadership" is that the wife is getting repeatedly sacrificed on the altar of male egocentricity. If the husband were to love his wife sacrificially, he would gladly surrender his claim in loving deference to his wife. Hurley has it turned around. The Bible places on the husband the burden of acting in love to the point of self-sacrifice, not on wives. Wives are only asked to submit to husbands. But husbands are to love their wives in a manner that encompasses and reaches far beyond mere submission, since they are to submit themselves to the point of death for their wives. Voluntary death implies death to self.

Hurley extends the same principle of male dominance to sexual relationships. He states "human physiology is such that, generally speaking, when both partners are expressive in their physical relationship, the man will still be the one taking the active initiative and the wife the one making active response. Neither initiative nor authority necessarily crushes or distorts self-expression or personal fulfilment" (p. 150).

The naïveté reflected in this outlook on the physiology of sex would be comical if the interpersonal implications of viewing the male as the initiator and the female as a sort of harem-girl, waiting to respond to her master's desire, were not tragic. One wonders what sense of mutual responsibility and what kind of sexual reciprocity can survive in a situation where the female partner's role consists in being available to respond to use by her mate whenever it becomes *his* pleasure to initiate rapport. One also wonders how such a male-centered view of sexual life can be reconciled with Paul's injunction that "husbands should love their wives as their own bodies" (Eph. 5:28), and with his statement about spouses having equal authority over each other's bodies in 1 Corinthians 7:4 (a text which is neither considered nor cited in Hurley's book).

42. Some commentators understand verse 4 to mean that Paul places the main responsibility for the discipline and instruction of children with the father as "head" or ruler of the family. However, it should be pragmatically observed that in most nuclear families, with the father in the marketplace and the mother as homemaker, the leading influence in the upbringing of children during the formative years of their lives is necessarily and ultimately exerted by the mother. Only a separation of mother from children or a substitution of roles between spouses might enable the father to assume the primary responsibility in the rearing of children. Some nontraditional families have actually effected such role reversals, with the father taking care of children and home, while the mother becomes the breadwinner. However, this is probably not a solution advocated by those commentators who insist on the husband acting as the governmental head of the family.

43. Hurley opts for a convenient compromise as he writes, "Paul intended that women should not be authoritative teachers in the church" (p. 201). Obviously, this definition creates a dilemma of its own. If women may not be "authoritative teachers," the assumption is that they could be nonauthoritative teachers. But then who, except for the innocent and the benighted, would want to sit under the ministry of a nonauthoritative teacher and thus run the risk of being led into error? Hurley's treatment of this passage is rather brief and disappointingly desultory.

44. Paul's argument may be cast in a contemporary setting (very inadequately) in this manner: "John enrolled in the course first. Jane came in later. John did not fail the examination, but Jane failed the examination and she flunked the course." Or again from a slightly different perspective: "Jim is a veteran teacher. Joan is an inexperienced teacher. Jim did not challenge the administration, but Joan challenged the administration and got the whole faculty in big trouble."

Some commentators arbitrarily separate verse 13 from verse 14, and attempt to transform Paul's single argument into two independent reasons for his prohibition. First reason: "For Adam was formed first, then Eve." Second reason: "And Adam was not deceived, but the woman was deceived and became a transgressor."

We reject such an approach on the basis of the following considerations:

(a) If verse 13 is to stand alone as a reason, Paul never explains why Adam's having been created first should constitute an advantage for man, nor does he draw any implications from it. The fact that Adam was created first is meaningless for the ministry of teaching in the church. Adam's having been first in line does not make an Ephesian male believer any more spiritual, more knowledgeable, more qualified, or a more apt teacher than his female fellow Christian.

(b) The fact that Adam was created first and then Eve is addressed only one other time in the Bible, by Paul himself as he shows that, because of her full human derivation from Adam in Eve, woman is better qualified than man to represent both herself and man in worship before God (1 Cor. 11:8–10). The chronological difference was used by Paul to woman's advantage, not restrictively.

(c) However, to prevent any speculation on the chronology of creation, Paul proclaimed a solemn disavowal (vv. 11–12), declaring the chronological primacy of man meaningless "in the Lord," that is, among Christians and for the life of the church. He stated that man and woman should be considered as being reciprocatively interdependent in terms of their origins, and that only God could claim original primacy. The proposition that Paul would flagrantly contradict himself in a later Epistle is inadmissible.

(d) The total absence of any conclusion drawn by Paul from his reference to the primacy of Adam indicates that chronology is not his concern in this passage. However, Paul's understanding of the primacy of Adam as a safeguard against deception shows that he is concerned with competency. The reference to Eve, who was created after Adam and who therefore was vulnerable to deception, provides further evidence that Paul is establishing a principle based not on chronology but on competency.

(e) The conjunction *and* at the beginning of verse 14 relates the statement that "Adam was not deceived" to verse 13 in an intangible bond, since verse 13 provides the explanation for the fact that "Adam was not deceived" (Paul easily uses *kai* as an explanatory connective: 4:4; 5:4–5; etc.). "Adam was not deceived" *because*, having been created first, he had received God's command in person. His chronological primacy did not make him more righteous but more knowledgeable and therefore less susceptible to deception.

(f) Verse 14 does not exonerate Adam as innocent of responsibility in the fall, and it does not say that Adam did not become a transgressor also. In fact, Paul places the responsibility for the fall upon Adam only (Rom. 5:12–14, 18–19; 1 Cor. 15:22). The point of this passage is deception. Adam was not deceived because, being first, he was better taught. Eve was deceived because she came later and did not have Adam's experience. Likewise, unqualified teachers bring a greater risk of deception and false teaching into the church.

(g) If a ban on teaching is to be interpreted as retribution for the fall, Paul's view of Adam's responsibility for the fall would require that men be punished more severely than women since, according to both Genesis and the apostle Paul, Adam carried the heavier burden of responsibility and he received the sentence of death. The logic of this position would require that men be barred from teaching.

(h) If a ban on teaching is to be viewed as retribution for the fall, the doctrine of salvation by grace and of the new creation would have to be reformulated with an exclusionary clause denying forgiveness to women because of Eve's self-deception.

(i) If a ban on teaching is to be viewed as retribution for the fall, there is no explanation for the choice of this particular ministry as a means of penalization, rather than the more significant and authoritative ministry of prophecy which was accessible to women in the early church.

(j) Apart from this text, Paul makes one more reference to Eve's being deceived by the serpent's cunning (2 Cor. 11:3). Again, Eve is cited as an illustration of the dangers of being led astray from devotion to Christ by unauthorized and unqualified teachers, posturing as superlative apostles. This passage provides another clear-cut instance for the use of Eve's deception as a negative illustration of the hazards of exposure to false teaching by unqualified persons who promote themselves into positions of authority.

On the basis of the foregoing observations, we conclude that the division of verses 13 and 14 into two independent units renders both inapplicable to the prohibition in verse 12, and puts both at odds with cognate teachings in the New Testament. However, when the unity of the passage is left inviolate by either punctuation (a period between verses 13 and 14 is thematically and grammatically unjustified because of the copulative conjunction *kai*) or interpretation, the passage gains coherence and relevance to the situation described in the Epistle, where a profusion of unqualified teachers were threatening the doctrinal integrity of the church. As a caveat, Paul proposes to make the archetypal illustration of Eve, who fell into error by taking a leadership initiative for which she was not qualified due to her comparatively limited background and training. Paul's prohibition does not suddenly absolve Adam of responsibility for the fall to place it upon Eve, nor does it exclude qualified women from holding positions of leadership that are authority-intensive. The prohibition establishes the principle of entrusting such positions to qualified personnel only. It is reiterated in Paul's personal injunction to Timothy, "Do not be hasty in the laying on of hands, and do not share in the sins of others" (5:22).

45. However, it is obvious that the particular problem of incompetent women vying for positions of prominence was not universal. It was particularly severe in Ephesus because of circumstances peculiar to that church in its environment. Paul does not hesitate to indicate that his teaching carries a universal application when this is the case. Thus, when he discusses the proper attitude that should be brought to prayer, and cautions against tonsorial ostentation and sartorial extravagance, he makes it clear that this teaching is valid "in every place" (2:8). No such reference accompanies the prohibition about women teachers.

A warning must be voiced against the selective legalism which universalizes a local situation such as the ban on unqualified women teachers in

Ephesus, but relativizes rules that are clearly given a universal relevance ("in every place"), such as hands lifted high in prayer and no braids, jewelry, and fine apparel (2:8–9). Referring to these rules, Hurley states "The specific examples offered here are, to a certain extent, culturally relative" (p. 198); but he eagerly universalizes the ban on women "in positions of authoritative teaching or exercising discipline over men" (p. 233). Consistency would require that both sets of ordinances be treated in the same manner, and that Hurley also universalize provisions that concern the enrollment of widows over sixty as church staff (5:9), the drinking of wine as a digestive aid (5:23), a lifestyle reduced to food and clothing (6:8), and the interdiction for Christians to be motivated by profit as a business incentive (6:9–10).

46. Both Timothy's assignment as troubleshooter in Ephesus and the writing of the Epistle to Timothy were occasioned by specific needs proper to the Ephesian situation (1 Tim. 1:3). The difficulties had resulted from "certain persons" who desired "to be teachers of the law" without understanding what they were talking about (1:6–7). Some of those false teachers, having "made shipwreck of their faith," had been confronted and excommunicated (1:19–20). Such radical action was justified by the fact that the heretics were "giving heed to deceitful spirits and doctrines of demons" (4:1). At times, the number of defections seemed overwhelming to Paul (2 Tim. 1:15, 4:14–15) because the heresies causing them were propagating like "gangrene" (2 Tim. 2:16–18). Among the prime targets of the false teachers were women who would listen to anybody and could never arrive at a knowledge of the truth (3:6–9), and people who did "not endure sound teaching but having itching ears" sought teachers who would "turn away from listening to the truth" (4:3–4). Evidently, the ban on teaching by women had been issued as one of several emergency measures during an extremely critical period in the history of the Ephesian church.

47. Paul had specifically assigned Timothy to remain in Ephesus so that he would oppose "certain persons" who were teaching "a different doctrine" (1 Tim. 1:3–4). He was to supervise the appointment of pastors and leaders according to carefully formulated standards designed to screen out people who "might fall into reproach and the snare of the devil" (3:1–13). Timothy was to put Paul's "instructions before the brethren" as a "good minister of Jesus Christ" (4:6–7), to "attend to the public reading of scripture, to preaching, to teaching" (4:13), and to "take heed" to himself and to his teaching in order to save both himself and his hearers (4:16). He was to denounce departures from "the sound words of our Lord Jesus Christ and the teaching which accords with godliness" of men who were "depraved in mind and bereft of the truth" (6:2b–5) and to avoid the false knowledge that caused some to leave the faith (6:20–21).

What Timothy had heard from Paul (himself a preacher, an apostle, and a teacher, 1 Tim. 2:7; 2 Tim. 1:11) before many witnesses, he was to entrust

to faithful men who would be able to teach others (2 Tim. 2:2) so that
opponents would be corrected with gentleness that "they may escape from
the snare of the devil after being captured to do his will" (2:23–26). Timothy
himself must continue in what he firmly believes, which was first taught
him by his grandmother Lois and his mother Eunice (3:14–15, 1:5), and he
must continue to "preach the word, be urgent in season and out of season,
convince, rebuke, and exhort, be unfailing in patience and in teaching" (4:2).

48. In this light, Hurley overstates his case when he writes, "Virtually all
are agreed that the role of the bishop, elder or presbyter [Greek word for
elder] is one which involves responsibility to direct the life of the flock, teaching with authority, and the exercise of disciplinary authority to guard the
faith" (p. 226). The use of the word *direct* and the dual mention of *authority*
in connection with elders do not correspond to the biblical data. Another
example will suffice to prove our point. In the Corinthian church, the whole
congregation was responsible for carrying out the functions listed by Hurley
as elders' authority prerogatives. According to 1 Corinthians, the church could
boast of having "ten thousand instructors in Christ" (4:15); excommunication
procedures were initiated by Paul (not elders) and carried out by the whole
congregation "assembled together" (5:4–5); Paul challenges "one wise man"
(not elders) to reconcile feuding brothers (6:5); the whole congregation designates its messengers to Jerusalem (16:3); and the whole congregation is
enjoined to be "subject" to the household of Stephanas (16:15–16). It is very
unlikely that all the elders of Corinth were members of the household of
Stephanas. Interestingly, the Corinthian believers were asked to "subject"
themselves not to elders, but to a household which must have included at
least one woman to merit the designation of "household"—unless, of course,
Paul is referring here to both Stephanas and his wife as the elders of the
Corinthian church.

49. Despite such overwhelming evidence, Hurley states, "The deacons of
Acts 6 did not teach and rule but served physical needs" (p. 228). He also
volunteers the following reflection, about which we charitably choose to with-
hold comment, "It is clear that the deacons of Acts 6 possessed a certain
amount of authority in their distribution of food. A question arises, however,
if we ask whether, for instance, this authority is of a sort which, if given to
women, would violate the restrictions upon them as set by Paul in 1 Timothy
2:11" (p. 226).

50. Concerning elders, Hurley writes "The office is specifically for men
as indicated by the requirement that they have but one wife [sic]" (p. 229).

51. If the intriguing reference to females in verse 11 is to be interpreted
as referring to wives, by necessity it concerns wives of elders and of deacons.
It is unthinkable that requirements at least as stringent not be laid on elders'
wives as for deacons' wives. By the same token, should verse 11 be interpreted
as setting requirements for deaconesses (for which Hurley presents convincing

arguments, pp. 230–31), this reference to female leaders applies to both women elders and deaconesses. It appears only in the section dealing with deacons, because women in Ephesus may have qualified as deaconesses but, at that point in time, they could not meet the qualification of "apt teacher" required of elders (v. 2). As shown in the previous section of this chapter, they were still in the learning stages. The disbalanced location of this text concerning women and its placement with deacons' qualifications rather than with elders' qualifications provides the most cogent argument against its interpretation as a reference to wives. Paul is enunciating qualifications for women leaders, deaconesses now, and for elders when they will have learned sufficiently to become "apt to teach."

52. Hurley is "right on" about this one: "Peter's example of Sarah is not to be cast in the military context of a private shouting, 'Yes, Sir!' to show blind, mindless obedience to his sergeant. Peter's comments make it very plain that when he refers to Sarah he is talking about a loving respect rather than blind, servile or fearful obedience" (p. 155).

53. The exact meaning of "weaker vessel" is intensely debated. It can be taken as a reference to anatomical differences between men and women or to the subservient state of women. The paradoxical injunction to "honor" the "weaker sex" suggests that the weakness Peter is referring to is not a generic trait but a handicap inflicted through oppressive stigmatization. Honor is to be rendered to equals or superiors ("all men," "the emperor" [1 Peter 2:18]). Persons of superior rank do not "honor" their subordinates or people in a position of weakness. The command to honor wives is intended to redress unjust treatment.

54. The writings of the church fathers indicate that the female identity of Junias was accepted without objection during the first twelve centuries of the church. However, a number of more recent translations endeavor to present both Andronicus and Junias as males. This is often done by translating the word for "relatives" or "compatriots" into the masculine "kinsmen." Since this rendering would result in the improbable occurrence of Paul's having six "kinsmen" in Rome at the same time (vv. 7, 11, 21), it is better to translate the word as "kinfolks" or "compatriots" and allow for Junias to remain female.

The meaning of "outstanding among the apostles" is also sometimes rendered as "well-known among the apostles," with the effect that the pair would not be apostles but that they would enjoy a high reputation among the apostles. In other words, Paul would be commending Andronicus and Junias to the Roman Christians because of their reputation among the other apostles. However, the references to the couple's imprisonment with him and to the time of their conversion indicate that Paul is competent to endorse the couple as "apostles" on the basis of his own involvement with them, and that he would have little interest in deferring to the opinion of others as a source of credentials. As in the case of Apelles and Rufus (vv. 10, 13), Paul is well qualified to recognize and commend outstanding Christian workers without having to invoke their reputation among other apostles. Both the context and the content of this verse require that it be read naturally as Paul's commendation of Andronicus and Junias, who were remarkable Christian workers, even among people commonly called "apostles" such as Silas, Timothy, and others.

55. Luther's suggestion that Apollos is the author of the Epistle to the Hebrews has much to commend it. Should this be the case, we would be indebted to Priscilla for many of the insights contained in that great document. Even more intriguing is the theory that Priscilla herself is the author of Hebrews (A. Harnack, A. S. Peake, O. Michel, etc.).

It is not inconceivable that Priscilla had been commissioned by some church leaders to address the issue of the relation of the two covenants. As a Jewish leader who had been associated with the now-deceased apostle Paul during his teaching ministry, she would be uniquely qualified to write authoritatively on an issue that they had confronted together repeatedly in their ministries to Jewish/Gentile churches. Because of the anti-female bias of the Judeo-Christian congregations, she may have been requested to write anonymously, with her identity known only by the local leaders who had given her the assignment. In this manner she would be able to address the issue from her expertise as a scholar of Jewish background, under the cover of apostolic authority derived from her close association with the apostle Paul and other worthies of the apostolic church. In so doing, she may also have set a precedent for non-apostles such as Mark, James, and Jude, but especially for Luke as he wrote the third Gospel and the Book of Acts, both anonymous in the text but authoritative for the church on the strength of Luke's association with Paul. This device of semi-anonymity would enable her to direct her exhortations at Christians wavering between the two covenants without her gender causing an obstacle for the acceptance of her message by the tradition-bound Judaizing believers.

This theory would help explain several baffling features of the Epistle:

(a) The absence of an authorial superscription, and the conspiracy of anonymity that surrounded its authorship in the ancient church. The lack of any firm data concerning the identity of the author in the extant writings of the church suggests a deliberate blackout more than a case of collective loss of memory.

(b) The assignment of such a task would explain the strange nature of this document, which is a cross between an Epistle and a treatise. The author would be writing a general tract without the concrete historical specificity that would implicate her identity but with the real needs of a congregation in mind.

(c) This theory would account for the tone of respectful deference extended to leaders among the readers, especially if the author had been commissioned by them to write the document incognito. The readers are called "holy brethren" (Heb. 3:1). They are exhorted to remember their leaders and to imitate their faith (13:17). In so doing, the author would place herself under the warrant of the leaders' authority for the acceptance of her message.

(d) The theory of Priscillan authorship would also provide an explanation for a number of semi-apologetic pleas for credibility found in the Epistle. Statements such as the following seem to address a hindrance that pertains to the status of the author without constituting a reason for disqualification as a doctor of the church.

> Pray for us, for we are sure that we have a clear conscience, desiring to act honorably in all things. I urge you the more earnestly to do this in order that I may be restored to you the sooner (Heb. 13:18–19, RSV).
>
> I appeal to you, brethren, bear with my word of exhortation, for I have written to you briefly (Heb. 13:22, RSV).

The theory would also account for the baffling remark made by the author prior to delving into high doctrine, "This we will do if God permits" (6:3). Rather than expressing confidence that death will not strike with the next dip of the pen, this statement seems to appeal to divine authority in pressing on to the exposition of the deeper dimensions of the Christian faith.

Likewise, the mention of the author's travel plans as a companion of Timothy would make sense for a woman teacher desirous of receiving from Paul's male disciple the guarantee of his advocacy as she would enter an alien and possibly unaccepting church situation (13:23).

Such references would constitute subtle hints of the author's understanding of the limitations pertaining to her status in a code language comprehensible to those readers aware of her identity. In this light, the gender of the participle *diēgoumenon* in 11:32 need not be anything more than an editorial masculine.

(e) The explicit references as well as several allusions to women as exemplars of faith in Hebrews 11 come into clearer focus under the pen of a female author. Doubting-Sarah (Gen. 18:12–15) becomes a claimant of the promise along with Abraham, the archetypal man of faith (11:11). Moses the deliverer of the people of God grows up into manhood as the son of Pharaoh's daughter (11:24). Rahab the harlot, another Gentile woman, makes possible the conquest of the land (11:31).

Verse 32 contains a list of six names in an order designed to cause puzzlement if not consternation. The list reads, "Gideon, Barak, Samson, Jephthah, David and Samuel." Placed in their proper chronological sequence, the names should read: Barak, Gideon, Jephthah, Samson, Samuel, David.

It should be noticed that the list consists of three pairs of names, each pair belonging to a distinct period of history. Thus Barak and Gideon belong together, Jephthah and Samson likewise, and obviously Samuel and David were contemporaries. Moreover, the names in each pair have been inverted by the author of Hebrews so as to place the more prominent figure in first position. Gideon was more significant than Barak, Samson than Jephthah, and David than Samuel. However, in each case, the lesser figure placed in second position against the historical sequence was the one who set a precedent for or heralded the ministry of the more dominant personage. Thus, Barak the warrior set a precedent for Gideon; likewise, Jephthah paved the way for Samson; and without Samuel's ministry there would have been no David.

Interestingly, the ministry of each lesser individual (Barak, Jephthah, Samuel) was made possible by a woman. Barak owed his victory to Deborah (Judg. 4–5), Jephthah to his daughter's sacrifice (Judg. 11), and Samuel owed his ministry to the dedication of his mother Hannah (1 Sam. 1). Indeed, by resorting to the subtle device of name inversions, the author of Hebrews seems to convey the message that God used the discreet ministries of women singularly chosen by Him to bring about history-shaping deliverances by the hand of Gideon, Samson, and David. Behind the spectacular accomplishments of the heroes of faith stood great women of faith.

The last reference to women in this chapter of Hebrews is to those who "received their dead by resurrection" (11:35). Although the reference is to the prophetic ministry in the old covenant (1 Kings 17:17–24; 2 Kings 4:17–37), this mention of the resurrection, coming as the culmination of the list of faith's victorious achievements, cannot but evoke the figure of Mary who gave the Messiah to the world and recovered Him after death by the resurrection.

These seven references to women, either explicit or allusive, illustrate the causalities of sacred history. At the origin of each phase of the unfolding story of redemption there was a woman used by God to implement His will.

Sarah originated the people of God.

The daughter of Pharaoh brought up Moses the liberator as her son.

Rahab made possible the entrance of the people into the promised land.

Deborah and Jephthah's daughter opened the way for the victories of Gideon and Samson.

Hannah was instrumental in the rise of David, whose descendant was to be the Savior.

And Mary gave Him to the world.

Obviously, a male author sensitive to God's activity in history across the sex difference would have been able to outline this noble epic. But the discreet development of the theme suggests the restrained hand of a woman.

(f) Finally, the nurturing, humane, compassionate tone of Hebrews has often been noted, along with a special interest in childhood (2:14; 5:8; 12:7–11). Such motifs are in line with J. Massyngberde Ford's assessment that "we gain [in Hebrews] glimpses of Jesus' character which do not appear elsewhere in the New Testament, qualities, we may add, which would be especially appealing to a woman—compassion, gentleness, and understanding of human weakness. No New Testament writing exhibits such a unique and delicate poise between the human and divine nature of Jesus or expresses his role as High Priest as does the Epistle to the Hebrews" ("The Mother of Jesus and the Authorship of the Epistle to the Hebrews," *The Bible Today*, February 1976, 82, p. 684).

At this stage of New Testament research, the Priscillan authorship of Hebrews remains a very tentative theory. But the sketchy remarks above may suggest that it is a theory worthy of consideration and of additional exploration. The same Priscilla who taught Apollos when he was already an eloquent man—well versed in the Scriptures, instructed in the way of the Lord, fervent in spirit, speaking and teaching accurately the things concerning Jesus (Acts 18:24–26)—could be the one who continues to nurture the life and thought of the church through this ageless portion of Scripture.

56. It is interesting to note how some versions of the New Testament soften the title "deaconess" to "servant" when it is applied to Phoebe, a woman (Rom. 16:1), but maintain the full force of the official title as "deacon" or "minister" when the same word is used for men (Eph. 6:21; Col. 1:7; 4:7; etc.).

In Phoebe's case, the title is indicated for the purpose of credentials, to identify her as a recognized leader in the Christian community. The point of Paul's commendation of Phoebe to the Romans is not to laud her for her "servant" spirit or for her dedication to others in the church of Cenchreae. Paul is writing a formal recommendation that requires recourse to Phoebe's title in order to establish her credentials as Paul's emissary to Rome on the basis of her appointive position of leadership as "*diakonon* of the church in Cenchreae." Obviously, neither Paul nor his fellow believers in Rome and Cenchreae found it unnatural for a woman to be a minister in the church of Jesus Christ.

Conclusion

Several studies have been conducted on the "metamorphic effects of power" in relationships where a partner controls the behavior of his or her companion. The studies indicate that "To the extent that power-holders (husbands or wives, politicians or executives) believe that they control another person's behavior, that other person is likely to be devalued. This sets the stage for subsequent exploitation of the less powerful" (p. 32). The findings of such

research also illustrate the principle "that dominance and power are nega-
tively associated with feelings of affection" (p. 32). Contrary to the belief that
the compliance and the obedience of one of the partners produce harmony
and love, the studies showed that "People who unilaterally controlled decision-making had a less satisfactory relationship than those who shared power"
(p. 32). The loss of love that results from the unilateral use of power in
marriage may happen imperceptibly. But "even if it is noticed, the loss of
affection can easily be blamed on the [assumed] increasing stupidity and
incompetence of the submissive partner" (p. 32). From David Kipnis, "The
View from the Top," *Psychology Today*, vol. 18, number 12, December 1984,
pp. 30–36.

In marital relationships governed by the authority/submission pattern, the
erosion of love becomes a constant threat as dominance generates devaluation, and devaluation degenerates into disdain. However, the biblical model
of mutual submission provides for the protection of the reciprocal esteem
and the personal self-respect of each spouse by involving both in the process
of sharing power and submission. The fact that the twin injunctions for wives
to respect their husbands and for husbands to honor their wives appear in
two texts dealing with mutual submission is not fortuitous (Eph. 5:33; 1 Peter
3:7). In marriage, love thrives on mutual respect, and mutual respect requires
mutuality in equality.

Introductory Reading List

This list consists only of a beginner's sampler for initiating research on the topic. Some of the books, such as Hurley's work, argue against the position presented in this study.

Books

Boldrey, R., and Boldrey J. *Chauvinist or Feminist? Paul's View of Women.* Grand Rapids: Baker, 1976.

Clark, Stephen B. *Man and Woman in Christ: An Examination of the Roles of Men and Women in Light of Scripture and the Social Sciences.* Ann Arbor: Servant, 1980.

Dayton, Donald W. "Evangelical Roots of Feminism." In *Discovering an Evangelical Heritage.* New York: Harper and Row, 1976.

DeJong, Peter, and Wilson, Donald R. *Husband and Wife: The Sexes in Scripture and Society.* Grand Rapids: Zondervan, 1979.

Gryson, R. *The Ministry of Women in the Early Church.* Collegeville, Minn.: Liturgical, 1976.

Gundry, Patricia. *Woman Be Free.* Grand Rapids: Zondervan, 1977.

—————. *Heirs Together: Mutual Submission in Marriage.* Grand Rapids: Zondervan, 1980.

Hestenes, Roberta. *Men and Women in Ministry: Collected Readings.* Pasadena: Fuller Theological Seminary, 1980.

Howe, E. Margaret. *Women and Church Leadership*. Grand Rapids: Zondervan, 1982.

Hurley, James B. *Man and Woman in Biblical Perspective*. Grand Rapids: Zondervan, 1981.

Jewett, Paul. *Man as Male and Female*. Grand Rapids: Eerdmans, 1975.

_____. *The Ordination of Women*. Grand Rapids: Eerdmans, 1980.

Lightfoot, N. R. *The Role of Women: New Testament Perspectives*. Memphis, Tenn.: Student Association Press, 1978.

Malcom, K. *Women at the Crossroads: A Path Beyond Feminism and Traditionalism*. Downers Grove: Inter-Varsity, 1982.

Otwell, J. H. *And Sarah Laughed: The Status of Women in the Old Testament*. Philadelphia: Westminster, 1977.

Pape, Dorothy R. *In Search of God's Ideal Woman*. Downers Grove: Inter-Varsity, 1976.

Sayers, Dorothy. *Are Women Human?* Downers Grove: Inter-Varsity, 1978.

Scanzoni, Letha, and Hardesty, Nancy. *All We're Meant to Be*. Waco: Word, 1976.

Siddons, Philip. *Speaking Out for Women—A Biblical View*. Valley Forge: Judson, 1980.

Stagg, E., and Stagg F. *Women in the World of Jesus*. Philadelphia: Westminster, 1978.

Stendahl, Krister. *The Bible and the Role of Women: A Case Study in Hermeneutics*. Philadelphia: Fortress, 1966.

Swidler, Leonard. *Biblical Affirmations of Women*. Philadelphia: Westminster, 1979.

Williams, Don. *The Apostle Paul and Women in the Church*. Ventura, Calif.: Regal, 1977.

Articles

Bartchy, S. Scott. "Power, Submission, and Sexual Identity among the Early Christians." In *Essays on New Testament Christianity*, edited by C. Robert Wetzel. Cincinnati: Standard, 1978.

Dayton, Donald W., and Sider, Lucille. "Women as Preachers: Evangelical Precedents." *Christianity Today*, May 23, 1973.

Hiebert, D. E. "The Apostle Paul: Women's Friend." *The Christian Reader*, June-July 1973.

Kaiser, Walter C. "Paul, Women, and the Church." *Worldwide Challenge*, September 1976.

Richardson, P. "Neither Male nor Female." In *Paul's Ethic of Freedom*. Philadelphia: Westminster, 1979.

Scholer, David M. "Hermeneutical Gerrymandering: Hurley on Women and Authority." *Theological Students Fellowship Bulletin*, May-June 1983.

Bibliography

This bibliography was compiled by my friend and colleague Alan F. Johnson, Professor of New Testament and Christian Ethics at Wheaton College. He has graciously made it available for inclusion in this book. It is our hope that the bibliography will be used as an instrument to facilitate further research on the topic of sex roles. An asterisk indicates a more or less (minimal, moderate, radical) nontraditional position. Other entries are traditional. Abbreviations are those followed in the *Religion Index* I, Periodicals.

Historical

Alexander, J. H. *Ladies of the Reformation.* Herts, England: Gospel Standard Strict Baptist Trust, 1978.

Allworthy, Thomas Bateson. *Women in the Apostolic Church.* Cambridge: Heffer, 1917.

Anders, S. "The Role of Women in American Religion." *Southern Journal of Theology* (Spring 1976).

Bahr, R. *Least of All Saints: The Story of Aimee Semple McPherson.* Englewood Cliffs, N.J.: Prentice-Hall, 1979.

Bainton, R. *Sex, Love, and Marriage.* Huntington, N.Y.: Fontana, 1958.

271

_____. *Women of the Reformation from Spain to Scandinavia*. Minneapolis: Augsburg, 1977.

_____. *Women of the Reformation in Germany and Italy*. Minneapolis: Augsburg, 1971.

Balsdon, J. P. V. D. *Roman Women*. New York: John Day, 1962.

Barstow, Anne. *Joan of Arc: Heretic, Mystic, Shamman*. Lewiston, N.Y.: Edwin Mellen, 1985.

Bartelt, Pearl Winter. "Women and Judaism." In *God, Sex, and the Social Project*, edited by James H. Grace. Lewiston, N.Y.: Edwin Mellen, 1978.

Beaver, R. Pierce. *American Protestant Women in World Mission*. Grand Rapids: Eerdmans, Rv. 1980.

Bell S. *Women: From the Greeks to the French Revolution*. Hartford: Wadsworth, 1973.

Bonar, Andrew. *A Commentary on Leviticus*. 1852. Grand Rapids: Baker, 1978.

Borresen, Kari Elisabeth. *Subordination and Equivalence: The Nature and Role of Women in Augustine and Thomas Aquinas*. Wolfe City, Tex.: University Press, 1981.

Brailsford, Mabel Richmond. *Quaker Women, 1650–1690*. London: Duckworth, 1915.

Brereton, V., and Klein, C. "American Women in Ministry." In *Women of Spirit: Female Leadership in the Jewish and Christian Traditions*, edited by Rosemary Reuther and E. McLaughlin. New York: Simon and Schuster, 1979.

Brooten, B. J. *Women Leaders in the Ancient Synagogue: Inscriptional Evidence and Background Issues*. Chico, Calif.: Scholar's Press, 1983.

Brown, J. P. "The Role of Women and the Treaty in the Ancient World." *Bib Z* 25: 1–28.

Bulloughs, Vern L. *The Subordinate Sex*. Champaign: University of Illinois Press, 1973.

Cameron A. "Neither Male nor Female." *Greece and Rome* 27 (1980): 60–68.

Cattan, L. *Lamps Are for Lighting: The Story of Helen Barrett Montgomery and Lucy Waterbury Peabody*. Grand Rapids: Eerdmans, 1972.

CBA Task Force on the Role of Women in Early Christianity. "Women and Priestly Ministry: The New Testament Evidence." *CBQ* 41 (1979): 608–13.

Christman, M. "Women of the Reformation in Strasburg, 1490–1530." *Archive for Reformation History* 63 no. 2 (1972): 143–67.

Clark, Elizabeth. *The Life of Melania the Younger*. Lewiston, N.Y.: Edwin Mellen, 1985.

Clark, Elizabeth A. *Women in the Early Church*. Message of the Fathers of the Church. Wilmington: Michael Glazier, 1983.

Clark, E., and Richardson, N. *Women and Religion*. New York: Harper and Row, 1977.

Clark, G. "Roman Women." *Greece and Rome* 28 (1981): 193–212.

Cohen, S. J. D. "Women in the Synagogue of Antiquity." *Conservative Judaism* 34 (1980): 23–29.

Cott, Nancy F. *The Bonds of Womanhood: "Women's Sphere" in New England 1780–1835*. New Haven: Yale University Press, 1977.

―――――. "Young Women in the Second Great Awakening in New England." *Feminist Studies* 3 (1975): 15–29.

Coyle, J. C. "The Fathers on Women and Women's Ordination." *Eglise Th* 9 (1978): 50–101.

Danielou, J. *The Ministry of Women in the Early Church*. London: Faith, 1961.

Davies, S. L. *The Revolt of the Widows*. Carbondale: Southern Illinois University Press, 1980.

Dayton, Donald W. "Evangelical Roots of Feminism." In *Discovering an Evangelical Heritage*. New York: Harper and Row, 1976.

Donaldson, J. *Woman: Her Position and Influence in Ancient Greece and Rome and in the Early Church*. New York: Gordon, 1973.

Douglas J. "Women of the Continental Reformation." In *Religion and Sexism*. New York: Simon and Schuster, 1974.

Eckenstein, L. *Woman Under Monasticism*. Cambridge, Mass.: Cambridge University Press, 1896.

Epstein, L. *Sex Laws and Customs in Judaism*. New York: Bloch, 1948.

Ferrante, Joan M. *Woman as Image in Medieval Literature from the Twelfth Century to Dante*. Durham, N.C.: Labyrinth, 1985.

Feuillet, A. "La dignite et le role de la femme d'apres' quelques textes pauliniens: comparison avec l'ancien Testament." *NT ST* 21 (1975): 157–91.

Fiorenza, Elizabeth Schussler. " 'You Are Not to Be Called Father,' Early Christian History in a Feminist Perspective." *Cross Currents* 29 (1979–80): 301–23.

―――――. "Word, Spirit, and Power: Women in Early Christian Communities." In *Women of Spirit: Female Leadership in the Jewish and Christian Traditions*, edited by Rosemary Reuther and E. McLaughlin. New York: Simon and Schuster, 1979.

Flexner, Eleanor. *Century of Struggle: The Woman's Rights Movement in the United States*. Cambridge, Mass.: Belknap, 1959.

Fraser, D. S. "Women in Ancient Israel." *Journal of Christian Brothers Research Fellowship* 26 (1974): 14–28.

Gies, F. *Women in the Middle Ages*. New York: Crowell, 1978.

Goodwater, L. *Women in Antiquity: An Annotated Bibliography*. Metuchen, N.J.: Scarecrow, 1975.

Grassi, Joseph A. *The Teacher in the Primitive Church and the Teacher Today*, 113–29. Santa Clara: University of Santa Clara Press, 1973.

Gryson, R. *Le Ministere Des Femmes Dans L'Eglise Ancienne*. Gembloux: Duculot, 1972.

―――――. *The Ministry of Women in the Early Church*. Collegeville, Minn.: Liturgical, 1976.

Hardesty, Nancy. " 'Your Daughters Shall Prophesy': Revivalism and Feminism in the Age of Finney." Ph.D. dissertation, University of Chicago.

Hardesty, Nancy, et al. "Women in the Holiness Movement: Feminism in the Evangelical Tradition." *Women of Light*. New York: Harper and Row, 1979.

Hardy, E. R. "The Priestess in the Greco-Roman World." In *Why Not? Priesthood and Ministry*, edited by M. Bruce et al. Nashville: Abingdon, 1976.

Herlihy, D. *Women in Medieval Society*. Houston: University of Saint Thomas, 1970.

Hosier, H. *Kathryn Kuhlman*. Old Tappan, N.J.: Revell, 1976.

Huber E. " 'A Woman Must Not Speak': Quaker Woman in the English Left Wing." In *Women of Spirit: Female Leadership in the Jewish and Christian Traditions*, edited by Rosemary Reuther and E. McLaughlin. New York: Simon and Schuster, 1979.

Hunt, Morton M. *The Natural History of Love*. New York: Knopf, 1959.

Irwin D. "The Ministry of Women in the Early Church: The Archaeological Evidence." *Duke Div R* 45 (1980): 76–86.

Irwin, Joyce L. *Womanhood in Radical Protestantism*. Lewiston, N.Y.: Edwin Mellen, 1979.

Jastrow, M. "Veiling in Ancient Assyria." *Revue Archeologique* 5th series 14 (1921): 209–38.

Jeremy, M. *Scholars and Mystics*. Chicago: Regnery, 1962.

Kahler, Else. *Die Frau in den Paulinishchen Briefen Unter Besonderen Berucksichtigung des Begriffes der Unterordnung*. Gotthelf-Verlag, 1960.

Kraemer, Ross S. "Women in the Religions of the Greco-Roman World." *Religious Studies Review* 9 (April 1983): 127–39.

La Porte, Jean. *The Role of Women in Early Christianity*. Lewiston, N.Y.: Edwin Mellen, 1982.

Lawson, Ellen. *The Three Sarahs: Documents of Black Antebellum College Women*. Lewiston, N.Y.: Edwin Mellen, 1985.

Lefkowitz, M. F., and Faut, M. B. *Women in Greece and Rome*. Toronto/Sarasota: Samuel-Stevens, 1977.

Leipoldt, J. *Die Frau in der ontiken Welt und in Urchristentum*. Gutersloh: Mohn, 1962.

Loewe, R. *The Position of Women in Judaism*. SPCK: London, 1966.

Maclean I. *The Renaissance Notion of Women*. New York: Cambridge University Press, 1980.

Macurdy, G. H. *Hellenistic Queens: A Study of Women-Power in Macedonia Seleucid Syria, and Ptolemaic Egypt*. The Johns Hopkins University Studies. Vol. 14. Baltimore: The Johns Hopkins University Press, 1932.

Macmullen, Ramsey. "Women in Public in the Roman Empire." *Historia* 28 (1980): 208–18.

Mancha, R. "Women of Authority: Calvin to Edwards." *Journal of Christian Reconstruction* 6 (Winter, 1979-80): 86–98.

Manners, E. *Elizabeth Hooten: First Quaker Woman Preacher.* New York: D. S. Taber, 1914.

McBeth. L. *Women in Baptist Life.* Nashville: Broadman, 1979.

McKeating, H. "Jesus ben Sira's Attitude to Women." *Expo T* 85 (1973): 85–7.

McKenna, M. *Women of the Church.* New York: P. J. Kennedy, 1967.

McLaughlin, E. "Equality of Souls, Inequality of Sexes: Woman in Medieval Theology." In *Religion and Sexism.* New York: Simon and Schuster, 1974.

―――――. "Woman, Power, and the Pursuit of Holiness in Medieval Christianity." In *Women of Spirit: Female Leadership in the Jewish and Christian Traditions,* edited by Rosemary Reuther and E. McLaughlin. New York: Simon and Schuster, 1979.

Meer, Haye van der, S. J. *Women Priests in the Catholic Church? A Theological-Historical Investigation.* Philadelphia: Temple University Press, 1973.

Meyer, Charles R. "Ordained Women in the Early Church." *J Ev TH S* 20 (1977): 337–52.

Meyers, Carol. "The Roots of Restriction: Women in Early Israel." *BA* 41 no. 3 (1978): 91–103.

Montgomery, H. *Western Women in Eastern Lands: Fifty Years of Woman's Work in Foreign Missions.* New York: Macmillan, 1910.

Morewedge, R. *The Role of Women in the Middle Ages.* London: Hodder and Stoughton, 1975.

Morris, J. *Against Nature and God: The History of Women with Clerical Ordination and the Jurisdiction of Bishops.* London: Mowbrays, 1973.

Morrow, T. *Early Methodist Women.* London: Epworth, 1967.

Myers, E. *A Century of Moravian Sisters.* New York: Revell, 1918.

Noonan, John T. *Contraception.* New York: Mentor, 1965.

Nunnaly-Cox, J. *Foremothers.* New York: Seabury, 1981.

O'Faolain, J. & Martines, L., eds. *Not in God's Image.* New York: Harper and Row, 1973.

O'Neill, William. *Eleanor Was Brave: The Rise and Fall of Feminism in America.* New York: Quadrangle, 1968.

Osiek, C. "The Church Fathers and the Ministry of Women." In *Women Priests: A Catholic Commentary on the Vatican Declaration,* edited by Leonard Swidler and Arlene Swidler. New York: Paulist, 1977.

―――――. "The Ministry and Ordination of Women According to the Early Church Fathers." In *Women and Priesthood,* edited by C. Stuhlmueller. Collegeville, Minn.: Liturgical, 1978.

Pagels, E. *The Gnostic Paul.* Philadelphia: Fortress, 1975.

Patterson, L. G. "Women in Early Church: A Problem of Perspective." In *Toward a New Theology of Ordination: Essays on the Ordination of Women,* edited by M. H. Micks and C. P. Price. Alexandria: Virginia Theological Seminary, 1976.

Peritz, Ismar J. "Woman in the Ancient Hebrew Cult." *JBL* 17 (1898): 111–48.

Perkins, P. *The Gnostic Dialogue: The Early Church and the Crises of Gnosticism.* New York: Paulist, 1980.

Pomeroy, Sarah B. *Goddesses, Whores, Wives, and Slaves: Women in Classical Antiquity.* New York: Schocken, 1975.

Power, E. *Medieval English Nunneries.* Cambridge, Mass.: The University Press, 1922.

Reuther, Rosemary. *Religion and Sexism: Images of Woman in the Jewish and Christian Traditions.* New York: Simon and Schuster, 1974.

Reuther, Rosemary, and Keller, R. *Women and Religion in America.* San Francisco: Harper and Row, 1981.

Rihbany, Abraham M. "Jesus and His Mother." In *The Syrian Christ.* New York: Houghton Mifflin, 1916.

————. "Women East and West"; "Paul and Women." In *The Syrian Christ.* New York: Houghton Mifflin, 1916.

Roelker, N. "The Role of Noblewomen in the French Reformation." *Archives for Reformation History* 63 no. 2 (1972): 168–95.

Ross, I. *Margaret Fell: Mother of Quakerism.* New York: Longman, 1949.

Rossi, Alice S., ed. *The Feminist Papers: From Adams to de Beauvoir.* New York: Bantam, 1973.

Smith, Charles Ryder. *The Bible Doctrine of Womanhood in Its Historical Evolution.* London: Epworth, 1923.

Spretnak, Charlene. *The Politics of Women's Spirituality: Essays on the Rise of Spiritual Power Within the Feminist Movement.* New York: Doubleday, 1982.

Stagg, E., and Stagg, F. *Women in the World of Jesus.* Philadelphia: Westminster, 1978.

Stuard, S. *Women in Medieval Society.* Philadelphia: University of Pennsylvania, 1976.

Swidler, L. *Biblical Affirmations of Women.* Philadelphia: Westminster, 1979.

————. *Women and Ministry in the New Testament.* Ramsey, N.J.: Paulist, 1980.

————. *Women in Judaism: The Status of Women in Formative Judaism.* Metuchen, N.J.: Scarecrow, 1976.

Tatum, N. *A Crown of Service: A Story of Women's Work in the Methodist Episcopal Church South 1878–1940.* Nashville: Parthenon, 1960.

Tavard, George H. *Woman in Christian Tradition.* Notre Dame, Ind.: University of Notre Dame Press, 1973.

Taylor, H. O. "Mystic Visions of Ascetic Women." In *The Medieval Mind.* New York: Macmillan, 1919.

Tertullian. "On the Apparel of Women." *The Ante-Nicene Fathers,* edited by Alexander Roberts and James Donaldson. Vol. 4. Grand Rapids, Eerdmans, 1956, 14–26.

Verdesi, E. "The Professionally Trained Woman in the Presbyterian Church." Ph.D. dissertation, Columbia University, 1975.

Welter, B. "The Feminization of American Religion, 1800–1860." In *Clio's Consciousness Raised*. New York: Harper Colophon, 1974.

Williard, F. *Women in the Pulpit*. Boston: D. Lathrop, 1888.

————. "Women and the Religious Communities." Whole issue of *Face to Face* 5 (1978): 32.

Wright, E. *Holy Company: Christian Heroes and Heroines*. New York: Macmillan, 1980.

Zinserling, Vincent. *Women in Greece and Rome*. New York: Abner Schram, 1972.

Biblical, Theological, and Sociological

Adeny, Walter F. *Women in the New Testament*. London: Nesbit, 1901.

Alexander, John W. "Headship in Marriage: Flip of a Coin?" *Chr T* (February 20, 1981): 23–26.

Almlie, G. L. "*Didaskalos*: The Office, Man and Woman in the New Testament." *Concor J* 8 (1982): 52–60.

Archer, G. L. "Does 1 Timothy 2:12 Forbid the Ordination of Women?" In *Encyclopedia of Bible Difficulties*. Grand Rapids: Zondervan, 1982.

Bailey, Derrick Sherwin. *Sexual Relations in Christian Thought*. New York: Harper, 1959.

*Balch, David Lee. "Let Wives Be Submissive." In *The Domestic Code in I Peter*. Chico, Calif.: Scholars Press, 1981. University Microfilms, 1974.

*Banks, R. "The Contribution of Women in Church." In *Paul's Idea of Community: The Early House Churches in Their Historical Setting*. Exeter: Paternoster; Grand Rapids: Eerdmans, 1980.

Bartchy, S. Scott. "Jesus, Power, and Gender Roles." *TSF Bulletin* (January-February 1984): 2–4.

*————. "Power, Submission, and Sexual Identity among the Early Christians." In *Essays on New Testament Christianity*, edited by C. Robert Wetzel. Cincinnati: Standard, 1978.

*Barth, Markus. *Ephesians*. The Anchor Bible. New York: Doubleday, 1974.

Bedale, Stephen. "The Meaning of *Kephale* in the Pauline Epistles." *J Ev Th S* (new series, May 1954): 211–215.

*Bianchi, Eugene C., and Reuther, Rosemary. *From Machismo to Mutuality*. Ramsey, N.J.: Paulist, 1972.

*Bird, Caroline. *The High Cost of Keeping Women Down*. New York: David McKay, 1968.

Birney, Leroy. *The Role of Women in the New Testament Church*. Christian

Brethren Research Fellowship, 1971. Reprinted *Journal of Christian Brothers Research Fellowship* 33 (1982): 1–23.

Bliss, Kathleen. *The Service and Status of Women in the Churches.* London: SCM, 1952.

Blitchington, W. Peter. *Sex Roles and the Christian Family.* Wheaton: Tyndale House, 1980.

Block, Berg. "The Liberated Wife." *Ref J* (October 1975): 17–19.

Bloesch, Donald. *Is the Bible Sexist?* New York: Cornerstone, 1982.

Blum, G. G. "The Office of Women in the New Testament." *Churchman* 85 (1971): 175–89.

*Boldrey, Richard, and Boldrey, Joyce. *Chauvinist or Feminist? Paul's View of Women.* Grand Rapids: Baker, 1976.

*_____. "Women in Paul's Life." *Trinity Studies* 2 (1972): 1–36.

*Booth, Catherine. *Female Ministry, or Woman's Right to Preach the Gospel.* London: Morgan and Chase, 1859.

*Boucher, Madeline. "Some Unexplored Parallels to I Cor. 11: 11–12 and Gal. 3:28: The NT on the Role of Women." *CBQ* 91 (1969): 50–58.

Brown, Raymond E. "The Meaning of Modern New Testament Studies for the Possibility of Ordaining Women to the Priesthood." In *Biblical Reflections on Crises Facing the Church.* New York: Paulist, 1975.

Brown, R. "Roles of Women in the Fourth Gospel." *Th St* 36 (1975): 688–99.

Bruce, Michael. "Heresy, Equality, and the Rights of Women." *The Churchman* 85:4 (Winter 1971): 246–62.

Bruce, Michael, and Duffield, G. E., eds. *Why Not? Priesthood and the Ministry of Women.* Marcham Manor Press, 1972.

Brunner, Peter. *The Ministry and the Ministry of Women.* St. Louis: Concordia, 1971.

Bruns, Edgar J. *God as Woman, Woman as God.* New York: Paulist, 1973.

*Buhirg, Marga. "Discrimination Against Women." In *Technology and Social Justice,* edited by R. H. Preston. Valley Forge: Judson, 1971.

*Burkhardt, Walter, ed. *Woman: New Dimensions.* Ramsey, N.J.: Paulist, 1975.

*Burtness, James H. "An Interview with the Rev. Barbara Andrews." *Dialog* 10 (1971): 123–29.

*Bushnell, Katherine C. *God's Word to Women.* Oakland: Katherine C. Bushnell, 1923.

Caird, George B. "Paul and Women's Liberty." *Bul J Rylands* 54 (1972): 268–81.

*Carmody, Denise Lardner. *Feminism and Christianity: A Two-Way Reflection.* Nashville: Abingdon, 1982.

*Carmody, Denise Lardner, and Carmody, John Tully. "Contemporary Feminist Theology." In *Christianity an Introduction.* Belmont, Calif.: Wadsworth, 1983.

Cartlidge, D. R. "1 Corinthians 7 as a Foundation for a Christian Sex Ethic." *J Rel* 55 (1975): 220.

*Cerling, C. E., Jr. "Women Ministers in the New Testament Church." *J Ev Th S* 19 (1976): 210–15.

*Christ, Carol P., and Plaskow, Judith. *Womanspirit Rising.* New York: Harper and Row, 1982.

Christenson, Larry. *The Christian Family.* Minneapolis: Bethany Fellowship, 1970.

Clark, Gordon. "The Ordination of Women." *The Trinity Review* 17 (January 1981): 1–6.

Clark, Stephen B. *Man and Woman in Christ: An Examination of the Roles of Men and Women in Light of Scripture and the Social Sciences.* Ann Arbor: Servant, 1980.

*Collins, Sheila D. "Toward a Feminist Theology." *Christian Century* 89 (August 2, 1972): 796–99.

Concerning the Ordination of Women. Geneva: World Council of Churches, 1964.

*Conn, Harvie M. "Evangelical Feminism: Some Bibliographical Reflections on the Contemporary State of the (Union)." *WTJ* 46 (1984): 104–24.

*Connor, James. "An Examination of I Corinthians 14:34–36. The Place of Women in Early Christian Assemblies." Master's thesis, Immanuel School of Religion, 1977.

*Culver, Elsie Thomas. *Women in the World of Religion.* Garden City, N.Y.: Doubleday, 1967.

Cunningham, Agnes. *The Role of Women in Ecclesial Ministry: Biblical and Patristic Foundations.* Washington, D.C.: United States Catholic Conference, 1976.

*Daly, Mary. *Beyond God the Father.* Boston: Beacon, 1974.

*————. *The Church and the Second Sex.* New York: Harper and Row, 1975.

*Davies, Steven L. *The Revolt of the Widows.* Carbondale: Southern Illinois University Press, 1980.

Davis, Elizabeth Gould. *The First Sex.* New York: G. P. Putman's Sons, 1971.

Davis, John Jefferson. "Some Reflections on Galatians 3:28, Sexual Roles, and Biblical Hermeneutics." *J Ev Th S* no. 3 (1976): 201–8.

*————. "Ordination of Women Reconsidered: Discussion of 1 Timothy 2:8–15." *Presbyterian Communique* (November-December 1979). Reprinted in *Women and Men in Ministry.* Pasadena: Fuller Theological Seminary, 1980. (Davis changed his view.)

*Dayton, Donald W., and Sider, Lucille. "Women as Preachers: Evangelical Precedents." *Chr T* (May 1973): 4–7.

*DeBeauvoir, Simone. *The Second Sex.* New York: Vintage Books, Random House, 1974.

de Fraine, J. *Women in the Old Testament.* De Pere, Wis.: St. Norberts Abbey Press, 1968.

*DeJong, Peter, and Wilson, Donald R. *Husband and Wife: The Sexes in Scripture and Society*. Grand Rapids: Zondervan, 1979.

Derrett, J. Duncan. "Religious Hair." *Studies in the New Testament*, vol. 1. Leiden: Brill, 1977.

Dumas, Francine. *Man and Woman: Similarity and Difference*. Geneva: World Council of Churches, 1966.

*Eller, Vernard. *The Language of Canaan and the Grammar of Feminism*. Grand Rapids: Eerdmans, 1982.

Elliot, Elisabeth. "Femininity." *Christian Herald* (March 1976): 57–8.

_____. *Let Me Be a Woman*. Wheaton: Tyndale House, 1976.

_____. "Why I Oppose the Ordination of Women." *Chr T* (June 6, 1975): 12–16.

*Ellis, E. Earle. "The Silenced Wives of Corinth." In *New Testament Textual Criticism*, edited by E. J. Epp and G. D. Fee. Oxford: Clarendon, 1981.

*Ellwood, Gracia Fay. "God Is a Virgin Mother." *RefJ* (April 1976): 19–22.

*_____. "Servants of One Another." *RefJ* (December 1975): 10–11.

*Ermarth, Margaret Sittler. *Adam's Fractured Rib*. Philadelphia: Fortress, 1970.

*Evans, Mary J. *Women in the Bible*. Downers Grove: Inter-Varsity, 1984.

Faxon, Alicia. *Women and Jesus*. New York: Pilgrim, 1973.

*Fiorenza, Elisabeth S. "Feminist Theology and a Critical Theology of Liberation." *Mission Trends No. 4, Liberation Theologies*, edited by Gerald H. Anderson and Thomas F. Stransky. Ramsey, N.J.: Paulist; Grand Rapids: Eerdmans, 1979.

*_____. *In Memory of Her: A Feminist Theological Reconstruction of Christian Origins*. Los Angeles: Crossroads, 1983.

*_____. "Toward a Biblical Hermeneutics: Biblical Interpretation and Liberation Theology." In *The Challenge of Liberation Theology: A First World Response*, edited by Brian Mahan and David Tracy. Maryknoll, N.Y.: Orbis, 1981.

*_____. "Women in the Pre-Pauline and Pauline Churches." *Union S* 33 (1978): 153–66.

*Fischer, Clare Benedicks; Brenneman, Betsy; and Bennett, Anne McGrew, eds. *Women in a Strange Land: Search for a New Image*. Philadelphia: Fortress, 1975.

Fitzmeyer, J. A. "A Feature of Qumran Angelogy and the Angels of 1 Corinthians 11:10." *NTS* 4 (1957–58): 48.

*Flanagan, N. M., and Snyder, E. H. "Did Paul Put Down Women in 1 Cor. 14:34–36?" *Bib Th Bul* 11 (1981): 10–12.

Foh, Susan T. "What Is the Woman's Desire?" *WTJ* 37–38 (Fall 1974/Spring 1976): 376–83.

_____. *Women and the Word of God*. Grand Rapids: Baker, 1979.

*Forbes, Cheryl. "Dorothy L. Sayers—For Good Work, for God's Work." *Christianity Today* 21:11 (March 4, 1977): 16–18.

*Ford, J. Massyngberde. "Biblical Material Relevant to the Ordination of Women." *J Ec St* 10 (1973): 669–94.

*Foster, A. Durwood. "God and Woman: Some Theses on Theology, Ethics, and Women's Lib." *Religion in Life* 42 (1973): 42–56.

Foster, J. "St. Paul and Women." *Expos T* 63 (1951): 376.

Franson, Fredrik. "Prophesying Daughters." *Cov Q* 34 (November 1976): 24–40.

*Fraser, David, and Fraser, Elouise. "A Biblical View of Women: Demothologizing Sexegesis." *Theology, News and Notes* (June 1975): 14–18.

*Friedan, Betty. *The Feminine Mystique.* New York: Dell, 1963.

*Gelpi, Donald L., S.J. *Experiencing God—A Theology of Human Emergence.* Ramsey, N.J.: Paulist, 1978.

Geng, Veronica. "Requiem for the Women's Movement." *Harpers* (November 1976): 49–68.

*Gerstenberger, E. S., and Schrage, W. Translated by Douglas Stott. *Woman and Man.* Nashville: Abingdon, 1981.

*Gibson, Elsie. *When the Minister Is a Woman.* New York: Holt, Rinehart and Winston, 1970.

*Giles, K. "The Order of Creation and the Subordination of Women." *Interchange* 23 (1978): 175–89.

*————. *Women and Their Ministry: A Case for Equal Ministries in the Church Today.* Australia: Dove Communications, 1977.

Gillquist, Peter E. *The Physical Side of Being Spiritual*, 57–67. Grand Rapids: Zondervan, 1979.

Goldberg, Steven. *The Inevitability of Patriarchy.* New York: William Morrow, 1973.

Goleman. Daniel. "Special Abilities of the Sexes: Do They Begin in the Brain?" *Psychology Today* (November 1978): 48–59.

*Gordon, A. J. "The Ministry of Women." *Missionary Review of the World* (new series) 7 (1894): 910–21.

*Gornick, Vivian, and Moran, Barbara K. eds. *Women in Sexist Society.* New York: Basic, Books, 1971.

Graebner, Alan. "Growing Up Female." In *Sociology: A Descriptive Approach*, edited by Jeffrey E. Nash and James P. Spradley. Chicago: Rand McNally College Publishing Co., 1976.

Greig, J. C. G. "Women's Hats—1 Corinthians 11:1–16." *Expo T* 69 (1958): 156.

*Gundry, Patricia. *Heirs Together: Mutual Submission in Marriage.* Grand Rapids: Zondervan, 1980.

*————. *Woman Be Free.* Grand Rapids: Zondervan, 1977.

*Hageman, Alice L., ed. *Sexist Religion and Women in the Church: No More Silence!* New York: Association, Press, 1974.

*Hanson, P. D. "Masculine Metaphors for God and Sex Discrimination in the Old Testament." *Ec R* 27 (1975): 316–24.

*Hardesty, Nancy. "Mutual Submission." *Chr T* (June 6, 1975): 39–41.

————. "The Status of Evangelical Women." *Ref J* (July/August 1973): 4–9.

————. "Women and Evangelical Christianity." In *The Cross and the Flag*, edited by Robert Clouse, Robert Linder, and Richard Pierard. Carol Stream, Il: Creation House, 1972.

————. *Women Called to Witness: Evangelical Feminism in the Nineteenth Century*. Nashville: Abingdon, 1984.

————. "Women: Second Class Citizens?" *Eternity* (January 1977): 14–29.

Harinck, C. "The Biblical View of Women in the Church." *The Banner of Truth* 39:5 (May 1973): 15–16.

*Harkness, Georgia. *Women in Church and Society*. Nashville: Abingdon, 1972.

*Harper, Joyce. *Women and the Gospel*. Middlesex, England: C.B.R.F. Publications, 1974.

*Hearn, Virginia. *Our Struggle to Serve*. Waco: Word, 1979.

Henry, Carl F. H. "Further Thoughts about Women." *Chr T* vol. 19, no. 18 (June 6, 1975): 36–37.

*Hestenes, Roberta, and Curley, Lois, eds. *Women and the Ministries of Christ*. Pasadena: Fuller Theological Seminary, 1979.

*————. *Women and Men in Ministry: Collected Readings*. Pasadena: Fuller Theological Seminary, 1980.

Heyer, Robert J., ed. *Women and Orders*. New York: Paulist, 1974.

*Heyard, Carter. "Speaking and Sparking, Building and Burning." *Chr Cris* (April 2, 1979): 66–72.

Hiebert, D. E. "The Apostle Paul: Women's Friend." *The Christian Reader* (June-July 1973): 1–5; (April-May 1973): 47–52.

*Hooker, Morna D. "Authority on Her Head: An Examination of I Cor. 11:10." *New Testament Studies* 10 (1963): 410–16.

Hommes, N. J. "Let Women Be Silent in the Churches." *Cal Th J* 4 (1969): 5–22.

*Hoover, K. W. "Creative Tension in 1 Timothy 2:11–15." *Breth Life* 22 (1977): 163–66.

*Hoppin, Ruth. *Priscilla: Author of the Epistle to the Hebrews*. New York: Exposition, 1969.

Hosie, Dorothea. *Jesus and Woman: Being a Study of the Four Gospels with Special Reference to the Attitude of the Man Jesus Christ Towards Woman*. London: Hodder and Stoughton, 1946.

House, Wayne H. "Paul, Women, and Contemporary Evangelical Feminism." *BS* 136 (January-March 1979): 40–53.

Howard, Thomas, and Dayton, Donald. "A Dialogue on Women, Hierarchy, and Equality." *Post-American* 4 (May 1975): 8–15.

Howard, Tom. "God Before Birth: The Imagery Matters." *Chr T* (December 17, 1976): 10–13.

*Howe, E. Margaret. "The Positive Case for the Ordination of Women." In *Perspectives on Evangelical Theology*, edited by Kenneth Kantzer and Stanley Gundry. Grand Rapids: Baker, 1979.

*_____. *Women and Church Leadership*. Grand Rapids: Zondervan, 1982.

Hurley, James B. "Did Paul Require Veils or the Silence of Women? A Consideration of 1 Cor. 11:2–16 and 1 Cor. 14:33b–36." *Westminster Theology Journal* 35 (1973): 190–220.

_____. *Man and Woman in Biblical Perspective*. Grand Rapids: Zondervan, 1981.

_____. *Man and Woman in 1 Corinthians*. Ph.D. dissertation. New York: Cambridge University Press, 1973.

*Janeway, Elizabeth. *Man's World, Woman's Place*. New York: Delta, 1971.

*Jaubert, Annie. "Le Voile des Femmes (I Cor. XI.2–16)." *N T St* 18 (1971–72): 419–30.

*Jewett, Paul. *Man as Male and Female*. Grand Rapids: Eerdmans, 1975.

*_____. *The Ordination of Women*. Grand Rapids: Eerdmans, 1980.

*_____. "Why I Favor the Ordination of Women." *Chr T* (June 6, 1975): 7–12.

*Jewett, Robert. "The Sexual Liberation of the Apostle Paul." *JAAR* 47 (1979) Supplement: 55–87.

*Johnston, Robert K. "The Role of the Woman in Church and Society." In *Evangelicals at an Impasse*. Atlanta: John Knox, 1978.

*Judge, E. A. "St. Paul as a Radical Critic of Society." *Interchange* 16 (1974): 191–203 (Section 3, 198–203, is on women.)

*Kaiser, Walter C. "Paul, Women, and the Church." *Worldwide Challenge* (September 1976): 9–12.

*Kantzer, Kenneth S. "Women's Role in Church and Family." *Chr T* (February 20, 1981): 10–11.

*Karris, R. J. "The Role of Women According to Jesus and the Early Church." *Women and Priesthood: Future Directions*, edited by C. Stuhlmueller. Collegeville, Minn.: Liturgical, 1978.

Keefe, Donald J. "The Ordination of Women: A Roman Catholic Assessment." *New Oxford Review* 47 (1980): 12–14.

*Kilmartin, Edward J., S.J. "Apostolic Office: Sacrament of Christ." *Th St* 36 (1975): 243–64.

Knight, George W. "*Authenteo* in Reference to Women in 1 Timothy 2:12." *NT St* (1984): 143–57.

_____. "Male and Female Related He Them." *Chr T* 21 (1976): 709–13.

_____. *The New Testament Teaching on the Role Relationship of Men and Women*. Grand Rapids: Baker, 1977.

_____. "The New Testament Teaching on the Role Relationship of Male and Female with Special Reference to the Teaching/Ruling Functions in the Church." *J Ev Th S* (Spring 1975) vol. 18, no. 2: 81–91.

──────. "The Ordination of Women: No." *Chr T* (February 20, 1981): 16–19.

*Kroeger, Catherine C. "Ancient Heresies and a Strange Greek Verb (1 Tim. 2:8–15," *RefJ* (March 1979): 12–10.

*Kroeger, Richard, and Kroeger, Catherine C. "May Women Teach? Heresy in the Pastoral Epistles." *RefJ* (October 1980) 14–18.

*Kross, Alfred C. "Permissiveness and Women's Liberation: The Case for Commitment" *RefJ* (November 1978): 10–12.

*──────. "Sexual Identity in Corinth: Paul Faces a Crisis" (I Cor. 11)." *RefJ* (December 1978): 11–15.

Kuhns, Dennis R. *Women in the Church*. Scottdale, PA: Herald Press, 1978.

*Lake, Alice. "Are We Born into Our Sex Roles or Programmed into Them?" *Woman's Day* (January 1976): 50.

*Lee, Luther. *Woman's Right to Preach the Gospel*. Syracuse, N.Y.: Luther Lee, 1853.

Leonard, Eugenie Andress. "St. Paul on the Status of Women." *CBQ* 12 (1950): 311–20.

*Leslie, William. "The Concept of Woman in the Pauline Corpus in the Light of Religious and Social Environment of the First Century." Ph.D. dissertation, Northwestern University, 1976.

Lewis, C. S. "Priestesses in the Church?" *God in the Dock*, edited by W. Hooper. Grand Rapids: Eerdmans, 1970.

*Liefeld, Walter L. "Women, Submission, and Ministry in First Corinthians." Paper read at the Oakbrook Consultation on Women and Ministry (October 1984). Responses by Alan F. Johnson and William H. Leslie.

*Lightfoot, N. R. *The Role of Women: New Testament Perspectives*. Memphis, Tenn.: Student Association Press, 1978.

Litfin, A. Duane. "Evangelical Feminism—Why Traditionalists Reject It." *BS* 136 (543, 1979): 258–71.

*Longenecker, Richard N. *New Testament Social Ethics for Today*. Grand Rapids: Eerdmans, 1984.

Longstaff, T. R. W. "The Ordination of Women: A Biblical Perspective." *ATR* 57 (1975): 322–27.

Mack, Wayne. *The Role of Women in the Church*. Easton, Penn.: Mack Publishing, 1972.

Maertens, T. *The Advancing Dignity of Woman in the Bible*. New York: St. Norberts Abbey Press, 1977.

Maier, Walter A. "Some Thoughts on the Role of Women in the Church." *The Springfielder* 33:4 (March 1970): 33–37.

Martin, Faith. "God's Image in the Christian Woman." *Covenanter Witness* 41:13 (June 18, 1975): 6–7.

*Martin, William J. "1 Corinthians 11:2–16: An Interpretation." In *Apostolic*

History and the Gospel, edited by W. W. Gasque and Ralph Martin. Grand Rapids: Eerdmans, 1970.

McGill, Arthur C. *Suffering: A Test of Theological Method.* Philadelphia: Westminster, 1982. Chaps. 3–5 are excellent on the "subordination" of Son to Father.

McGrath, Sister Albertus Magnus, O.P. *What a Modern Catholic Believes about Women.* Chicago: The Thomas More Press, 1972.

*Mead, Margaret. *Male and Female.* New York: Morrow, 1949.

*Meeks, Wayne. "The Image of the Androgyne: Some Uses of a Symbol in Earliest Christianity." *Hist Rel* 13 (1974): 165–208.

*Mercadante, Linda. *From Hierarchy to Equality.* Vancouver: G-M-H Regent College, 1978.

*————. "The Male-Female Debate: Can We Read the Bible Objectively?" *Crux* no. 2, vol. 15 (June 1979): 20–25.

*————. "Women's Realities: A Theological View." *TSF* 8 (1984): 8–10.

Meyer, Charles R. "Ordained Women in the Early Church." *Chicago Studies* (1965).

*Mickelsen, Berkeley, and Michelson, Alvera. "Does Male Dominance Tarnish Our Translations?" *Chr T* (October 5, 1979) 23–29. Response to article, *Chr T* (November 16) 8–9.

*————. "The 'Head' of the Epistles." *Chr T* (February 20, 1981): 20–23.

*————. *Women and the Bible.* Downers Grove: Inter-Varsity, 1985.

*Miles, Herbert J., and Miles, Fern Harrington. *Husband Wife Equality.* Old Tappan, N.J.: Revell, 1978.

*Miles, Judith. *The Feminine Principle.* Minneapolis: Bethany Fellowship, 1970.

*Millett, Kate. *Sexual Politics.* New York: Avon, 1969.

Mitchell, John. "Was Phoebe a Deacon—No?" *The Presbyterian Guardian* 42 (November 1975): 134–35.

*Mollenkott, Virginia. "A Challenge to Male Interpretation: Women and the Bible," *Sojourners* 5:2 (February 1976): 20–25.

*————. "Church Women, Theologians, and the Burden of Proof." *Ref J* (July/August 1975): 18–20.

*————. *The Divine Feminine: The Biblical Imagery of God as Female.* New York: Crossroad, 1983.

*————. "Evangelicism: A Feminist Perspective." *Union Seminary Quarterly Review* 32 (1977): 95–103.

*————. "Interpreting Difficult Scriptures." *Daughters of Sarah* 5:2 (March/April 1979): 16–17.

*————. *Speech, Silence, Action! The Cycle of Faith.* Nashville: Abingdon, 1980.

*————. "Women and the Bible: A Challenge to Male Interpretations." *Mission Trends No. 4, Liberation Theologies,* edited by Gerald H. Anderson

and Thomas F. Stransky. Ramsey, N.J.: Paulist; Grand Rapids: Eerdmans, 1979.

*————. *Women, Men, and the Bible.* Nashville: Abingdon, 1977.

*Mollenkott, Virginia, et al. "Exegeting Implications." *Chr T* (June 4, 1976): 24–25. (Letter to the editor).

Montgomery, Helen Barrett. *Centenary Translation of the New Testament.* Philadelphia: American Baptist, 1924.

Moo, Douglas, J. "1 Timothy 2:11–15: Meaning and Significance." *Trinity J* 1/1 (1980): 62–63.

————. "The Interpretation of 1 Tim 2:11–15: A Rejoinder." *Trinity J* 2 (1981): 198–222. See P. Payne, a response.

*Morgan, Marabel. " 'Preferring One Another': An Interview." *Chr T* 20:24 (September 10, 1976): 12–15.

————. *The Total Woman.* Old Tappan, N.J.: Revell, 1973.

*Morgan, Robin, ed. *Sisterhood Is Powerful.* New York: Random House, 1970.

*Morris, Joan. *The Lady Was a Bishop.* New York: Macmillan, 1973.

Morris, Leon. "The Ministry of Women." *Women and the Ministries of Christ,* edited by Roberta Hestenes and Lois Curley. Pasadena: Fuller Theological Seminary, 1979.

*Morrison, Melanie. "Even Paul Was Ambivalent." *Sojourners* (January 1978): 29–34.

*————. "Three Books on the Biblical View of Women." (Review of Boldrey's, Mollenkott's and Otwell's books.) *Sojourners* (January 1978): 29–34.

*Mount, Eric. "The Feminine Factor." *Soundings* 53:4 (Winter 1970): 379–97.

*Neal, Sister Marie Augusta. "Sociology and Sexuality: A Feminist Perspective." *Chr Cris* no. 8, vol. 39 (May 14, 1979): 118–22.

*Nyce, Dorothy Yoder. "Remembering God Who Gave Us Birth." *Daughters of Sarah* vol. 5, no. 3 (May/June 1979): 3–6.

*Odell-Scott, D. W. "Let the Women Speak in Church: An Egalitarian Interpretation of 1 Cor. 14:33b–36." *Bib Th Bul* 13 (1983): 90–93.

*Olthius, James H. "An Appendix: Paul on Women." In *I Pledge You My Troth: A Christian View of Marriage, Family, Friendship.* New York: Harper and Row, 1975.

*————. "Mankind: Male and Female." In *I Pledge You My Troth: A Christian View of Marriage, Family, Friendship.* New York: Harper and Row, 1975.

Osborne, Grant R. "Hermeneutics and Women in the Church." *J Ev Th S* vol. 20, no. 4 (December 1977): 337–52.

Osburn, C. D. "Aythenteo (1 Timothy 2:12)." *Restoration Q* 25 (1982): 1–12.

*Otwell, J. H. *And Sarah Laughed: The Status of Women in the Old Testament.* Philadelphia: Westminster, 1977.

*Pagels, Elaine. "Paul and Women: A Response to Recent Discussion." *JAAR* vol. 42 (1974): 538–49.

Panning, Armin J. "Authentein—A Word Study." *Wisconsin Lutheran Quarterly* 78 (1981): 185–91.

*Pape, Dorothy R. *In Search of God's Ideal Woman.* Downers Grove: Inter-Varsity, 1976.

*Payne, Phillip. "Libertarian Women in Ephesus: A Response to D. Moo's Article 'First Tim 2:11–15: Meaning and Significance.'" *Trinity J* 2 (1981).

*Penn-Lewis, Jessie. *The Magna Charta of Women.* Minneapolis: Bethany Fellowship, 1975.

*Plaskow, Judith. *Sex, Sin, and Grace: Women's Experience and the Experience and the Theologies of Reinhold Niebuhr and Paul Tillich.* Washington, D.C.: University Press of America, 1980.

Powers, B. W. "Women in the Church: The Application of 1 Timothy 2: 8–15." *Interchange* 17 (1975): 55–59.

*Proctor, Priscilla and Proctor, William. *Women in the Pulpit—Is God an Equal Opportunity Employer?* New York: Doubleday, 1976.

*Prohl, Russell C. *Woman in the Church: A Study of Woman's Place in Building the Kingdom.* Grand Rapids: Eerdmans, 1957.

Quebedeaux, Richard. *The Young Evangelicals.* New York: Harper, 1974.

*Reumann, John. "What in Scripture Speaks to the Ordination of Women?" *Con Th M* 44–45 (1973–74): 6–30.

*Reuther, Rosemary. "Feminism and Peace." *Chr Cent* 100 (1983): 771–76.

*————. "Guarding the Sanctuary: Sexism and Ministry" and "Witches and Jews: The Demonic Alien in Christian Culture." In *New Woman, New Earth: Sexist Ideologies and Human Liberation.* New York: Seabury, 1975.

*————. *Sexism and God-Talk: Toward a Feminist Theology.* Boston: Beacon, 1983.

*————. "The Sexuality of Jesus: What Do the Synoptics Say." *Chr Cris* (May 1978): 134–37.

Reynolds, Stephen M. "Hair in Scripture: A Critique of Two Recent Studies and a Proposed Solution to the Problem." *The Reformation Review* 21:21 (January 1974): 65–71.

————. "On Head Coverings." *W TH J* 36 (1973): 90–91.

*Richardson, P. "Neither Male nor Female." In *Paul's Ethic of Freedom.* Philadelphia: Westminster, 1979.

*Ridderbos, Herman. "Women." In *Paul: An Outline of His Theology.* Translated by J. R. DeWitt. Grand Rapids: Eerdmans, 1975.

Roberts, Benjamin Titus. *Ordaining Women.* Rochester, N.Y.: Earnest Christian, 1891.

*Roberts, Mark D. "Woman Shall be Saved; A Closer Look at 1 Timothy 2:15." *Ref J* 33 (1983): 18–22.

*Romero, Joan. "Karl Barth's Theology of the Word of God: Or How To Keep Women Silent and in Their Place." In *Women in Religion*, edited by Judith

Plaskow and Joan Romero. American Academy of Religion and Scholars Press, 1984.

*Russell, Letty M. *Human Liberation in a Feminist Perspective: A Theology.* Philadelphia: Westminster, 1974.

_____. "Women and Freedom." *Mission Trends No. 4, Liberation Theologies,* edited by Gerald H. Anderson and Thomas F. Stransky. Ramsey, N.J.: Paulist; Grand Rapids: Eerdmans, 1979.

_____, ed. *The Liberating Word—A Guide to Nonsexist Interpretation of the Bible.* Philadelphia: Westminster, 1976.

Ryrie, Charles. *The Place of Women in the Church.* New York: Macmillan, 1958.

Sampley, J. *And the Two Shall Become One Flesh.* New York: Cambridge University Press, 1971.

Saucy, Robert L. "The Negative Case Against the Ordination of Women." In *Perspective on Evangelical Theology,* edited by Kenneth Kantzer and Stanley Gundry. Grand Rapids: Baker, 1979.

*Sayers, Dorothy. *Are Women Human?* Grand Rapids: Eerdmans, 1971.

Scaer, David P. "May Women Be Ordained as Pastors." *The Springfielder* 36:2 (September 1972): 89–109.

*Scanzoni, John. "Assertiveness for Christian Women." *Chr T* (June 4, 1976): 16–18.

*_____. "Authority in Christian Marriage." *Ref J* (November 1974): 20–23.

*_____. *Love and Negotiate: Creative Conflict in Marriage.* Waco: Word, 1979.

*Scanzoni, Letha. "The Feminists and the Bible." *Chr T* 2 (February 1973): 10–15.

*_____. "The Great Chain of Being and the Chain of Command." *Ref J* (October 1976): 14–18.

*_____. "How to Live with a Liberated Wife." *Chr T* (June 4, 1976): 6–9.

*Scanzoni, Letha, and Hardesty, Nancy. *All We're Meant to Be.* Waco: Word, 1974.

*Schelkle, K. H. *The Spirit and the Bride: Women in the Bible.* Translated by M. J. O'Connell. Collegeville, Minn.: Liturgical, 1979.

Schmidt, Ruth A. "Second-Class Citizenship in the Kingdom of God." *Chr T* (January 1, 1971): 13–14.

*Scholer, David M. "Exegesis: 1 Timothy 2:8–15." *Daughters of Sarah* 1:4 (May 1975): 7–8.

*_____. "Hermeneutical Gerrymandering: Hurley on Women and Authority." *TSF Bulletin* (May-June 1983): 11–13.

*_____. "Women's Adornment: Some Historical and Hermeneutical Observations on the New Testament Passages." *Daughters of Sarah* 6:1 (January/February 1980): 3–6.

*_____. "Women in Ministry, Session Seven: 1 Timothy 2:8–15." *Covenant Companion* 73:2 (February 1984): 14–15.

*Schweizer, E. "Traditional Ethical Patterns in the Pauline and Post-Pauline Letters and Development (Lists of Vices and House-Tables)." In *Text and Interpretation: New Testament Studies Presented to Matthew Black*, edited by Ernest Best and R. Wilson. New York: Cambridge University Press, 1979.

*Scroggs, Robin. "Paul and the Eschatological Woman." *JAAR* 40 (1972): 283–303.

*_____. "Paul and the Eschatological Woman: Revisited." *JAAR* 42 (1974): 532–37.

*_____. "Paul: Chauvinist or Liberationist?" *Chr Cent* 89 (1972): 307–9.

*Siddons, Philip. "Paul's View of Women." *Chr T* (February 10, 1978): 40–42.

*_____. *Speaking Out for Women—A Biblical View*. Valley Forge: Judson, 1980.

*Sigountos, James G., and Shank, Myron. "Public Roles for Women in the Pauline Church: A Reappraisal of the Evidence." *J E Th S* 26 (1983): 283–95.

*Snodgrass, K. "Paul and Women." *Cov Q* 34 (1976): 3–19.

*Snodgrass, Karen, and Hardesty, Nancy. " 'Head': What Does It Mean?" *Daughters of Sarah*, vol. 2 (July 1976): 1–5.

*Spencer, Aida Dina Besancon. "Eve at Ephesus (Should Women be Ordained as Pastors According to the First Letter to Timothy 2:11–15?)." *J Ev Th S* (1974): 215–22.

_____. "Paul, Our Friend and Champion." *Daughters of Sarah* 2:3 (May 1976): 1–3.

Stanton, Elizabeth Cady, ed. *The Woman's Bible*. 2 vols. New York: European, 1898.

Starr, Lee Anna. *The Bible Status of Women*. New York: Revell, 1926.

Stedman, Elaine. *A Woman's Worth*. Waco: Word, 1975.

*Stendahl, Krister. *The Bible and the Role of Women: A Case Study in Hermeneutics*. Philadelphia: Fortress, 1966.

*_____. "Women in the Churches: No Special Pleading." *Soundings* 53:4 (Winter 1970): 374–378.

*Stephens, Shirley. *A New Testament View of Women*. Nashville: Broadman, 1980.

*Stob, George. "The 'Man/Woman' Question." *Ref J* (July-August 1976): 21–28.

*Stouffer, Austin H. "The Ordination of Women: Yes." *Chr T* (February 20, 1981): 12–15.

Surburg, Raymond F. "The Place of Woman in the Old Testament." *The Springfielder* 33:4 (March 1970): 27–32.

*Swarthley, Willard M. *Slavery, Sabbath, War, and Women*. Scottdale, Penn.: Herald Press, 1983.

*Swidler, Arlene. *Woman in a Man's Church*. Paramus, N.J.: Deus, 1972.

*Swidler, Leonard. "Jesus Was a Feminist." *Catholic World* 212 (1970–71): 177–83.

*Taber, Charles R., ed. "Sexism and Mission: A Dialogue on Contextualization." *Gospel in Context* 2 (1979): 2–40.

*Tanner, Leslie B., ed. *Voices for Women's Liberation.* New York: Signet, 1970.

Taylor, G. "Women in Creation and Redemption." *Journal of Christian Brothers Research Fellowship* 26 (1974): 14–28.

*Terrien, Samuel. "Toward a Biblical Theology of Womanhood." *Religion in Life* 42:3 (Autumn 1973): 322–33.

Tetlow, Elizabeth M. *Women and Ministry in the New Testament.* Ramsey, Paulist, 1980.

Thebeau, Duane. "What the Scriptures Say about Women's Ordination." *Foundations* (October 1975): 6–9.

*Thielicke, Helmut. *Theological Ethics,* vol. 3, *Sex.* Grand Rapids: Eerdmans, 1979.

Thomas, W. D. "The Place of Women in the Church at Philippi." *Expos T,* vol. 83 (1971/1972): 117–20.

Thrall, Margaret E. *The Ordination of Women to the Priesthood.* London: SCM, 1958.

Tiemeyer, Raymond. *The Ordination of Women.* Minneapolis: Augsburg, 1970.

*Tolbert, Mary Ann, ed. *The Bible and Feminist Hermeneutics.*

Tremain, Rose. *The Fight for Freedom for Women.* (New York: Ballantine, 1973).

*Trible, Phyllis. "Depatriarchalizing in Biblical Interpretation." *JAAR* 41 (1973): 30–48.

*———. "Eve and Adam: Genesis 2–3 Reread." *Andover Newton Quarterly* 13:4 (March 1973): 251–58.

*———. "Feminist Hermeneutics and Biblical Studies." *Chr Cent* (February 3, 1982): 116–18.

*———. *God and the Rhetoric of Sexuality.* Philadelphia: Fortress, 1978.

*———. "Good Tidings of Great Joy: Biblical Faith without Sexism." *Chr Cris* 34:1 (February 4, 1974): 12–16.

Trompf, G. W. "On Attitudes Toward Women in Paul and Paulinist Literature: I Corinthians 11:3–16 and Its Context." *CBQ* 4–2 (2, 1980): 196–215.

Ulanov, Ann Belford. *Receiving Woman: Studies in the Psychology and Theology of the Feminine.* Philadelphia: Westminster, 1981.

Vogels, W. "It Is Not Good That the 'Mensch' Should Be Alone: I Will Make Him/Her a Helper Fit for Him/Her." *Eglise Th* 9 (1978): 9–35.

Vos, Clarence J. *Woman in Old Testament Worship.* Delft: Judels and Brinkman, 1968.

*Walker, W. O., Jr. "1 Corinthians 11:2–16 and Paul's Views Regarding Women." *JBL* 94 (1975): 94–110.

Waltke, B. J. "1 Corinthians 11:2–16: An Interpretation." *Bibliotheca Sacra* 135, 537 (1978): 46–57.

Weeks, Noel. "Of Silence and Head Covering." *West Th J* 35 (1972–73): 21–27.

Weidman, Judith L. *Christian Feminism: Visions of a New Humanity.* San Francisco: Harper and Row, 1984.

*Williams, Don. *The Apostle Paul and Women in the Church.* Ventura, Calif.: Regal, 1977.

*Wilson-Kastner, Patricia. *Faith, Feminism, and the Christ.* Philadelphia: Fortress, 1983.

Witherington, Ben III. "Rite and Rights for Women—Galatians 3:28." *NT St* 27: 593–604.

*Wolterstorf, Nicholas. "The Bible and Women: Another Look at the Conservative Position." *Ref J* 29 (1979): 23–26.

————. "On Keeping Women Out of Office: The CRC Committee on Headship." *Ref J* 34 (1984): 8–14.

Yates, Gayle Graham. *What Women Want: The Ideas of the Movement.* Cambridge, Mass.: Harvard University Press, 1975.

Yoder, Perry, and Yoder, Elizabeth. *New Men, New Roles.* Newton, Kans.: Faith and Life, 1977.

Zerbst, Fritz. *The Office of Woman in the Church.* St. Louis: Concordia, 1955.

Bibliographical

Cerling, C. E., Jr. "An Annotated Bibliography of the New Testament Teaching about Women." *J Ev Th S* (Winter 1973): 47–53.

Scholer, David M. *Introductory Reading List for the Study of the Role and Status of Women in the New Testament.* David Scholer, 1981: 1–4.

Storrie, Kathleen. "Contemporary Feminist Theology: A Selective Bibliography." *TSF Bulletin* 7 (May-June 1984): 13–15. Mostly on feminine theologies and sociological studies.